VMware
vSphere®
Performance

VMware vSphere® Performance

Designing CPU, Memory, Storage, and Networking for Performance-Intensive Workloads

Matt Liebowitz

Christopher Kusek

Rynardt Spies

SYBEX®
A Wiley Brand

Acquisitions Editor: Mariann Barsolo

Development Editor: Alexa Murphy

Technical Editor: Jason Boche

Production Editor: Christine O'Connor

Copy Editor: Judy Flynn

Editorial Manager: Pete Gaughan

Vice President and Executive Group Publisher: Richard Swadley

Associate Publisher: Chris Webb

Book Designers: Maureen Forys, Happenstance Type-O-Rama, Judy Fung

Proofreader: Louise Watson, Word One New York

Indexer: Robert Swanson

Project Coordinator, Cover: Todd Klemme

Cover Designer: Wiley

Dear Reader,

Thank you for choosing *VMware vSphere Performance: Designing CPU, Memory, Storage, and Networking for Performance-Intensive Workloads*. This book is part of a family of premium-quality Sybex books, all of which are written by outstanding authors who combine practical experience with a gift for teaching.

Sybex was founded in 1976. More than 30 years later, we're still committed to producing consistently exceptional books. With each of our titles, we're working hard to set a new standard for the industry. From the paper we print on to the authors we work with, our goal is to bring you the best books available.

I hope you see all that reflected in these pages. I'd be very interested to hear your comments and get your feedback on how we're doing. Feel free to let me know what you think about this or any other Sybex book by sending me an email at contactus@sybex.com. If you think you've found a technical error in this book, please visit http://sybex.custhelp.com. Customer feedback is critical to our efforts at Sybex.

Best regards,

Chris Webb
Associate Publisher, Sybex

I dedicate this book to Jonathon Fitch. Sadly, Jonathon, one of the original authors of this book, lost his battle with cancer in April 2013. He wrote chapters during his treatments and showed remarkable courage. This book was important to him, and he was dedicated to getting it completed. Many of the words you read in this book were his. I hope his family can read these words and take some comfort in remembering how smart and talented Jonathon was. He will be missed.

I'd also like to dedicate this book to my family, especially my wife, Joann, for supporting me in this effort. My children, Tyler and Kaitlyn, are my life and the reason why I work so hard. I love you all so much!

—Matt Liebowitz

This book is dedicated to Jonathon Fitch and a labor of love for him and his family. We lost a great person in our community, in the world of virtualization, and in our worldwide family. May we all remember the efforts of Jonathon and the impact he has had on our community and our lives. He was taken from us too soon. He will be missed.

As I've spent the last year in Afghanistan, this is a special dedication to all of the troops: The soldiers on the ground in war-torn countries. The veterans who have served their time and are underappreciated. The heroes who protect our freedom and secure our future.

And last, I'd like to dedicate this book to my family: my best friends, Emily and Chris Canibano; my silly cats; my son, Alexander; and my godchildren, Erehwon and Isabelle.

—Christopher Kusek

When I was approached by the editors at Sybex to help write this book, Jonathon Fitch was the first of the authors that I was introduced to. He was one of the three original authors of this book and wrote many of the words in the storage and networking chapters. The success of this book was really important to Jonathon, as he wanted to dedicate it to his mother, who passed away shortly after work commenced on the first chapters of the book.

Sadly, Jonathon lost his battle with cancer in April 2013. I therefore dedicate this book to Jonathon and hope that his family can take comfort in knowing that through his hard work and dedication to this project, his words and his name will forever live within its text.

I would also like to dedicate the book to my family. My wife, Sarah, and my children, Lanie and Zachariah, have supported me unconditionally throughout this long project. You are my life and I love you all very much.

—Rynardt Spies

Acknowledgments

I first became involved with this book back in December 2011 in the role of technical editor. Numerous delays and subsequent releases of VMware vSphere caused the schedule to get pushed back further and further. In March 2013, Jonathon Fitch, one of the original authors of the book, told me that his health had deteriorated and he would be unable to finish his chapters. I agreed to take over for him and ensure that his ideas remain in the book. Sadly, Jonathon passed away in April 2013, but much of his original content still remains in these chapters.

Thank you to my two co-authors, Christopher Kusek and Rynardt Spies. Both of you have put up with me for over two years, first as a technical editor and then as a co-author. I'm glad we got a chance to work together on this and finally bring it to press. Thanks for your efforts!

Writing a book from scratch is difficult enough, but taking over and revising and updating someone else's chapters makes it that much harder. Thanks to Mariann Barsolo and Pete Gaughan from Sybex for their support as we made this transition. You both put up with schedule changes and numerous other requests from me with ease and you made this process much simpler for me. Thank you and the rest of the Sybex team for everything!

Technical books like this need to be accurate, and we were very lucky to have one of the best in the virtualization industry, Jason Boche, as our technical editor. Thanks so much, Jason, for keeping us honest and making sure we got everything right. Your advice and insight were greatly appreciated! Anytime you're ready to switch hats and take on the author role, I'll happily be your technical editor.

I'd also like to thank some friends and colleagues who have encouraged me along the way. Dave Carlson, thanks for your support throughout the years, both personally and professionally. Michael Fox, thanks for encouraging and supporting me on all of my book projects. I've also been driven to be better by colleagues past and present, including Joe Hoegler, Rob Cohen, Dave Stark, Robin Newborg, Ahsun Saleem, Amit Patel, and Ryan Tang. Thank you all for helping me get where I am today.

Finally, I want thank my family for their support on my latest book project. Thank you to my wife, Joann, for your support throughout this process, including getting up with the kids when I had been up late writing. To my Bean and Katie Mac, I love you both so much, and even though you won't understand the words on these pages, know they are all for you!

—*Matt Liebowitz*

Google defines acknowledgment as "the action of expressing or displaying gratitude or appreciation for something," and to that end, I want to acknowledge that a book like this cannot be produced by one person alone. To all those involved, I thank you. I would like to thank my co-authors, Matt Liebowitz and Rynardt Spies, and our rock-star technical editor, Jason Boche. And I'd like to extend a special thanks to Jonathon Fitch for all his efforts. We worked diligently to ensure that his memory would live on forever.

This wouldn't have been possible without our amazing team from Sybex—Mariann Barsolo, Pete Gaughan, Jenni Housh, Connor O'Brien, Christine O'Connor, and especially Alexa Murphy for sending me files via email because FTP doesn't work so well from Afghanistan!

I'd like to thank some friends and colleagues: Chad Sakac, because you live in a landlocked country in Central Africa. John Troyer and Kat Troyer, because you rock and rock so hard! John Arrasjid, because we shot green lasers at Barenaked Ladies at PEX. Mike Foley, because not only do you rock, but you were one of the last people I ate dinner with before coming to Afghanistan. Scott and Crystal Lowe, because you are the power couple of virtualization. Ted Newman and Damian Karlson, may you survive the madness that is virtualization. My fellow #vExperts of Afghanistan: William Bryant Robertson, Brian "Bo" Bolander, and our fearless associates Brian Yonek and Stacey McGill.

And last, thanks to my family because they rock.

—*Christopher Kusek*

It would simply be impossible to name all the people that I would like to acknowledge and thank for their contributions to this book and to my career. Without their input, I would not have been able to even begin contributing to a book such as this.

I would like to thank the team at Sybex: Mariann Barsolo, Alexa Murphy, Jenni Housh, Connor O'Brien, Pete Gaughan, and the rest of the Wiley team that worked so hard to get this book published. It's been a pleasure working with you all.

To my co-authors, thank you both for putting up with me for so long. Christopher, you were there from the start as an author, and I would like to thank you for your hard work and professionalism. Matt, I know that it's not always easy to pick up a project from someone else. Thank you for your contributions and guidance as the original technical editor and for taking over from Jonathon as a co-author when you were already busy with another book project.

To our technical editor, Jason Boche, thank you for keeping us honest. With you on the team, I was safe in the knowledge that even as I was trying to make sense of my own writing in the early hours of the morning, you were there to iron out any inaccuracies.

I would like to extend a special thanks to Professor Mendel Rosenblum, a co-founder of VMware. Thank you for taking time out of your busy schedule to help me understand some of the inner workings of x86 CPU virtualization. At a time when I had read hundreds of pages of conflicting technical documents on the topic, your helping hand ensured that the readers of this book are presented with accurate information on x86 CPU virtualization.

To VMware, thank you for creating such an awesome product in vSphere! Thank you to the performance engineers at VMware who were always willing to point me in the right direction whenever I needed information.

Thank you to Scott Lowe for your assistance throughout the course of writing this book and for putting me in touch with the relevant people at VMware. Your contributions are much appreciated. Mike Laverick, thank you for always being supportive and offering guidance to a first-time author on how to approach a project such as this.

To the rest of my friends in the virtualization community, thank you for making the virtualization community the best community to be a part of. Tom Howarth, thank you for all the input that you've had in my career. I appreciate your friendship. Thank you to Tyrell Beveridge for supplying me with some lab hardware on which I did a lot of the testing for this book.

Also, thank you to my colleagues at Computacenter for your support and professionalism. As always, it's a privilege and a pleasure for me to be working with you all.

I would not have been able to write this book without input from others into my technical career in IT. I would like to thank Paul Liversidge for throwing me in at the deep end with ESX 2 back in 2005. It was the start of it all. Thank you for mentoring my technical path back in 2005. Thanks to Philip Damian-Grint, for your mentorship and the technical input you had throughout my career. Thank you for the numerous conversations we had during the course of writing this book and your words of encouragement.

I would like to say a special thank-you to my family for their support and words of encouragement throughout this project. To my wife, Sarah, thank you for putting up with me during this project. The late nights with a laptop have finally come to an end. To my kids, Lanie and Zachariah, thank you for being such good kids and bringing so much joy to my life. You are the best and I love you all very much.

To my parents, brothers, and sisters, I really could not have asked for better people to be part of a family with. Thank you for all your prayers and always believing in me. Even though some of us live thousands of miles apart, know that you are always in my heart and I love you all.

Most important, I thank God, the author and finisher of my faith (Hebrews 12:2). When medically, there was little hope, He answered my parents' prayers. Today, I can only say that it's by grace and grace alone that I live.

—Rynardt Spies

About the Authors

Matt Liebowitz is an architect with over 11 years of experience in the virtualization industry. Today Matt provides thought leadership and strategy as the Virtualization Discipline Lead for EMC Global Services.

Matt is the author of *Virtualizing Microsoft Business Critical Applications on VMware vSphere* (VMware Press, 2013) and was a contributing author on *Mastering VMware vSphere 5.5* (Sybex, 2013). He is also a frequent contributor to the VMware Technology Network (VMTN) and has been an active blogger on virtualization since 2009. Matt has also authored articles for several industry publications on various virtualization topics. He has presented on the topic of virtualization at numerous industry events and his local VMware User Group in New Jersey.

Matt is very honored to have been named a VMware vExpert each year since 2010 as well as an EMC Elect in 2013. He also holds numerous industry certifications from VMware and Microsoft. Matt maintains a VMware virtualization–focused blog at www.thelowercasew.com and is active on Twitter at @mattliebowitz.

When Matt is not out trying to spread the virtualization love, he's happily playing with his two young kids, Tyler and Kaitlyn, and spending time with his wife, Joann.

Christopher Kusek had a unique opportunity presented to him in 2013: to take the leadership position responsible for theater-wide infrastructure operations for the war effort in Afghanistan. Leveraging his leadership skills and expertise in virtualization, storage, applications, and security, he's been able to provide enterprise-quality service while operating in an environment that includes the real and regular challenges of heat, dust, rockets, and earthquakes.

Christopher has over 20 years of experience in the industry, with virtualization experience running back to the pre-1.0 days of VMware. He has shared his expertise with many far and wide through conferences, presentations, #CXIParty, and sponsoring or presenting at community events and outings, whether Storage, VMworld, or cloud-focused.

Christopher is the author of *VMware vSphere 5 Administration Instant Reference* (Sybex, 2012). He is a frequent contributor to VMware Communities Podcasts and vBrownbag and has been an active blogger for over a decade.

A proud VMware vExpert and huge supporter of the program and the growth of the virtualization community, Christopher continues to find new ways to do outreach and spread the joys of virtualization and the transformative effect it has on individuals and businesses alike. Christopher was named an EMC Elect in 2013 and 2014 and continues to contribute to the storage community, both directly and indirectly, with analysis and regular review.

Christopher continues to update his blog with useful stories of virtualization and storage and his adventures throughout the world, which currently include stories of his times in Afghanistan. You can read his blog at http://pkguild.com or, more likely, catch him on Twitter (@cxi).

When Christopher is not busy changing the world one virtual machine at a time or FaceTiming with his family on the other side of the world, he's trying to find awesome vegan food in the world at large or somewhat edible food for a vegan in a war zone.

Rynardt Spies is a virtualization consultant with nine years of experience in the virtualization industry. His main focus today is on private and hybrid cloud infrastructures.

Rynardt is a frequent contributor to the VMware Technology Network (VMTN) and has been an active blogger on virtualization and other IT-related topics since April 2008. For his contributions to the VMware virtualization community, he has been named a VMware vExpert 2009, 2010, 2013 and 2014.

Rynardt holds VCP (VMware Certified Professional) certifications for VMware Virtual Infrastructure 3, vSphere 4, and vSphere 5. He also holds both administration and design VCAP (VMware Certified Advanced Professional) certifications on vSphere 4.

Rynardt maintains a virtualization-focused blog at `http://www.virtualvcp.com` and is active on Twitter at @rynardtspies.

Aside from virtualization, Rynardt has interests in aviation and flight simulation. When he is not playing with technology, he spends his time with his wife, Sarah, and two young kids, Lanie and Zachariah.

Contents at a Glance

Contents

Introduction

It's hard to believe how far we've come in the virtualization industry. What was once considered a niche technology used only for development and testing is now used for production workloads and even business-critical applications. The VMware vSphere platform is capable of supporting nearly any virtualized workload with very few obstacles standing in the way of close to 100 percent virtualization.

Today's workloads are more demanding than ever before. Email servers frequently require large amounts of memory and CPU resources in order to handle the large volume of email that we all deal with on a daily basis. Database servers often require large amounts of memory and storage resources, from a capacity perspective as well as performance, to meet the demands of a business. And newer technologies, such as virtual desktop infrastructure (VDI), have introduced significant demand for resources in vSphere environments.

To address the growing demand for more powerful virtual machines, VMware has continuously improved the vSphere platform. Virtual machines on vSphere can now have up to 64 virtual CPUs and 1 terabyte of memory, and vSphere has numerous storage enhancements to help deliver excellent storage performance. VMware has tested and proven that many large-scale workloads—like those associated with Microsoft Exchange Server, SQL Server, and Java— can perform as well or in some cases even better when virtualized than when deployed on physical servers.

People tend to remember the negative longer than they remember the positive, however, and that is true with the performance of virtual machines. If you tried to virtualize a big workload back in 2005 with VMware ESX 2.x, you may not have gotten the performance you got when it was on a physical server. Does that mean that it will still perform poorly today on vSphere 5.5? We know that you'll get much better performance, yet many choose to use stories of poor performance as a rationale for keeping workloads physical.

It's for this reason that we decided to write this book. We are in the trenches helping customers with their virtualization initiatives. We have seen with our own eyes that nearly all workloads can be virtualized and that the vSphere platform is capable of delivering performance close to or equal to bare metal deployments. The vSphere platform can scale to meet the challenge of today's largest workloads, and we intend to show you how.

This book covers the information you'll need to make sure your virtual machine performance meets the demands of your applications and your business. We hope that once you're through reading the book, you'll be convinced that concerns about performance should not hold you back from virtualizing any workload.

What Is Covered in This Book

This book covers the performance of your virtual infrastructure in two ways: the conceptual aspects and the practical aspects of performance.

We'll cover conceptual aspects by focusing on the design elements that are important to consider when creating your virtual infrastructure and virtual machines. We'll also show you how to troubleshoot performance problems, an important topic when virtualizing performance-critical applications. In addition, we'll cover a common set of tools you can keep in your "toolbox" that can help you benchmark performance, diagnose problems, and monitor ongoing performance in your environment.

We'll also cover the practical aspects of performance in your virtual infrastructure. This includes the specific considerations you'll need to understand when allocating CPU, memory, network, and storage to your virtual machines. Understanding these elements and properly allocating these resources can have a profound impact on the performance of all virtual machines in your environment. In each chapter, we'll also cover common troubleshooting methodologies you can use to diagnose and resolve CPU, memory, network, and storage performance problems.

Here is a glance at what's in each chapter:

Chapter 1: Performance Design   This chapter starts by focusing on the often overlooked design considerations necessary in making today's datacenters perform in a virtual environment. It covers principles to architect your applications using the resources already available in your datacenters while using real-world design examples.

Chapter 2: Building Your Toolbox   This chapter provides an in-depth look at the useful tools in every virtualization admin's toolbox. It covers capacity planning, performance benchmarking, simulation, and tools native to vSphere. This chapter provides insight into what these tools are used for and when to use them for troubleshooting, benchmarking, or analyzing performance.

Chapter 3: The Test Lab   In this chapter, you'll learn when and why to build a test lab. In addition, the chapter provides insight into tools and resources available to augment a lab. The information here is a self-contained solution set for your lab and troubleshooting needs.

Chapter 4: CPU   This chapter describes the basics of CPU scheduling in the ESXi platform and the hardware virtualization enhancements in today's modern processors. It also covers the CPU sizing that's recommended so you can provide good performance for virtual machines. Techniques for troubleshooting CPU performance problems are also covered.

Chapter 5: Memory   This chapter provides an overview of the various methods that VMware ESXi uses to manage memory, including how memory is shared among workloads and reclaimed from VMs in times of contention. It also covers the memory sizing that's recommended to provide good performance for virtual machines. Techniques for troubleshooting memory performance problems are also covered.

Chapter 6: Network   This chapter provides valuable insights into designing both physical and virtual networks to support your vSphere environment, including how host selection impacts your networking options. It also covers the recommended network allocations and configurations you'll need to know to provide good performance for virtual machines. Techniques for troubleshooting network performance problems are also covered.

Chapter 7: Storage   This chapter provides guidance on designing physical and virtual storage to meet performance demands. VMware has introduced numerous storage enhancements into the vSphere platform, and this chapter covers each of them and how they can be used to deliver good performance to virtual machines. Techniques for troubleshooting storage performance problems are also covered.

Who Should Buy This Book

This book is aimed at virtualization administrators, system administrators, and consultants/architects who are looking to learn how to get superior performance out of their virtual machines running on VMware vSphere. With that in mind, we have made some assumptions about the knowledge level of the reader—basic concepts of virtualization are not covered. To get the most out of this book, the reader should have the following knowledge and experience:

- A basic understanding of VMware vSphere, including features like vMotion and Distributed Resource Scheduler

- A basic understanding of networking and storage concepts

- Experience installing and configuring VMware vSphere, because many basic configuration tasks are not covered

- Experience designing, managing, and administering vSphere environments, because that will help provide a basis for the information provided in this book

If you are new to VMware vSphere, we highly recommend the book *Mastering VMware vSphere 5.5* (Sybex, 2014), which will provide you with all you need to know to become a vSphere expert.

How to Contact the Authors

We welcome feedback from you about this book or about books you'd like to see from us in the future.

You can reach Matt by email at matt.liebowitz@outlook.com, on Twitter at @mattliebowitz, or by visiting Matt's blog at www.thelowercasew.com.

You can reach Christopher by email at Christopher.kusek@pkguild.com, on Twitter at @cxi, or by visiting Christopher's blog at www.pkguild.com.

You can reach Rynardt by email at rynardt.spies@virtualvcp.com, on Twitter at @rynardtspies, or by visiting Rynardt's blog at www.virtualvcp.com.

Chapter 1

Performance Design

In the early days of VMware virtualization, we were all subscribed to one core set of beliefs: virtualization was a great tool to run multiple instances of nonimportant workloads on a single server. The stories always tended to start like this: "We tried virtualization with our mission-critical and performing workloads years ago and it ran horribly, so we don't virtualize those." Not everyone is willing to state exactly what year it was, but in pretty much every case they're talking about the first couple of releases of VMware. This particular distinction is important for two reasons: perception is reality, and people don't forget.

Digressing from virtualization for a moment, let's take a trip down memory lane back to the track and field of 1954. Those days weren't all that much different, with one minor exception: breaking the 4-minute mile record was an impossibility. Hundreds of years had passed with the belief that running the distance of one mile took a minimum of 4 minutes. Then on May 6, 1954, Roger Bannister did the impossible, breaking the 4-minute mile barrier.

But what does this have to do with virtualization, let alone performance considerations of designing VMware systems? We've gone our entire careers with the understanding that virtualization and performance were at odds with each other, a sheer impossibility. The whole concept of virtualizing mission-critical applications was not even a possibility to be pondered. We tried it in 2005 and it didn't work, or we know someone who tried it and they said, "No, it doesn't work; it's impossible."

Here's the good news: those barriers have been broken—shattered in fact. Virtualization is now synonymous with performance. In fact, virtualization can help drive even further levels of performance the likes of which would cause your physical systems to whimper. This book will help you take those old beliefs to your peers, colleagues, associates, and bloggers and put it all into perspective and context.

In the following chapters, we'll go through the depth and breadth of these perceived notions of performance-limiting areas so that we dispel old beliefs about virtualization and performance and focus on the reality of today with VMware vSphere. Most important, with discrete lessons, examples, and valuable scenarios of how to achieve performance within your virtualization environment, you'll walk away with information you won't forget, enabling you to experience virtualization and all its wonders for your most miniscule and most performance-critical and mission-critical applications.

In this chapter we look at:

◆ Starting simple

◆ Establishing a baseline

◆ Architecting for the application

◆ Considering licensing requirements

◆ Integrating virtual machines

◆ Understanding design considerations

Starting Simple

When it comes to design, people often begin by focusing on how difficult it is and start by over-complicating things. Designing for performance in a VMware vSphere environment is no different. As with any design, there are a number of components that when treated together can be seen as a complex model likely to leave one overwhelmed by the challenges at hand. But you'll find that when broken up into discrete components such as CPU, memory, network, and storage, the entire architecture and ultimately its performance can be far more manageable. But where do we get started?

Determine Parameters

The first challenge when it comes to designing your environment for performance is determining what the parameters of the environment require in order to fulfill your needs. This is often translated into performance service-level agreements (SLAs) but may carry with it a number of other characteristics. Poorly defined or nonexistent SLAs commonly provision the maximum available resources into virtual machines, which can result in wasted resources, ultimately impacting your performance and the ability to meet any established SLAs.

For example, the typical behavior when provisioning SQL Server in a virtual machine is to allocate two or four virtual CPUs (vCPUs); 4, 8, or 16 GB of RAM; a sufficient amount of disk space on a RAID 1 set; and multiple 1 Gb NICs or 10 Gb interfaces. This is considered acceptable because it's often how physical machines will be deployed and provisioned. With little regard for what the application profile is, this typical configuration will spread from vSphere cluster to vSphere cluster, becoming a baseline established and set forth by database administrators (DBAs).

Not to disregard applications that truly meet or exceed that usage profile, but that should not be the de facto standard when it comes to an application profile design. Based on the latest VMware Capacity Planner analysis of >700,000 servers in customer production environments, SQL Server typically runs on two physical cores with an average CPU utilization of <6 percent (with 85 percent of servers below 10 percent and 95 percent of servers below 30 percent). The average SQL Server machine has 3.1 GB of memory installed with only 60 percent used, using an average of 20 I/O operations per second, or IOPS (with over 95 percent of servers below 100 IOPS), and last, an average network usage of 400 kilobytes per second (KBps) in network traffic.

Suffice it to say you could comfortably get by with a majority of your SQL Server installations running with 1vCPU, 2 GB of RAM, and on SATA disk. This is not to say that all of your servers will meet these criteria, but most of them likely will. This becomes important as you start to set the criteria for the starting "default template" to work from for a majority of your application profiles.

Continuing on the theme of starting simple, there are a few lessons that can help you get started down the road to meeting and exceeding your performance needs without having to invest months and months into testing. When working with a particular application, start by referring to vendor support policies, recommendations, and best practices. "Sure," you're thinking, "Isn't that what this book is for, to give me recommendations and best practices?" Yes and no. Vendor support and best practices can change, often in response to updates, new releases, announcements, advances in hardware, and so on. So the best practices and recommendations for an AMD Opteron processor may differ from those for the latest Intel Xeon processor. Be sure to use these principles as a guide to ensure that you're asking the right questions, looking down the right paths, and applying the right rules when it comes to your architectural design, and with that knowledge in hand, you can easily handle the latest update to a CPU or a network card.

Architect for the Application

The second lesson when it comes to starting simple is to architect for the application and not for the virtualization solution, but to keep it scalable as projects require. Today's architectural decisions impact future flexibility necessary for growth. We'll go into greater depth on this later in this chapter, but we want to stress how relevant and important it is to remember that virtualization without application is just data consolidation with no value. In the end you're virtualizing applications into discrete containers that carry with them their own use cases and requirements, not building a comprehensive virtualization factory and cluster to hopefully house whatever you put into it.

Assess Physical Performance

The third thing you'll need to do is to sit back and pretend you're doing everything physically, and then do it virtually. A lot of people blindly enter into virtualization either assuming the system will be slower because it's "virtual" or expecting it to operate the same as it would if it were physical, and they unintentionally undersize and underarchitect things. Both of these choices can lead you down a dangerous path that will result in hair loss and virtualization regret. If you are able to garner a certain level of performance out of your application when running it physically but you give it fewer resources virtually, you're likely to get diminished results. Thus, understand the profiles of your applications and your servers, what their actual requirements are, and how they perform before you virtualize them instead of relying on perception after the fact with few or no metrics to help quantify.

Start with Defaults

And last, in the effort of keeping things simple, the fourth step to getting started is defaults, defaults, defaults, and best practices. They exist for a reason: garden variety simplicity. Designing with both in mind will help prevent unnecessary support cases. Unless you have a critical application that requires very unique and specific optimization that you gleaned by following the best practices and recommendations from lesson one, start with defaults. You can always modify the defaults and go from there when you have an unknown and untested application or use case. Operating within the realm of defaults enables you to begin to establish a baseline of the performance characteristics of your cluster and of your design. Don't hesitate to test things, but it shouldn't take you months to go through those iterative tests.

We cannot stress enough that establishing a baseline of predictability to meet your SLAs is important for your application profiles, but start small and work your way up larger as opposed to deploying large and trying to scale back from there.

Establishing a Baseline

The preceding sections provided examples of guidelines used for establishing a baseline. What exactly is a baseline, though, when it comes to VMware vSphere? A baseline is a series of predictable characteristics based upon what infrastructure you have in place for your CPU, memory, network, and storage.

Something you may realize quickly after designing and architecting your application is that once you start to establish a baseline, you've overprovisioned. Don't let the fact that you will likely overprovision 99 percent of your environment discourage you; the fact that you're reading this book is a sure sign that you're trying to get help for this!

There is no right or wrong baseline for your virtual machine and your applications. The exception is when you have anomalous conditions that should be treated as just that, an anomaly that, depending upon the characteristics, this book should help you identify and resolve. So without further ado, let's get down to the business of your baseline.

Baseline CPU Infrastructure

From an infrastructure standpoint, you are typically choosing your servers based upon the number of cores and CPUs it will support and the number of memory slots it can handle. From these architectural decisions you're able to dictate the maximum number of vCPUs your VMware vSphere cluster can support as well as the maximum amount of memory that will be available to your virtual machines. It will be these decisions that enable you to establish what the maximum configurations of a virtual machine will support.

As an example, if you're repurposing older equipment that has a maximum of four cores available per server and is maxed out at 16 GB of RAM, you can reliably guarantee that you'll be unable to provision a single virtual machine with 32 vCPUs and 64 GB of RAM. So quickly, at a glance, your virtual configuration can only fall short of the resources available in your largest vSphere host—remember, vSphere and the overhead it reserves for VMs requires available resources as well.

Once you've established the maximum you're able to support, you'll quickly start to realize that your acceptable minimum is typically leaps and bounds below what you believe it to be. In the process of establishing a baseline of your applications, you will more often than not find that the "manufacturer suggested best practices" are conservative at best—and downright fraudulent at worst!

Let's take this example down into the weeds a moment if we can. How many times have you been told that an application requires a certain amount of resources because it is going to be ever so busy, only to find when you dive down into it that those resources go underutilized?

So does this imply that there is a best configuration when it comes to defining how many vCPUs you should assign to your application? Let's dig a little deeper into what exactly the characteristics of vCPU data can mean. You may notice in Figure 1.1 that the primary relevant data surrounding CPUs are number of CPUs, CPU capacity, CPU shares, CPU limit, and CPU reservations. Left to its own devices, your infrastructure can comfortably focus on the number of CPUs you assign a host and whether you specify any shares or limits; in most cases you can get by entirely on paying attention to the number of CPUs you assign the host and its workload.

FIGURE 1.1
Workload overview

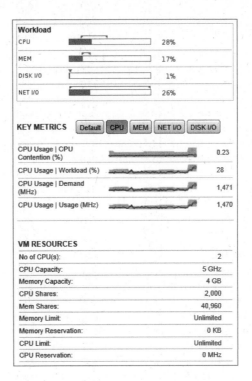

Analyzing CPU usage, contention, and workload can help to establish your application baseline. It is an important distinction to point out that in fact a watched CPU *will* spike, so it is best to have data collected passively over time using a monitoring tool like esxtop, vCenter Operations Manager, or the built-in performance tool in vCenter. We've seen many users report that their application is underprovisioned because they loaded up Windows Task Manager and it showed the CPU spike; not only is that bound to happen, it is expected.

Now the most important part of monitoring your CPU utilization is going to be sitting back and *not* tweaking, modifying, or touching the number of shares or cores you have allocated. We know that's like being offered a cookie and being told to wait, but it is important to be patient in order to understand just what your application's use-case baseline is.

Author Christopher Kusek shared a little story about how he went about testing out these very steps to baseline an application. As engineers and architects we like to be extremely conservative in our estimates, but by the same token we want to use only the resources that are required. He had an application that can be pretty intensive, a monitoring tool that would collect data from his over 100 vCenter servers and the thousands of ESXi hosts that operated within those datacenters. Because it was fairly hefty, he felt that the initial two vCPUs and 8 GB of memory he allocated it was not up to snuff. So as this was an IT tool that could afford an outage whenever he deemed fit, he increased the number of vCPUs to eight and the memory up to 16 GB.

What this enabled was the ability to see at what peak the system would operate over a period of time (establishing the baseline) without impacting the performance of the application. He chose to take advantage of historical data collection and reporting, leveraging vCenter

Operations Management and the Performance tab of vCenter to collect this data. Something VMware vSphere is particularly good about is figuring out what it needs and sticking with it. In a short amount of time with this unpredictable application, it was established that the system would operate efficiently with a maximum of five vCPUs and 12 GB of memory.

At this point, Christopher tuned the system down to those requirements, and with his baseline set, he knew not only what the operational workload was, but also what the expected peaks were. He was then able to expect, without undersizing and impacting performance and without oversizing and wasting resources, what it really took to run this particular application.

What you will find is that allocation of vCPUs can be one of the most important aspects of your virtualization environment, especially when you consider the CPU scheduler covered in Chapter 4, "CPU." This is definitely one area not to skimp on in terms of aggregate MHz but at the same time not to be wasteful in terms of number of provisioned logical vCPUs (coscheduling complexity of >1 or 2 vCPUs = +++%RDY%) because it truly is a finite asset that cannot be "shared" without performance implications.

Memory

Memory is an infinite resource that we never have enough of. When it comes to establishing your memory baseline, you're typically going to see a pretty consistent pattern. All things being equal, you will find that if your application, workload, and use case do not significantly change, the amount of memory consumed and required will begin to be predictable.

Knowing the importance of memory in an infrastructure, VMware has made numerous investments over the years. Whether through memory overcommit, compression, or ballooning, this is one resource that is designed to be allocated. But it bears mentioning that just because you can allocate 128 GB of RAM on a system with only 64 GB of RAM doesn't mean you always should. What this means for your applications is that establishing baseline memory is a delicate balance. If you prescribe too little memory, your system ends up swapping to disk; if you prescribe too much memory, you end up overprovisioning the system significantly. This delicate balance is often seen as the sweet spot of memory allocation. For most people this tends to be pretty arbitrary, depending upon the application and the operating system. This was pretty easily done when running 32-bit applications because the system would be unable to address beyond 3 to 4 GB of RAM, encouraging a fairly consistent design of 4 GB of memory being allocated.

When it comes to 64-bit operating systems and applications capable of using large amounts of memory, there is a tendency to design as if you were running it physically and assign arbitrary amounts of resources. As a result, a virtual machine that may only require 512 MB or 768 MB of RAM will often be allocated with 1, 2, 4, or more GB of RAM. A step further than that when it comes to overarchitected and overprescribed applications like Exchange 2010, the minimum may come in at 12, 24, or even 36 GB of RAM.

Figure 1.2 shows a sample workload of an Exchange 2003 server with 4 GB of memory allocated to it.

FIGURE 1.2
Memory overall workload percentage

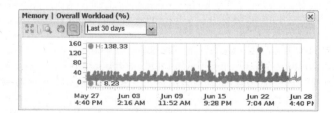

While analyzing and establishing the baseline of this application over the course of 30 days, the low at ~327 MB and an average high would peak at approximately 1.6 GB of memory allocated. All workloads may experience a "spike" as this system did, demanding well over 5.6 GB of the available 4 GB, but anomalies are just that, and they can be expected to sometimes be well outside of the norms.

Fortunately for us, the method in which VMware employs its memory enhancements (see Chapter 5, "Memory") allows us to take an unexpected spike, as it did on June 22 (see Figure 1.2), without it having a devastating impact upon the operations of the virtual machine and the underlying application.

One area VMware does not skimp on is providing you with more than enough insight into whether you're making the right decisions in your architecture and what the metrics of those decisions are. Within vCenter, you're able to get down to the details of just how much memory the application you're running is using, as shown in Figure 1.3.

FIGURE 1.3

vCenter memory usage

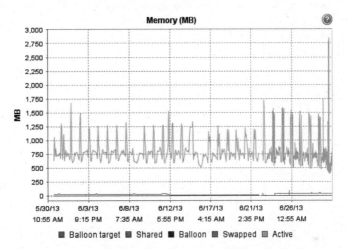

At first glance you'd be able to pretty readily tell that your application over the prior 30 days has been running well under 2 GB of usage even at its high points. Use these tools at your disposal, such as the Performance tab, on your VMs within vCenter to get a comfortable feel for your baseline. Unlike having physical servers, where procurement is required to make critical changes with virtualization, you can simply shut down your host, add additional memory, and bring it back online if you happened to underprovision it in the first place.

It is important to identify that you can never be "wrong" when it comes to allocating your memory to your virtual machines. You might provision too little, or you might considerably overprovision the memory to a particular guest, but none of those decisions is set in stone. If you need to go back and either increase or decrease the amount of memory you provided, that should be the least of your worries.

Network

Knowing what your limits are when it comes to networking is especially important. It's extremely important to start with a solid foundation when it comes to your network. Taking advantage of features such as VLAN trunking (802.1q) and static link aggregation (802.3ad) when possible will help you keep your network infrastructure more virtual and reliable.

Whether you're building your networking infrastructure from scratch or repurposing existing gear, we cannot stress enough the importance of knowing your limits. If your application is latency sensitive, throwing more virtual NICs at the problem may not solve it as much as co-locating the servers that are communicating with each other on the same cluster and vSwitch. Networking can often make or break an infrastructure due to misconfiguration or general misunderstanding. Know what the aggregate potential of your VMware vSphere cluster is, including what the lowest common denominator is. You can readily establish a network baseline of "1 Gb links" if you find that the majority of your workloads are barely using less than 1 Mb, let alone a full 1 Gb link.

Often, networking problems can be overlooked when troubleshooting or understanding some troubles. Author Christopher Kusek recalls that he once worked with a VMware cluster where backups were running quickly except for on a few virtual machines used to back up large databases. A request was made to provision additional backup servers because the backups were running slowly and the client wanted to split the load up, assuming it would make it faster. It turned out that virtual machines being backed up that were co-located with the backup server were moving "super fast" because they were operating across the same vSwitch and able to transfer at 10 Gb, but the other virtual machines resided on separate nodes in the cluster and had to go across a slower 1 Gb link.

When it comes to networking in VMware, your network will often be limited by and only as fast as its weakest link. For example, due to misconfiguration, you may end up using a management network interface at 1 Gb or slower or a networking configuration on an uplink switch. However, if you follow a few standard rules and practices, you can prevent these problems on your network.

Networking tends to differ pretty heavily from decisions you make around CPU and memory because you are usually deciding how many MHz and MB you're assigning an application from a "pool" of available computing power. The decision around networking is only how many interfaces to assign an application. Unless your application requires access to multiple networks with different routes and VLANs, the answer to that will almost always be one interface.

What this translates into, as seen in Figure 1.4, is that unlike your memory and CPU workloads, which in peak moments can exceed 100 percent, network has a hard ceiling after which everything leveraging the network in the VM will either slow down or just drop the packets. Simply throwing more NICs at the virtual machine will usually not resolve this, especially if it is network bound by the ESXi host.

FIGURE 1.4
Network workload percentage and network usage rate

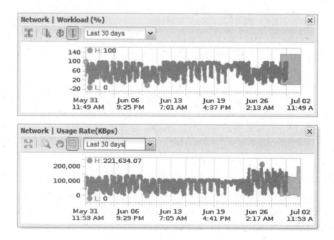

This particular file server was under pretty significant network stress continuously. When additional network links were introduced on the ESXi host system, the virtual machine was not only able to relieve some of that stress, it also had real-world user implications. At peak times, network bandwidth would drop to less than 1 KBps for end users, after providing the additional links even under the same peak stress as before the performance would soar to MB/s speeds, as you can see in Figure 1.5.

FIGURE 1.5
Networking file copy example

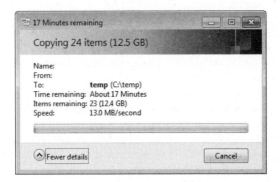

Networking will continue to be a challenge we all suffer through, usually limited more by our physical architecture than we ever will by our virtual design decisions. All you can do is make the best of what you have and identify what will benefit your applications best. In Chapter 6, "Network," we'll show you how to better make those decisions on how to work with what you have and how to identify situations where taking into account locality of reference and co-location of virtual machines will serve you better than merely throwing more hardware at the situation.

Storage

When it comes to establishing the baseline of a virtualized environment, one of the most over-looked areas is often storage. One of the greatest misconceptions is that because you switched from physical servers to virtual servers you should be able to skimp on the number of spindles required to handle the IO profile. Quite the opposite is typically the case.

While most physical servers will use less than 5 percent of their CPU potential and only a portion of their physical memory, and only touch the surface of their network cards, if a physical server was using 1,900 IOPS to perform its workload, it will continue to use 1,900 IOPS when it is switched to the virtual. Establishing your baseline when it comes to storage is even more impor-tant. Identify just how many IOPS you were using before, decide if there are characteristics of your applications that have particular special needs, and make sure that is reflected in the datas-tores supporting the storage for the apps.

While many of the characteristics of your configuration may change as you make design con-siderations for virtualization, how you design for storage isn't likely to change nearly as much as you think.

The same is true if your application was using 10 IOPS when it was physical; it will continue to use just as few in the virtual world. This also encourages you to cram a whole bunch of low-I/O and low-utilization previously physical machines into even fewer virtual machines. With the exception of some aggressive applications and workloads like databases, you'll come to find the demands of the majority of applications are often more space constrained than IOPS constrained.

VMware has made a number of investments and development into storage over the years, recognizing its extreme importance to the delivery of operational workloads. Features such as Storage DRS (SDRS), Storage vMotion, VAAI, VASA, VSA, vFlash, VSAN, Storage I/O Control (SIOC), and multipathing policies take simple SAN or NAS provisioned disks to the next level for your virtual infrastructure.

With these virtualization-enhanced storage capabilities, you're able to maximize on-demand and online modifications of your virtual machine environment. What this truly enables you to do is establish your lowest tier of storage as the "default" for virtual machines and then move up a tier on a disk-by-disk basis if required by taking advantage of Storage vMotion online without application downtime.

When it comes to identifying the baseline of your application, operating systems tend to have a much lower set of requirements than performance-driven applications. Take the graph in Figure 1.6, for example. The 21 operating systems running against this single disk tend to be averaging around 10 IOPS apiece, running as high as 16 IOPS at their peak. That's hardly anything to be overly concerned about when it comes to storage design to meet the performance needs of these application OS disks.

FIGURE 1.6
OS aggregate IOPS

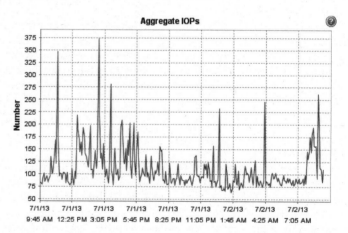

But the story tends to get a bit murkier when it comes to the baseline of applications that the business is reliant upon. In the graph shown in Figure 1.7, the average lows are below those of the operating systems seen in Figure 1.6, but the peak workload is significantly higher, requiring an extensive storage architecture to be able to respond to the demands of the application.

The architecture and design of storage is very similar to networking because these investments are usually not made lightly. Storage architecture, whether designed well or not, will usually stick with you for a minimum of three to five years, depending upon your organization's depreciation and refresh cycle.

Fortunately, the intelligence of the storage capabilities within VMware and guidance identified in Chapter 7, "Storage," can help you to take your storage architecture to the next level, whether through redesign and re-architecture or by simply making some slight modifications to take advantage of your existing investment.

FIGURE 1.7
Application aggregate IOPS

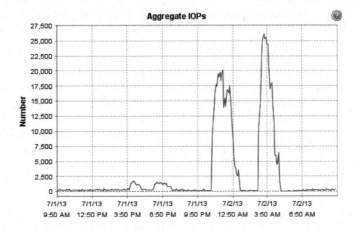

Architecting for the Application

You've gone through the effort to build a VMware vSphere cluster and have established a baseline of the capabilities of your ESXi servers. Now you're ready to start populating it, right? Not exactly.

It is important at this point that you ensure that your architecture and even your templates are designed with the applications in mind and not the solution. The reason you do not architect solely based on your architecture is that given the ability, your application owners will request the maximum available that your solution supports. In other words, if they knew they could get a 32-vCPU server with 1 TB of RAM and 64 TB of disk space, even if only to host a 32-bit server that can't support more than 4 GB of RAM, they will. Then the requests would never stop coming in and your system would collapse in inefficiency.

At this point it becomes extremely important to define the applications and start characterizing their workloads. This matters whether you're deploying a web server, a highly performing database server, a utility server, or an AppDev vApp consumed by your development team; the characteristics of performance can be predictable and the expectation of the template standardized upon.

To begin, people will often establish a catalog of the services they offer to their end users, similar to that mentioned previously. Then from within this catalog a breakdown is established to meet the most likely characteristics as needed by the user community in the form of CPU, memory, network, and storage needs. As necessary, some of these workloads will be broken up into subsets of small, medium, large, or custom, as in the following examples:

Small: 1 vCPU, 2 GB of RAM
Medium: 2 vCPU, 4 GB of RAM
Large: 4 vCPU, 8 GB of RAM
Custom: Up to 64 vCPU with 1 TB of RAM

The rules about characterizing your applications and workloads aren't set in stone, but should be determined through your design and architectural considerations. Using tools like VMware Capacity Planner, Microsoft Assessment and Planning Toolkit, VMware vCenter

Operations Manager, and some of the native tools like the vCenter Performance tab and Perfmon, can help you take these characteristics from smoke and mirrors or app owners' mad dreams to cold, hard operational facts.

It is important to remember that if you undersize a virtual machine and an application—whether because you were unsure of the workload or because the number of users of a system increased, demanding additional resources—you can correct that by simply taking the system down and adding additional resources. We've yet to meet an app owner who complained when we visited them and said, "I noticed your application is actually underperforming and could use additional memory or another vCPU. Would you mind if I shut down your server and provide you with more resources?" They usually jump at the chance and establish a hard and fast downtime window for you to make those changes, if not let you do it immediately.

Yet, visit that same application owner and try to reclaim six of those eight vCPUs you allocated them and not only will they never find the time to shut down the system, they'll stop taking your calls! To head this issue off at the pass, you may want to hot-add on all of your virtual machines. Unfortunately, not all operating systems support hot-add of CPU and memory, and there are numerous caveats to consider, covered in Chapter 4 and Chapter 5, respectively.

Considering Licensing Requirements

The first thing you might be thinking of is what does licensing have to do with the design phase of your virtual infrastructure? Licensing has everything to do with the architecture and design of your vSphere environment. As you make decisions about how many virtual CPUs you want to allocate to your templates and ultimately to your applications, this can have a direct impact on how much you'll be paying in licensing to support that particular application.

When you have an application that is licensed on a per-vCPU basis, if you're able to meet and exceed the SLAs of that application with fewer vCPUs, you will be saving hard dollars, which translates into a more cost-effective and efficient infrastructure. The following table gives you a sense of hard vCPU limits when it comes to license versions.

	VSPHERE ESSENTIALS KITS		VSPHERE WITH OPERATIONS MANAGEMENT ACCELERATION KITS		
	Essentials	Essentials Plus	Standard	Enterprise	Enterprise Plus
Includes					
vSphere	6 CPUs	6 CPUs	6 CPUs	6 CPUs	6 CPUs
vCenter Server	1 instance vCenter Server Essentials	1 instance vCenter Server Essentials	1 instance vCenter Server Standard	1 instance vCenter Server Standard	1 instance vCenter Server Standard
vSphere Data Protection Advanced				6 CPUs	6 CPUs
Entitlements per CPU License					
vCPU	8-way	8-way	8-way	32-way	64-way
Features					
Health Monitoring and Performance Analytics			•	•	•
Capacity Management and Optimization			•	•	•
Operations Dashboard and Root Cause Analysis			•	•	•
Hypervisor	•	•	•	•	•
vMotion		•	•	•	•
High Availability		•	•	•	•
Data Protection and Replication		•	•	•	•
vShield Endpoint		•	•	•	•
vSphere Storage Appliance		•			
Fault Tolerance (1 vCPU)			•	•	•
Storage vMotion			•	•	•
Distributed Resource Scheduler and Distributed Power Management				•	•
Storage APIs for Array Integration, Multipathing				•	•
Distributed Switch					•
Storage DRS and Profile-Driven Storage					•
I/O Controls (Network and Storage) and SR-IOV					•
Host Profiles and Auto Deploy					•

Source: www.vmware.com/files/pdf/vsphere_pricing.pdf

This can really start to make sense when you move beyond consolidation and simple virtualization of your nonessential applications and focus on your mission-critical apps, which have greater demands and needs. Consider the demands and needs of virtualizing your MSSQL, Exchange, Oracle, and SAP servers. You may be able to get away with fewer than eight vCPUs in some of those application profiles, and you wouldn't want to be without vMotion, HA, Data Protection, and vSphere Replication.

As your environment moves beyond simple consolidation and into a full-blown, highly available virtualized architecture, it is inherently beneficial to review and identify what business needs align with feature sets available in only the more advanced versions of vSphere. In later chapters you'll find discussions of features that are only available in certain versions of vSphere. This will help provide justification to align your business needs to the feature sets.

Integrating Virtual Machines

As we dive into the points of integration of virtual machine scalability, we take a deeper look at some of the technologies that have made VMware ESX a market leader for the past decade. Three key aspects of that success have been the use of the technologies VMware vMotion, Distributed Resource Scheduler (DRS), and High Availability (HA).

Virtual Machine Scalability

We've touched on the topic of virtual machine scalability in various sections as individual discussions. The topic of how many vCPUs and how much memory to assign and how the licensable implications and limitations will drive that ultimate scalability has been discussed briefly. In a majority of situations you'll find the topic of your virtual machines needing scalability insignificant. Where this tends to rear its ugly head is when an application has needs beyond what you're able to support or provide.

Often scalability is a demand under the circumstances of misconfiguration or negligence, such as, for example, a database server with poorly written queries that execute far more work than necessary or a mailbox server designed and architected to operate with 1,000 mailbox users and is overallocated to have 5,000 users. In some of these conditions, throwing more resources at the server may help, but there is no guarantee that solution will solve the problem.

Whether you're provisioning guests at the bare minimum required for them to operate or providing them the maximum resources available in a single ESXi host, the tools are in the box to allow you to grow and shrink as your applications demand. Some of the tools that make that a possibility are explained in the following sections.

vMotion

VMware vSphere's vMotion remains one of the most powerful features of virtualization today. With vMotion, you can perform various infrastructure maintenance tasks during business hours rather than having to wait until the wee hours of the morning or weekends to upgrade BIOS or firmware or do something as simple as add more memory to a host. vMotion requires that each underlying host have a CPU that uses the same instruction set, because after all, moving a running virtual machine (VM) from one physical host to another without any downtime is a phenomenal feat.

VMware VMs run on top of the Virtual Machine File System (VMFS) or NFS. Windows still runs on New Technology Filesystem (NTFS), but the underlying filesystem is VMFS-5 or VMFS-3. VMFS allows for multiple access, and that is how one host can pass a running VM to another host without downtime or interruptions. It is important to realize that even momentary downtime can be critical for applications and databases. Zero downtime when moving a VM from one physical host to another physical host is crucial.

Unfortunately, there is no way to move from Intel to AMD or vice versa. In the past, there were even issues going from an older Intel CPU to a newer Intel CPU that since have been mitigated with the introduction of Enhanced vMotion Compatibility (EVC), shown in Figure 1.8.

FIGURE 1.8
The Change EVC
Mode dialog box

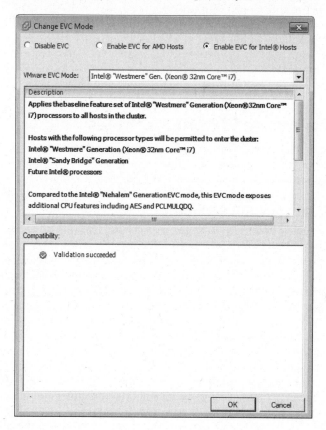

vMotion technology requires shared storage, but the virtual machine files do not move from that shared storage during the logical transition. If, for example, you have to change the virtual machine's physical location, you must first power down the VM and then "migrate" it from one logical unit number (LUN) or hard drive to another LUN or hard drive. Or you can use Storage vMotion, allowing the virtual machine to move between hosts and storage.

A caveat to vMotion is that traditional intrusion detection systems (IDSs) and intrusion prevention systems (IPSs) may not work as originally designed. Part of the reason for this is that the traffic of VMs that are communicating with one another inside a host never leaves the host and therefore cannot be inspected. Virtual appliances are developed to address this concern. They have the ability to run side-by-side VMs.

Since uptime is important, VMware developed Storage vMotion so that the physical location of a running virtual machine's storage can be changed, again without any downtime and without losing any transactional information. Storage vMotion is very exciting because one of the reasons that virtualization is the hottest technology in IT today is the flexibility and mobility it brings to applications in the datacenter (compared with running servers the traditional way in a physical environment).

There are other ways to leverage the technology. Virtual machines can be moved on the fly from shared storage to local storage if you need to perform maintenance on shared storage or if LUNs have to be moved to other hosts. Imagine moving a server with no downtime or sweat on your part by simply dragging a virtual machine onto another server in the cluster.

Made available in vSphere 5.1 was the ability to use vMotion without shared storage, with a few caveats and considerations:

◆ Hosts must be ESXi 5.1 or later.

◆ It does not work with DRS.

◆ It counts against the limits for both vMotion and Storage vMotion, consuming a network resource and 16 datastore resources.

Distributed Resource Scheduler

Distributed Resource Scheduler (DRS) helps you load-balance workloads across a vSphere cluster. Advanced algorithms constantly analyze the cluster environment and leverage vMotion to migrate a running VM from one host to another without any downtime. You can specify that DRS perform these actions automatically. Say, for instance, that a VM needs more CPU or memory and the host it is running on lacks those resources. With the automatic settings you specify, DRS will use vMotion to move the VM to another host that has more resources available. DRS can be set to automatically make needed adjustments any time of day or night or to issue recommendations instead. Two circumstances that often trigger such events are when an Active Directory server is used a lot in the morning for logins and when backups are run. A DRS-enabled cluster shares all the CPU and memory bandwidth as one unified pool for the VMs to use.

DRS is extremely important because in the past, VMware administrators had to do their best to analyze the needs of their VMs, often without a lot of quantitative information. DRS changed the way the virtualization game was played and revolutionized the datacenter. You can now load VMs onto a cluster and the technology will sort out all the variables in real time and make necessary adjustments. DRS is easy to use, and many administrators boast about how many vMotions their environments have completed since inception (see Figure 1.9).

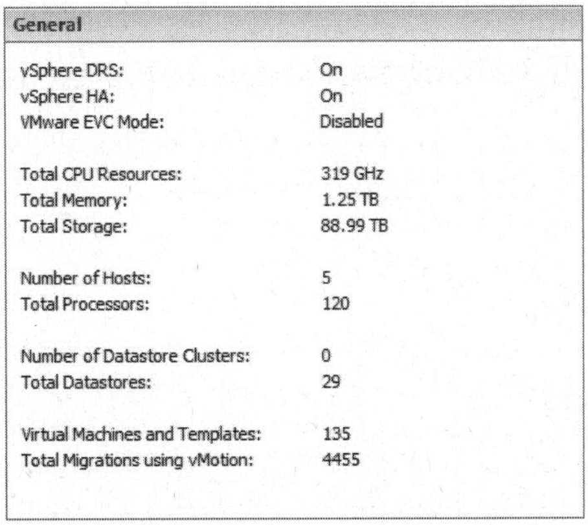

FIGURE 1.9
This depicts all vMotions, including those invoked by DRS

General	
vSphere DRS:	On
vSphere HA:	On
VMware EVC Mode:	Disabled
Total CPU Resources:	319 GHz
Total Memory:	1.25 TB
Total Storage:	88.99 TB
Number of Hosts:	5
Total Processors:	120
Number of Datastore Clusters:	0
Total Datastores:	29
Virtual Machines and Templates:	135
Total Migrations using vMotion:	4455

For example, let's say an admin virtualizes a Microsoft Exchange server, a SQL server, an Active Directory server, and a couple of heavily used application servers and puts them all on one host in the cluster. The week before, another admin virtualized several older Windows servers that were very lightweight; because those servers used so few resources, the admin put them on another host. At this point, the two hosts are off-balanced on their workloads. One has too little to do because its servers have low utilization and the other host is getting killed with heavily used applications. Before DRS, a third admin would have had to look at all the servers running on these two hosts and determine how to distribute the VMs evenly across them. Administrators would have had to use a bit of ingenuity, along with trial and error, to figure out how to balance the needs of each server with the underlying hardware. DRS analyzes these needs and moves VMs when they need more resources so that you can attend to other, more pressing issues.

High Availability

When CIOs and management types begin learning about virtualization, one of their most common fears is "putting all their eggs in one basket." "If all our servers are on one server, what happens when that server fails?" This is a smart question to ask, and one that VMware prepared for when it revealed the HA, or High Availability, feature of VMware Infrastructure 3. A virtual infrastructure is managed by vCenter, which is aware of all of the hosts that are in its control and all the VMs that are on those hosts. vCenter installs and configures HA, but at that point, the ESXi hosts monitor heartbeats and initiate failovers and VM startup. This is fundamentally important to understand because vCenter can be one of the VMs that has gone down in an outage and HA will still function, providing a master HA host, aka failover coordinator, is still available.

VMware recommends a strategy referred to as an N+1 (as a minimum, not an absolute), dictated by architectural requirements. This simply means that your cluster should include enough hosts (N) so that if one fails, there is enough capacity to restart the VMs on the other host(s). Shared storage among the hosts is a requirement of HA. When a host fails and HA starts, there is a small window of downtime, roughly the same amount you might expect from a reboot. If the organization has alerting software, a page or email message might be sent indicating a problem, but at other times, this happens so quickly that no alerts are triggered. The goal of virtualization is to keep the uptime of production servers high; hosts can go down, but if servers keep running, you can address the challenge during business hours.

Understanding Design Considerations

In this last part of the chapter, we go on to look into what you've learned in the previous sections and apply those principles to choosing a server and determining whether you ought to scale up or scale out.

Choosing a Server

When it comes to choosing a server, there is no right or wrong answer, but hopefully with a little guidance you can take the appropriate steps to end up with the best solution for your infrastructure. The question of reusing versus replacing your servers will often come up, and the answer can entirely depend upon the age, warranty, and capability of the servers you plan to reuse. Thus, here are some cardinal rules to follow when it comes to determining your virtual architecture:

♦ Stay within the same CPU family or risk losing performance.

♦ Just because you have hardware to use doesn't mean you should.

♦ If it's out of warranty or not supported on the HCL, replace it.

Earlier we mentioned CPUs and CPU families in relation to EVC, and the discussion of CPU-aware load balancing in Chapter 4 will express the importance of CPU considerations when it comes to nonuniform memory access (NUMA). Keeping your CPU family the same will enable you to have VMs vMotion throughout the cluster without any complication or efforts on your part. By reusing older hardware, which may require EVC, you may be introducing more problems and need to troubleshoot more issues in your environment than if you had a more uniform virtual infrastructure. There is by no means anything wrong with reusing older hardware; you just need to consider whether the benefit of repurposing outweighs that of replacing it in power, cooling, performance, and space.

It is understandable if you found an old cache of 4xPort 1 Gb NICs that you don't want to go to waste, but given the choice of a single 10 Gb converged network adapter (CNA) or 10 1 Gb interfaces, for numerous reasons you should adopt the CNA. As you find yourself ripping out and replacing older infrastructure and servers, you'll find that your requirements for the number of cables and cards will greatly diminish. Physical servers that were required for resiliency of storage and connectivity to have a minimum of two 4xPort 1 Gb NICs and two 2xPort Fibre Channel connected to separate fabrics can now be replaced with a single pair of CNAs to provide both storage and network connectivity. Not only are the implications of power and cooling greatly reduced with fewer ports drawing power, but you also significantly reduce the number of cables required to be run and come out of your servers.

Last, if it is out of warranty or no longer on the Hardware Compatibility List (HCL), just replace it. Chances are, by the time that hardware has had the opportunity to drop out of warranty, or if it's somehow no longer on the HCL, it is not going to be a suitable candidate to be running your mission-critical infrastructure. Yes, it may be an acceptable fit for your lab (as we'll discuss in Chapter 3, "The Test Lab"), but this is not the time to try to get by with something you wouldn't relegate as a replacement for an otherwise equivalent physical workload.

Scaling Up vs. Scaling Out

Scaling up and scaling out takes the decisions you make choosing your server to the next level, partly deciding how many baskets you want to keep your eggs in but at the same time deciding how many different kinds of eggs you're talking about. You can ask 10 different people their opinion on whether you should scale up or out and you'll get 77 different answers. And that's perfectly okay; they're all completely right and yet likely wrong at the same time.

Whether to scale up or out really will fall into architectural decisions that you've made, haven't made, and do not have under your control. If you have many extremely high CPU and memory performance applications that require large amounts of both, you'll want to lean toward scaling up, whereas if your workload is pretty easily met and you have a good balance and load across your cluster, you may want to consider scaling out. It's important to consider that the more you scale out the more network and storage ports you'll need available, and if your environment is full or nearing full, the costs of scaling out might outweigh the benefits versus simply scaling up.

All things being equal though, consider the example of two clusters, one scaled up (Figure 1.10) and the other scaled out (Figure 1.11).

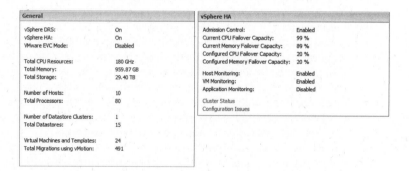

FIGURE 1.10
Scaled up

General		vSphere HA	
vSphere DRS:	On	Admission Control:	Enabled
vSphere HA:	On	Current CPU Failover Capacity:	98 %
VMware EVC Mode:	Disabled	Current Memory Failover Capacity:	61 %
		Configured CPU Failover Capacity:	20 %
Total CPU Resources:	319 GHz	Configured Memory Failover Capacity:	20 %
Total Memory:	1.25 TB		
Total Storage:	88.99 TB	Host Monitoring:	Enabled
		VM Monitoring:	Enabled
Number of Hosts:	5	Application Monitoring:	Disabled
Total Processors:	120		
		Cluster Status	
Number of Datastore Clusters:	0	Configuration Issues	
Total Datastores:	29		
Virtual Machines and Templates:	135		
Total Migrations using vMotion:	4455		

FIGURE 1.11
Scaled out

General		vSphere HA	
vSphere DRS:	On	Admission Control:	Enabled
vSphere HA:	On	Current CPU Failover Capacity:	99 %
VMware EVC Mode:	Disabled	Current Memory Failover Capacity:	89 %
		Configured CPU Failover Capacity:	20 %
Total CPU Resources:	180 GHz	Configured Memory Failover Capacity:	20 %
Total Memory:	959.87 GB		
Total Storage:	29.40 TB	Host Monitoring:	Enabled
		VM Monitoring:	Enabled
Number of Hosts:	10	Application Monitoring:	Disabled
Total Processors:	80		
		Cluster Status	
Number of Datastore Clusters:	1	Configuration Issues	
Total Datastores:	15		
Virtual Machines and Templates:	24		
Total Migrations using vMotion:	491		

The availability of additional hosts provides a wealth of benefits, including having a greater percentage of CPU and memory failover capacity. While in this example the scaled-up system has nearly twice as much CPU resources, their memory requirements, due to the increased number of memory slots, enable having the same or an even larger pool of addressable memory.

Without truly understanding your usage profile, application use cases, and more, no one can make an educated decision about whether scaling up or scaling out is appropriate for you, though fortunately, today's availability of high compute and large memory systems will often mean you need not choose.

Summary

This chapter started out by discussing the implications of architecting and designing your virtualization environment for performance, but if you're not new to virtualization, chances are you build your environments with consolidation in mind. These two need not be mutually exclusive. In fact, what started out as an experiment in consolidating your infrastructure may have accidentally evolved into a virtual infrastructure being used as a consolidation point, irrespective of the end state.

Hopefully, by this point you have a pretty stable foundation of what it will take to adapt your existing infrastructure or architect a new infrastructure to the point that it is capable of running your business's IT infrastructure. Over the next several chapters, we'll dive deeper into the specifics of what will make your infrastructure performance soar.

Chapter 2

Building Your Toolbox

At this point you should have a sense of design and architecture in mind and some methodologies to help you go about solving problems. The next step is to identify a series of tools that will not only help you validate what you know but also augment and improve the quality of your experience.

Some believe you're only as good as the tools in your toolbox, while others believe that experience trumps all. The fact is, great experience with a powerful set of tools will make you a force to be reckoned with. This chapter will cover various tools that you can use for monitoring utilization, measuring performance, and simulating load.

In this chapter we look at:

◆ Capacity planning tools

◆ Performance analysis tools

◆ Performance benchmarking tools

◆ Performance simulation tools

Capacity Planning Tools

Capacity planning is multifaceted, comprising planning for what to provision in your environment, analyzing what already exists as your environment grows, and scaling your capacity to meet changing demands. The following tools will help provide some insight into your environment as it grows and scales.

VMware Capacity Planner

VMware Capacity Planner is a useful tool that you can use to gain insight into resource utilization and develop a plan for server and service consolidation. To enable administrators to work with the VMware Capacity Planner, a data collector is installed onsite at the datacenter to collect hardware, software, utilization, and metrics information. This agentless data collection can then be scrubbed and made anonymous before being transmitted to a centralized information warehouse and presented via a dashboard.

One of the benefits of sending this data to the centralized host is that the Capacity Planner dashboard is able to provide reference data comparisons of like applications across the industry. This allows you to compare performance and workloads of applications to ensure that they'll continue to maintain the levels of performance expected when virtualized.

Through dashboards like this, the VMware Capacity Planner is able to provide extensive analysis and insights into your server's performance, which can help assist in determining what your long-term capacity needs will be.

While invaluable, the Capacity Planner is not a panacea for all problems; analysis and insight are still required to make sense of the data and how it impacts your organization. That is one of the reasons it cannot simply be downloaded by end users or administrators and used. To download and use VMware Capacity Planner, you must either engage a VMware Partner or, if you are a VMware Partner, you must go through a VMware Education course to be authorized to download and work with the tool.

Microsoft Assessment and Planning Toolkit

Microsoft Assessment and Planning Toolkit (MAP) is an agentless, automated, multiproduct planning and assessment tool for quicker and easier desktop, server, and cloud migrations. MAP is a free tool that is easy to deploy and use. You can use this tool to scan Microsoft operating systems and Microsoft applications, certain Linux distributions, Oracle, and VMware vCenter and ESXi.

MAP is able to provide detailed readiness assessment reports and executive proposals with extensive hardware and software information and actionable recommendations. For the purpose of this book, we'll be focusing on information relevant when assessing servers and applications that will run on a vSphere infrastructure.

One of the intrinsic benefits of the MAP tool is the comprehensive technical details and executive overviews the reporting features provide. MAP produces reports that show the utilization of all of the monitored servers over the monitoring period, breaking down the utilization into not only minimum, maximum, and average utililization but also 95th percentile utilization. The 95th percentile utilization is the utilization of the server 95 percent of the time during the monitoring period. Oftentimes if you take the average utilization for sizing purposes, you'll size your virtual machines either too low or too high. By using the 95th percentile for sizing, you get a more accurate picture of how the server performs most of the time and consequently a more accurately sized virtual machine.

Another benefit of MAP over using VMware Capacity Planner is that this tool assesses more than just physical and virtual machines; it can also review and assess application performance and viability of upgradability between versions of applications and operating systems. It is for this reason that these two tools are complementary and should be used in conjunction with each other instead of each by itself.

Finally, perhaps one of the best benefits of using MAP is that it is a completely free product. While VMware Capacity Planner requires that you go through VMware or a certified partner, MAP can be downloaded for free by anyone. MAP is also frequently updated, often receiving an update whenever a new version of Windows or any Microsoft enterprise product is released.

Using Capacity Planning Tools

Many of you are likely familiar with capacity planning tools, especially those who have taken on large server virtualization projects. Though these tools may have gained in popularity for server consolidation, they can be extremely useful for maintaining good performance of virtual machines in vSphere.

The following list provides some examples of where you can use these tools in your own environment:

♦ Use capacity planning tools before virtualizing any physical servers. By knowing the actual utilization of your physical servers, you can properly size them when migrating them to virtual machines. Don't simply take a server and virtualize it using the same configuration you would use if it were physical. If you have a physical server with eight CPU cores and 16 GB of RAM but it only actually uses two CPUs and 4 GB of RAM, why create a virtual machine that matches the physical configuration? Doing so would hurt consolidation ratios or, worse, potentially impact the performance of other virtual machines. Use capacity planning tools to understand the utilization and size the virtual machines accordingly.

♦ When virtualizing business-critical applications, the application owners may be hesitant to move forward or may make unreasonable demands for resources. Let's say you want to virtualize Microsoft SQL Server and the application owner demands four virtual CPUs and 24 GB of RAM. You've done a capacity assessment and see that the server really only uses two CPUs and 8 GB of RAM. Capacity planning tools can be used to show the application owner exactly how many resources the server is actually using, making it easier to have the discussion about resizing the server when it is virtualized. In the event that more resources are required, they can often be added on the fly without any downtime, making it easier to negotiate sizing with application owners.

♦ Capacity planning tools can also be used on servers that have already been virtualized. In situations where you are migrating to another vSphere cluster or environment with different hardware, having useful utilization data can be key to maintaining good performance. Ongoing capacity management tools, discussed next, are more suited for this job, but not all organizations have access to them.

♦ If applications are experiencing performance problems, capacity planning tools can often provide valuable insight into how the application is actually running. Relying solely on statistics in vCenter does not provide you with the full picture. Both MAP and Capacity Planner can evaluate and report on utilization at the guest OS level and down to the application level, and they can do so over time to show trends. These tools can provide visibility into performance that you can't get from vCenter alone.

Capacity planning tools are great to keep in your toolbox. Whether you're looking to virtualize physical servers or you're troubleshooting performance of virtual machines, these tools can provide you with data that can help you be successful.

Ongoing Capacity Management

Most virtual environments are not short term and as a consequence will require regular upkeep, maintenance, and extensive capacity management. The tools in the following sections will help you take your environment from simply being operated to being maintained and sustained.

VMWARE VCENTER OPERATIONS MANAGER

VMware vCenter Operations Manager, or vCOPs, provides great levels of insight into your environmental conditions in real time as well as information for planning and analysis across the full extent of your infrastructure.

vCenter Operations Manager's primary dashboard, seen in Figure 2.1, is broken up into three sections: Health, Risk, and Efficiency. Badges are used to identify the health of your environment today and going forward. The dashboard is color coded so you can quickly see at a glance where there may be issues in your vSphere environment.

FIGURE 2.1

VMware vCenter
Operations dashboard

In addition to the primary dashboard, vCOPs has a dashboard that can help you predict the future growth of your current infrastructure. The dashboard is based upon your actual utilization, using the performance data vCOPs has collected over time to make its recommendations. The predictive capabilities of vCenter Operations, as shown in Figure 2.2, will not only assess how much time you have left before you exhaust your physical resources, it will also provide an assessment of how many virtual machines you can support. This type of ongoing capacity management is crucial to maintaining good performance of existing virtual machines while providing visibility into when you may run out of resources. Once resources have been exhausted, your environment will likely begin to experience performance degradation.

One of the main benefits of using vCenter Operations Manager as a capacity planning tool in your environment is that it maintains a view of the past, the present, and the predicted future of your virtual machines and applications, as seen in Figure 2.3. As discussed in Chapter 1, when an application generates metrics and performance is measured, vCenter Operations will maintain a historical picture through the life cycle of the virtual machine and the virtual infrastructure.

Whether you're running a small infrastructure with a handful of servers and a small number of VMs or you're monitoring thousands of hosts and virtual servers, this tool will give historical insight and predictability up to half a year in the future. Hardware procurement cycles can often take a long time, so knowing well in advance when you'll need to purchase new ESXi hosts can help you stay out in front of your capacity demands.

Another benefit of vCOPs is its pluggable adapter integration with other infrastructure components in the datacenter, such as storage. Vendors with this adapter can essentially bring their platform-specific objects into vCOPs, presenting more of an end-to-end view of the datacenter while taking advantage of the powerful analytics engine. Storage vendors, for example, can provide plug-ins to provide visibility into storage performance from within vCOPs. Work with your server, storage, and networking vendors to see if they provide any plug-ins for vCOPs.

FIGURE 2.2
Time and capacity remaining

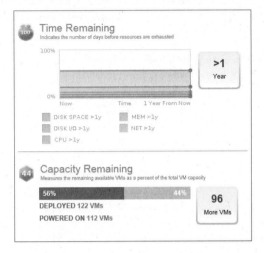

FIGURE 2.3
Resource trends over time

vCOPs can also be extended to include application-level visibility when using vCenter Hyperic, part of the vCenter Operations Management Suite, providing you with a view into over 80 enterprise applications. This provides one single location to monitor your physical and virtual environment as well as individual enterprise applications. This combination of capabilities makes vCOPs a powerful tool, not only for ongoing capacity planning but also for monitoring and maintaining good performance in your environment.

VMware vCenter Log Insight

VMware recently introduced vCenter Log Insight, a tool that integrates into vCenter Operations Manager and provides visibility into syslog data in a simple-to-use interface. Syslog data, which can be important when you're troubleshooting complex problems, is often presented in a format that makes working with it difficult at best. vCenter Log Insight helps to reduce that problem by aggregating syslog data from multiple sources into a single interface, allowing administrators to get access to syslog data quickly and easily. Less time spent finding logs from multiple sources means you can spend more time actually troubleshooting the problem.

While not a replacement for other tools, vCenter Log Insight augments your ability to collect logs through automation, aggregation, analytics, and search capabilities. There are several vSphere infrastructure components that have native capability to export logs to a syslog collector. Aggregation of these logs across datacenter components allows vCenter Log Insight to filter or present corresponding events from a specific time period, which in turn can aid in "connecting the dots." This can help administrators find a resolution faster.

Performance Analysis Tools

Performance analysis tools allow you to monitor the performance of your ESXi host or virtual machines and produce detailed data to help you understand or troubleshoot your environment. Some of these tools are built into ESXi, while others are available as stand-alone utilities. The tools described in the following sections are commonly used to monitor and analyze performance of ESXi hosts and virtual machines.

esxtop

If you decide to master only one tool discussed in this chapter, esxtop should be that tool. esxtop is a performance monitoring tool built into ESXi that provides you with real-time visibility into the performance of the host. For those that are familiar with Microsoft Windows, esxtop is most similar to Performance Monitor (often referred to as "perfmon"). For those with Linux experience, esxtop is similar to the "top" tool.

esxtop is accessible either by logging into the console of an ESXi host or by connecting remotely via tools like the vSphere command line interface (CLI) or the vSphere Management Assistant (vMA). Once launched, esxtop provides real-time visibility into each of the four key resources on an ESXi host: CPU, memory, storage, and network. It provides performance metrics from each of these resources, at the host level as well as at the individual guest level.

INTERACTIVE MODES

When you first launch esxtop, it is launched in interactive mode. You are able to change the views to show different performance counters simply by pressing the appropriate key. Table 2.1 shows the modes and the keys that must be pressed to enable them.

TABLE 2.1: esxtop interactive modes

KEY	MODE	DESCRIPTION
c	CPU panel	The CPU panel displays server-wide statistics as well as statistics for individual world, resource pool, and VM CPUs.
m	Memory panel	The Memory panel displays server-wide and group memory utilization statistics; similar to the CPU panel.
d	Storage Adapter panel	The Storage Adapter panel is aggregated per storage adapter by default.
u	Storage Device panel	The Storage Device panel displays server-wide storage utilization statistics.
v	VM Storage panel	The VM Storage panel displays VM-centric storage statistics.

TABLE 2.1:   esxtop interactive modes

KEY	MODE	DESCRIPTION
n	Network panel	The Network panel displays server-wide network utilization statistics.
i	Interrupt panel	The Interrupt panel displays information about interrupt vectors.
p	Power panel	The Power panel displays CPU power utilization statistics.
V	Virtual machine view	Toggles between View All and View VM Only views in the CPU panel and Memory panel. The View VM Only view clears away all processes that are not virtual machines, making the display easier to view and manipulate.

Now that you're into the tool and you see the various interactive modes, there are some features you can use to help dive down into specifics and troubleshoot problems. Depending upon which interactive mode you've selected within esxtop, you can use the Field Select command (f) to turn on and off columns of information to be presented to you.

For example, let's say you wanted to look at queue statistics in the storage adapter view. These stats are not displayed by default, but by first typing **d** to enter this view and then **f** to select stats, you can choose the QSTATS field by typing **d**, as shown in Figure 2.4.

FIGURE 2.4
Selecting fields in esxtop

With the QSTATS field selected, you can now see the counter AQLEN displayed in esxtop, as shown in Figure 2.5. This field is not displayed by default, but it (and many others) can be added to the display to help you view the performance data that you're looking for.

BATCH MODE

In addition to looking at performance statistics in real time, another very useful mode in esxtop is known as batch mode. In batch mode, you run esxtop for a set period of time and allow it to gather performance data automatically. The data is written to a CSV file, which can then be fed into a tool like Performance Monitor in Windows, which many administrators are familiar with.

Running esxtop in batch mode is useful because you can see how your ESXi host or virtual machines are performing over a defined period of time. You can specify which statistics to monitor and how often data should be gathered and written to the CSV file. The more statistics you include and the more frequently you tell esxtop to write data to CSV, the larger the output file will be.

FIGURE 2.5
Viewing nondefault fields in esxtop

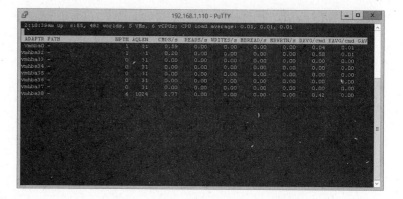

In batch mode, you specify the interval between when esxtop will gather statistics and when it will write them to the CSV file. You also specify the number of iterations that you want to run before automatically stopping. These configurations are passed to the esxtop command in order to run esxtop in batch mode. Table 2.2 lists the parameters that can be passed to esxtop.

TABLE 2.2:   esxtop parameters

KEY	DESCRIPTION
a	Displays and gathers all esxtop statistics.
b	Runs esxtop in batch mode.
d	The delay, in seconds, between data gathering snapshots. The default value is 5 seconds.
n	The number of iterations that esxtop will run and write data to the CSV file.

For example, let's say you wanted to run esxtop for a total of 5 minutes; you want it to gather data once every 5 seconds for a total of 100 iterations, include all esxtop statistics, and output the data to a CSV file named results.csv. To do that, issue the following command:

```
Esxtop -a -d 5 -n 100 >results.csv
```

Once esxtop has run in batch mode, you can take the resulting CSV file and load it into Performance Monitor in Windows. Simply copy the file to your Windows computer and do the following:

1. In Performance Monitor, type Ctrl+L to bring up the Source tab in the Performance Monitor properties.

2. Select the radio button labeled Log files and then click Add.

3. Browse to your CSV file, select it, and click Open.

4. Click the Apply button to load the CSV file data into Performance Monitor.

5. Select the Data tab, and then click the Add button to choose the performance counters you wish to view.

6. Find the counters that you'd like to view, and click the Add button to display them in Performance Monitor, as shown Figure 2.6. Click OK, and then click OK again to view your data.

FIGURE 2.6

Selecting esxtop performance counters to view in Performance Monitor

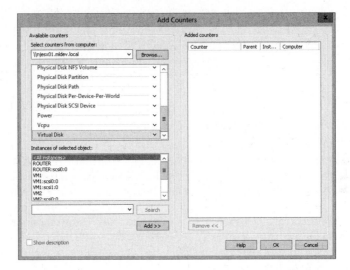

Now that the data you've gathered is visible in Performance Monitor, you can see the graphs. The longer you monitor for, the more data you'll gather and can graph over time. An example of the output of esxtop data in Performance Monitor is shown in Figure 2.7.

FIGURE 2.7

Viewing esxtop data in Performance Monitor

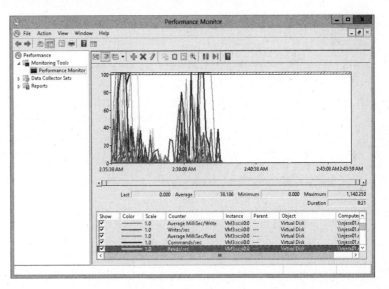

BE CAREFUL WITH THE -A OPTION IN ESXTOP

It might be tempting to use the -a option in esxtop whenever you run it in batch mode. You may think, "Why not have all statistics available to me when I view the data in Performance Monitor?" While that argument does have merit, the reality is that esxtop can gather *a lot* of data.

Only use the -a option when you really need to view all possible data gathered from esxtop. Using this option will not only increase the size of the CSV output file, it will also make it cumbersome to use because you'll have many more performance counters to choose from, and many sound duplicative or are just completely unnecessary for your current task.

Unless you're sure, don't use -a. You'll likely end up spending more time trying to find the right performance counter than actually doing anything with the data you've gathered.

WHEN TO USE ESXTOP

A common question among administrators is, "Why do I need to use esxtop when I have real-time statistics within vCenter?" While it's true that vCenter does have the option of displaying real-time statistics, remember that in vCenter, real-time statistics are still delayed by 20 seconds. esxtop, on the other hand, can display data as frequently as you want.

It often makes sense to start your data analysis within vCenter when performance problems are occurring. vCenter uses a database to store historical performance data, which makes it useful for reporting purposes and to see trends. If you determine that there is a performance event occurring and you need more detailed data or more frequent updates, then you should switch over to esxtop.

esxtop is one of the most powerful performance tools you can have in your toolbox. If you are not already well versed in esxtop, take the time to learn and understand how it works so that you can use it to troubleshoot performance problems. vSphere performance specialists often rely on this tool heavily when analyzing performance problems, and you should too.

We'll cover specific esxtop counters that are relevant to CPU, memory, storage, and networking in later chapters in this book.

GO DEEPER INTO ESXTOP

You can find more information on esxtop, including detailed descriptions of the performance statistics available, at `https://communities.vmware.com/docs/DOC-9279`.

VMware also provides a Fling called VisualEsxtop, which provides a graphical interface to esxtop. It is a very useful tool for administrators who are not comfortable with connecting to the console of an ESXi host. You can download VisualEsxtop at `http://labs.vmware.com/flings/visualesxtop`.

---

vscsiStats

Another important tool for your performance toolbox is called vscsiStats. This tool is built into ESXi and allows you to gather individual virtual machine I/O statistics. When compared to esxtop, which gathers real-time data at the ESXi host level, vscsiStats is used solely to gather disk information all the way down to the individual virtual disk level. Also, since esxtop is not only used for storage performance monitoring, it does not give a full view into the storage performance of a virtual machine.

The vscsiStats tool can be used to troubleshoot performance problems as well as for benchmarking and performance testing purposes. It can return information about the size of I/Os in a virtual machine, latency statistics, and whether the I/O being generated by the VM is random or sequential. You can get all of this information without having any firsthand knowledge of what is running inside the virtual machine. In fact, it doesn't matter what guest OS is running or what application is installed. Since vscsiStats simply gathers storage performance data, you can gather this information without being an expert in the application or guest OS running in the virtual machine. Table 2.3 lists the types of histogram data that vscsiStats can gather.

TABLE 2.3:   vscsiStats histogram performance data

NAME	DESCRIPTION
ioLength	Displays information about the size of the I/O commands issued in the virtual machine.
seekDistance	Displays the distance, in logical block numbers (LBNs), that the disk head travels when executing a read or a write. Small numbers indicate sequential I/O operations and larger numbers indicate random I/O operations.
outstandingIOs	Displays I/O queuing data. High values here are likely to represent performance problems.
latency	Displays storage latency statistics for the virtual disk.
interarrival	Displays the amount of time in between the disk commands issued by the virtual machine.

vscsiStats is run at the ESXi console similar to the way you run esxtop. Running vscsiStats -l will provide a list of all of the virtual machines running on the ESXi host, including both the wordGroupID of each VM and the handleID of each individual virtual disk. This data is useful if you're looking to gather storage performance statistics on a single virtual hard disk of a VM that has multiple virtual hard disks. The output of vscsiStats -l looks like the following:

```
Virtual Machine worldGroupID: 95174, Virtual Machine Display Name: VM1, Virtual
    Machine Config File: /vmfs/volumes/707a93d0-63f06c9b/VM1/VM1.vmx, {
```

```
Virtual SCSI Disk handleID: 8197 (scsi0:0)
Virtual SCSI Disk handleID: 8198 (scsi1:0)
```

Now that you have both the worldGroupID and the handleID of each virtual hard disk, you can configure vscsiStats to run and gather the data you're looking for. To enable vscsiStats data collection, record the worldGroupID from the previous example (in this case, 95174) and enter it into the following command. In this example, you'll gather statistics on each virtual hard disk, but you could also include the handleID to specify which virtual hard disk to monitor:

```
vscsiStats -s -w 95174
```

By default, vscsiStats will run for only 30 minutes. If you need to run it for longer than 30 minutes, simply enter the previous command again and it will run for another 30 minutes. This type of data gathering can be resource intensive, so don't run it for too long or you could impact the performance of other VMs on the host.

Once the 30-minute period has completed, you can view the data that you've gathered. You just need to pick the histogram data that you want to report against and issue a command to view it. To view vscsiStats latency data, for example, issue the following command:

```
vscsiStats -w 95174 -p latency
```

By default, vscsiStats will simply print the output to the screen, as shown in Figure 2.8. This view may not be entirely useful, especially if you're dealing with a lot of data. As with esxtop, you can output the data from vscsiStats to a CSV file so that it can be manipulated in more familiar tools like Microsoft Excel.

FIGURE 2.8
Default output of vscsiStats

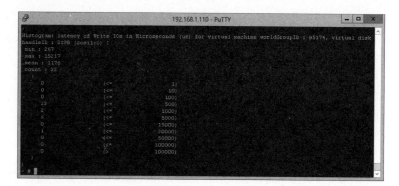

To export the vscsiStats data to Excel, you just need to enter a configuration parameter into the command along with your desired histogram data. For example, let's say you want to view the latency statistics for your virtual machine and save it to a CSV file called latency.csv. To view the latency statistics and export them to a CSV file, issue the following command:

```
vscsiStats -w 95174 -p latency -c >latency.csv
```

After you've opened the data in Excel, expand columns A and B to find the data that you're looking for. Suppose you want to see the I/O latency of all reads during the monitoring period. In the CSV, look for "Histogram: latency of Read IOs in Microseconds (us)" in column A. Under that, you'll see "Frequency" in column A and "Histogram Bucket Limit" in column B, as highlighted in Figure 2.9.

FIGURE 2.9

vscsiStats output in Microsoft Excel

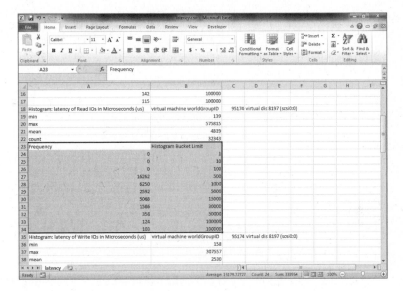

If you select everything under Frequency and Histogram Bucket Limit and insert a graph, unfortunately the graph will be incorrect because Excel will not properly choose the horizontal and vertical axes. It's easy to fix, however. Use the following procedure to produce an appropriate graph of vscsiStats data in Excel:

1. Select the data that you want to graph (highlighted in Figure 2.9), switch to the Insert tab on the ribbon, select Column, and choose either a 2D or 3D column graph.

2. After the graph has been inserted, right-click on it and choose Select Data.

3. Under Legend Entries (Series), click Histogram Bucket Limit and click Remove.

4. Click the Edit button under Horizontal (Category) Axis Labels, select only the data values (numbers) under Histogram Bucket Limit, and click OK.

5. Once you have only Frequency displayed under Legend Entries (Series) and only the data from the Histogram Bucket Limit selected under Horizontal (Category) Axis Labels, as shown in Figure 2.10, click OK to display the proper graph.

FIGURE 2.10

Setting up horizontal and vertical axes for a graph of vscsiStats data

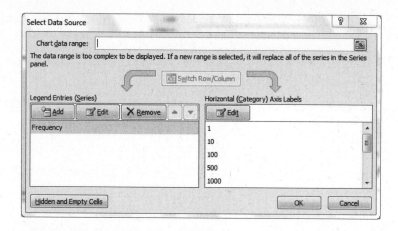

As you can see, vscsiStats is a powerful tool for understanding detailed storage performance characteristics of your virtual machines. This tool is especially useful when using vFlash Read Cache in vSphere 5.5, which is covered in more detail in Chapter 7.

Performance Benchmarking Tools

Performance benchmarking tools let you take your existing or proposed infrastructure and determine where your maximum capabilities exist. Benchmarking tools are useful for providing a baseline of how your hardware is capable of performing. They can provide insight into what kind of performance you might expect from new hardware before introducing it into your environment.

VMmark

VMmark is a benchmark tool by VMware designed specifically to quantify and measure performance of virtualized datacenters. This tool and its output can help identify the right server solution for your datacenter.

Because it was developed as a tool for hardware vendors and system integrators to evaluate system performance, many customers will not run the tool itself. Fortunately, the results from hardware vendors and their configurations are published to aid in determining the appropriate platform to choose. Figure 2.11 shows an example of the output of VMmark comparing the performance of different server vendors.

The VMmark tool includes collections of diverse workloads called tiles, which represent common workloads found in today's datacenters. The latest version of VMmark includes the ability to test for performance, server power consumption, and server and storage power consumption during load testing.

You should use this tool if you find yourself working with custom performance-sensitive applications. This tool helps ensure that you have the capability to assess what infrastructure they should run on and provides hard metrics to point back to changes in hardware, configuration, or infrastructure.

FIGURE 2.11
VMware benchmark
performance results

Date	Submitter	Score	System Description	Total Hosts	Total Cores	Matched Pair	Uniform Hosts	VMmark Version
10/05/2012	Hewlett-Packard *hp*	59.99 @ 62 tiles Download Disclosure	ProLiant BL465c Gen8 VMware ESX 4.1 U2 / vCenter 5.0	16 Total Hosts 32 Total Sockets	512 Total Cores 512 Total Threads	No	Yes	2.1.1
11/13/2012	Fujitsu FUJITSU	46.22 @ 40 tiles Download Disclosure	Fujitsu PRIMERGY BX924 S3 VMware ESX 4.1 U3 / vCenter 5.1	8 Total Hosts 16 Total Sockets	128 Total Cores 256 Total Threads	No	Yes	2.1.1
09/11/2012	Cisco CISCO	42.79 @ 36 tiles Download Disclosure	Cisco UCS B200 M3 VMware ESXi 5.1 / vCenter 5.1	8 Total Hosts 16 Total Sockets	128 Total Cores 256 Total Threads	No	Yes	2.1.1

Due to the strain this may put on your production system, you should leverage this tool in your lab environment or on dedicated test systems. Initially, you can check if your server vendor has already run the tool and see how the VMmark score compares to other vendors or your own test.

NOTE   For more information on VMmark, including the opportunity to view the results from various hardware vendors or to download the tool yourself, go to www.vmware.com/a/vmmark/.

vBenchmark

Benchmarking does not simply have to be about determining how much performance you can get out of a piece of physical hardware. You can also use benchmarking tools to actually try to quantify the benefits of virtualization across a number of important factors. VMware has released a Fling called vBenchmark that can do just that.

The goal of vBenchmark is simple: quantify the benefits of virtualization to management. You can, for example, quantify the amount of physical RAM that you're saving by deploying virtual machines instead of physical servers. vBenchmark will also show you averages across your environment, such as the average configured amount of RAM per VM or GB of storage consumed. You can also compare your data to that of the community by allowing vBenchmark to upload an anonymous version of your data to its community site. It can be useful to compare yourself to others, especially if you're trying to show the benefits of virtualization to management or application owners.

Once vBenchmark is deployed, the dashboard provides an at-a-glance view of your environment, showing you data such as average vCPUs per VM, configured vRAM per VM, or GBs of storage per VM, as shown in Figure 2.12. From here you can choose the Compare your results to your Peers option to send data to VMware, which allows you to see what similar environments average out to. The Share tab provides the option to export the data to a CSV file so you can ensure that no proprietary or sensitive information is being shared.

vBenchmark is not only a one-time use tool for point-in-time data; instead, it is persistent over time and provides insight that you can go back to visit and revisit regularly. The longer you let it run, the more likely it is to produce data that you can use to quantify the benefits of virtualization to management.

NOTE To learn more about vBenchmark and download a copy, go to `https://labs.vmware` `.com/flings/vbenchmark`.

FIGURE 2.12
VMware vBenchmark
dashboard results

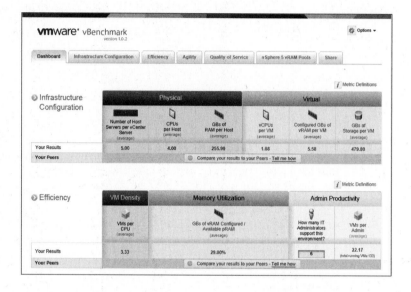

Performance Simulation Tools

Performance simulation tools allow you to generate synthetic load inside virtual machines. You can use these tools to generate high amounts of CPU, memory, disk, or network utilization on one or more virtual machines to tax the resources of your ESXi hosts. These tools can be useful in your lab or even before putting servers into production to determine how applications will behave under load or to test features like vSphere DRS.

In the following sections, we'll review tools that you can use to simulate CPU, memory, disk, and network load in your environment.

CPU/Memory

Generating both CPU and memory load is useful to test vSphere features or to see how applications perform under load. Though there are numerous tools to generate this load, using a single tool to accomplish both can simplify your testing.

PRIME95

One of the oldest tools available to simulate CPU and memory load is a tool called Prime95. The tool was originally designed to help find prime numbers (and still serves that purpose today), but it also is useful as a load simulation tool.

When you first run Prime95, you'll be prompted to run a torture test with certain characteristics. You can choose, for example, to stress the CPU but not RAM, or you can choose to stress both resources. Figure 2.13 shows the options for the torture test, with "Blend (tests some of everything, lots of RAM tested)" selected as the test parameter. This is the test that should be used to test both CPU and memory.

FIGURE 2.13

Configuring a torture test in Prime95

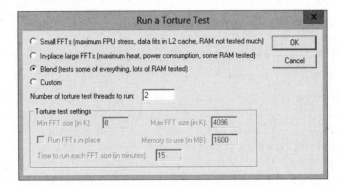

It is important to note the field Number of torture test threads to run in Figure 2.13. This indicates how many CPUs will be stress tested as part of the test. If you have four vCPUs and select only two threads, Prime95 will only tax the CPU to 50 percent capacity. To test all vCPUs, make sure the value in this field matches the number of configured vCPUs.

There are several reasons you might want to heavily stress test the CPU and memory of one or multiple virtual machines. The following list provides some common examples, but there may be many others depending on your individual requirements:

◆ Using Prime95 on multiple virtual machines at once can be a good way to stress test the physical hardware of your ESXi hosts. If you configure virtual machines to utilize all available CPU and memory resources, using Prime95 can stress your physical CPUs and memory and potentially find faulty hardware before putting the server into production. This is commonly referred to as a "burn-in" test.

◆ Introducing artificial CPU and memory load into an environment can be useful to determine how virtual machines will perform under load. For example, if an application's baseline performance metric (such as database queries per second, for example) is met under normal conditions, Prime95 can introduce load and subsequently CPU or memory contention. You can then see how your application performs under this load to get an idea of how well it will perform if this scenario were to occur in production.

◆ Generating CPU and memory load can be a great way to test features like vSphere DRS. You can simulate load to make sure DRS will automatically migrate virtual machines to balance out that load. You can also use it to validate that CPU and memory reservations are being met. Perhaps most important, you can observe if your virtual machines are receiving the resources that you believe they are entitled to based on their configured limits, reservations, or shares. This can be especially important when resource pools are used to allocate CPU and memory resources to virtual machines. The concept of allocating resources to resource pools is covered in more detail in Chapter 4.

There can be many reasons you'd want to generate artificial CPU and/or memory load in your environment. Whatever your reasons are, Prime95 is a good tool to use to simulate that load.

NOTE To learn more about Prime95 and download a copy, visit `www.mersenne.org/freesoft`.

Storage

As we talk about in Chapter 7, storage often has the largest impact on overall virtual machine performance. An organization can buy servers with the most powerful CPUs and huge quantities of RAM, but if the storage isn't capable of meeting the performance requirements, then all virtual machines will suffer. It is for that reason that it is important to have a set of tools you can use to test and validate the performance of your storage platform before putting it into production.

Iometer

Perhaps the best known tool for generating storage I/O is called Iometer. Iometer is well liked because it is capable of generating specific kinds of I/O to mimic the workload profile of applications. You can configure the I/O to be random or sequential, reads or writes, and you can also choose the specific block size to use. That makes Iometer a tool that can not only generate I/O activity, it can generate I/O activity that closely mimics the I/O that an actual application will generate. And since it's just an application that runs on Windows or Linux, Iometer is portable and can be used on physical or virtual servers.

Iometer works by generating a test file inside your virtual machine and then running I/O tests against that file. The test file you create is defined in sectors, so you'll need to convert gigabytes to sectors before starting your test. Enter the appropriate number of sectors in the box labeled Maximum Disk Size, as shown in Figure 2.14. In this example, we're using 16,777,216 sectors to generate an 8 GB test file. Make sure to select the appropriate disk under Targets (if your virtual machine has more than one virtual disk) and choose the appropriate number of workers. Each worker is a thread in which I/O will be generated and the total number of workers shouldn't exceed the number of vCPUs assigned to the virtual machine.

THE SIZE OF YOUR IOMETER TEST FILE MATTERS

It's very important to choose the proper size for your Iometer test file when running a test. A common mistake when running Iometer is to create a test file that is too small, which can result in inaccurate results. When an operating system like Windows reads a file, it copies portions of the file (or the entire file) into RAM for faster access. In the case of an Iometer test, this can skew the results by causing the reads to occur from RAM instead of disk.

A general rule of thumb would be to create an Iometer test file size that is at least double the size of the amount of configured RAM. This eliminates the possibility of the operating system caching the file in RAM and skewing the results.

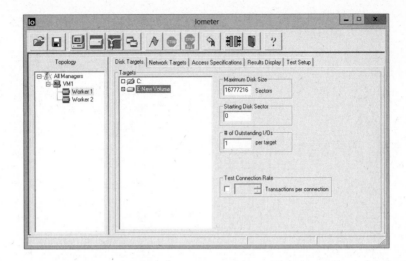

Next, define access specifications for the test to determine the types of I/O you want to generate. For example, in Figure 2.15, we're creating a new access specification using a 16 KB block size, with a read/write ratio of 60 percent writes and 40 percent reads. Those I/Os are broken down in 60 percent random and 40 percent sequential. If this I/O profile matches what you expect in your environment, then running this test can show you exactly how well your storage will perform under the expected load. You can also adjust the queue depth to match whatever is appropriate for your particular storage array. We cover queue depth in more detail in Chapter 7.

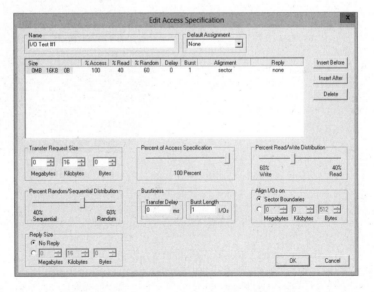

Once your test has been configured, you can simply select the green flag at the top of the screen to start them. Select the Results Display tab to view the results in real time. Moving the Update Frequency slider down to a lower level, like 1 or 2, will allow you to see a more real-time view of the results of your test, as shown in Figure 2.16. For a more graphical (and admittedly fun) view, select the > button at the end of each row to bring up a speedometer view of your results, as shown in Figure 2.17.

FIGURE 2.16
Viewing the real-time results of the Iometer test

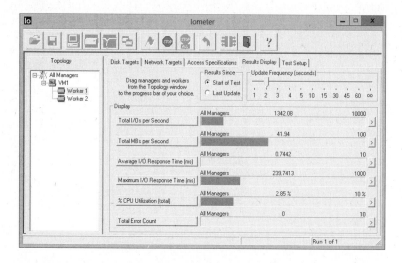

FIGURE 2.17
The Iometer speedometer view

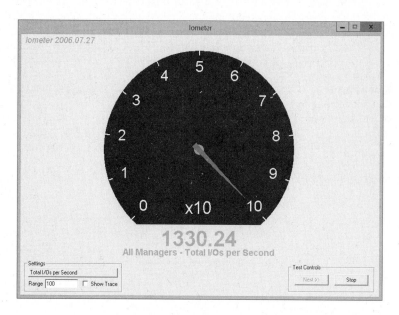

Iometer comes with several default access specifications, but it is best to create one that most closely matches your environment. Though it is possible to run a test that simply generates as much I/O as possible to see the limits of your storage infrastructure, there is likely not a lot of value in that test unless you're trying to sell storage arrays. After all, if the test does not accurately match what your actual storage I/O profile will look like, the data is not useful.

Once the test has completed, you can get an idea of not only the amount of IOPS you were able to generate but also what latency was recorded. Generally speaking, the higher the IOPS value recorded, the better the performance, as long as the IOPS are delivered within a reasonable amount of latency. Acceptable latency values vary depending on the type of storage in use, but typically 5–10 milliseconds (ms) of latency is acceptable for most workloads.

All applications are not created equal, and I/O workloads may vary based upon application type. It is very important to have a true sense of your expected I/O profile before using Iometer. Your output will only be as good as your test data, so try to get an accurate picture of the expected I/O profile before using Iometer. If you're unsure of what the I/O profile will look like, work with application owners or software vendors to get an idea of the values to use in your test. Or if you simply want to test the bounds of your storage array, you can configure Iometer to try to drive the maximum amount of IOPS out of your storage.

NOTE   For more information on Iometer and to download the tool, visit `www.iometer.org`.

I/O Analyzer

I/O Analyzer is a virtual appliance created by VMware designed to measure storage performance in a virtual environment. I/O Analyzer uses Iometer, discussed in the previous section, to generate I/O loads. It can also take storage I/O traces as input to generate an automated load or to more closely match a real application workload.

I/O Analyzer provides a simple, easy-to-use graphical interface for running Iometer tests in your virtual infrastructure. It extends the functionality of Iometer by allowing you to play back traces of actual workloads and also has scheduling capabilities to allow you to schedule tests to occur at certain times of the day.

Another way in which I/O Analyzer is different from simply running Iometer is that it can have visibility into esxtop. If you provide ESXi host credentials, I/O Analyzer can show you not only the output of the Iometer test but the relevant esxtop counters as well. Having this visibility into the results from two tools in a single location can be a big time-saver and is a big benefit of using I/O Analyzer.

The ease with which you can run Iometer tests and view the results are key benefits of I/O Analyzer. The tool is provided free of charge from VMware, has a VMware Labs Fling, and is a handy tool to keep in your performance toolbox.

NOTE   For more information and the link to download I/O Analyzer, visit `http://labs .vmware.com/flings/io-analyzer`.

Network

Network utilization is often not the first thing that administrators think of when talking about generating artificial load. After all, today's networks are not frequently the cause of performance bottlenecks, even when IP-based storage is used. There can be a need, however, to generate network performance in order to validate that an application's requirements can be met. Today many applications rely on synchronous replication for high availability, and that can generate large amounts of network traffic. Simulating load to ensure that these requirements can be met is important for validating that the application will perform as well as expected.

IPERF

When it comes to investigating your virtual network infrastructure for issues involving networking, look no further than Iperf. Iperf is a tool to measure maximum TCP bandwidth and change window size, and it can report on bandwidth, delay jitter, and datagram loss. At an architectural level, Iperf has both a client and a server and can measure the total network throughput between them. This allows you to measure how two virtual machines, for example, will perform when communicating over the network.

TIP VMware has a Knowledge Base article that discusses troubleshooting virtual machine performance issues. It discusses using Iperf to determine if network latency is causing performance problems with virtual machines. You can view the Knowledge Base article at `http://kb.vmware.com/kb/2001003`.

Iperf has numerous configuration options that can be tuned in order to create a test that accurately reflects your virtual machine's network workload profile. Remember, as we discussed with tools like Iometer, the results of a test with Iperf is only as accurate as the data you put in. Work with application owners or software vendors to determine the network requirements before running a test.

NOTE For more information on Iperf and to download the version that is compatible with your chosen operating system, visit `https://code.google.com/p/iperf/`.

Summary

The tools in your toolbox can help make your job easier and make you more effective. Having a solid set of tools to call upon for different situations is essential for designing, implementing, and maintaining a virtual infrastructure.

First, we covered capacity planning tools that you can use prior to virtualizing a server. These free tools are available from both VMware and Microsoft and can give you a view into the actual utilization of a server regardless of how many resources are configured. These tools are also useful for getting detailed analyses of application-specific performance counters. Once the servers have been virtualized, you can use tools like vCenter Operations Manager and Log Insight to keep an eye on the overall capacity, performance, and operations of your virtual machines.

Next, we covered performance monitoring tools like esxtop that are essential for viewing the real-time performance statistics of your virtual infrastructure. If you master only one tool from this chapter, make sure it is esxtop because it is one of the most important tools in diagnosing and troubleshooting performance problems. We also covered vscsiStats, a tool that provides detailed storage performance analysis of virtual machines or even individual virtual disks.

Performance benchmarking tools are useful to see how your selected hardware matches up against similar hardware from multiple vendors. VMware provides VMmark, a benchmarking tool designed to help hardware vendors benchmark their equipment against a virtual infrastructure. VMware also provides a tool called vBenchmark to help validate the benefits of virtualizing your infrastructure.

There is more to performance tools than simply monitoring performance, however. There is often a need to generate artificial loads in order to simulate the performance of applications in your environment. Tools like Prime95 allow you to introduce CPU or memory load, which can be useful for seeing how your virtual machines will perform under load or to validate that your resource allocations work as expected. Tools for simulating storage load like Iometer or VMware I/O Analyzer can help you benchmark and test your storage to determine if it will meet your requirements. Finally, tools like Iperf can simulate network utilization between two virtual machines to help you determine if your network can meet the demands of your applications.

In most cases, at least one tool is required to perform essential troubleshooting steps such as automating the process, isolating the symptoms, and ultimately diagnosing the problem. While some of these tools may be familiar to you and others may be brand new, it's important to have a good understanding of them so you can use them when the need arises. In later chapters we'll refer to using these tools in the context of evaluating CPU, memory, storage, and network performance.

Chapter 3

The Test Lab

At this point you should have a firm grasp of architectural and design constructs and troubleshooting methodologies, reinforced with a toolbox to make you a force to be reckoned with. Now it's time to get serious and apply these rules to a lab environment. If you've been using VMware for virtualization as long as we have, you'll recall that VMware got its start by being the test lab. The irony of this fact should not be taken for granted. As your virtualization infrastructure has taken on a much more mission-critical role, the need to validate in a test bed has never been more important.

Not all test labs are created equal—and justifiably so. Your test lab should be built with a combination of use case, function, and purpose in mind. Thus, while a six-node ESXi cluster with dual 10 Gigabit Ethernet (10GbE) switches with Metro clustered storage may sound like an awesome lab, it is of little value to you if all you're doing is testing the reliability of an ESXi upgrade or merely applying the latest Microsoft patch. That said, there is value in replicating a production environment in the lab if possible. Some of the benefits are the ability to test datacenter infrastructure changes, perform proofs of concept, including incorporating new design ideas, and migrations.

Whether you are looking to replicate production applications or providing sandboxes for your DevOps team to create the next-generation business applications, the test lab will provide the vehicle to make that possible. The test lab will take on many different guises for your environment through various stages of an application's and infrastructure's life cycles. We'll dive into these use cases so you can use your test lab to the max without compromising the value that it provides.

In this chapter we look at:

◆ Why build a test lab

◆ Strategies for a successful lab

◆ How to build your lab

Why Build a Test Lab?

The rationale for building a lab in the first place is often questioned. Gone are the days when a lab platform was required to get experience working with virtualization. We now have solutions like VMware's Hands-On Labs Online and vSphere AutoLab by LabGuides to produce a lab environment with minimum effort. Make no mistake: these tools provide useful education depending on what your needs are, but there is still much value in building a test lab.

The principles we'll be discussing next will help you identify what kind of environment you want to be testing and running this lab from. While many are known to have fairly comprehensive home labs, the same can be said of the need to facilitate your production business needs, whether for testing, benchmarking, troubleshooting, or more. So without further ado, let's start diving into the lab!

Test Changes before Applying in Production

It has never been more important in the world of virtualization than now to test, test, test any changes that will impact production. One situation that will come up often is when you want to improve performance in production vMotion by putting it on a dedicated VLAN with a maximum transmission unit (MTU) setting of 9000, as seen in Figure 3.1. When done correctly and perfectly, this can work out very well; however, if configured incorrectly, it could do something as simple as break HA or even go so far as to bring production to a screeching halt.

FIGURE 3.1
Managing virtual adapters

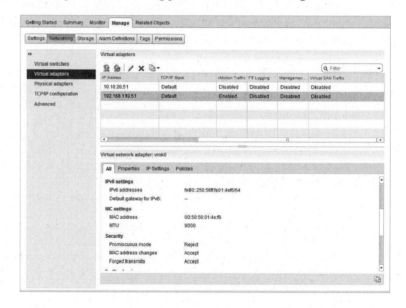

The lab offers you the ability to vet minor changes before applying them in production. It also provides a vehicle to test, validate, deploy, and roll back changes. Depending upon your environment, change management rules may be rather daunting or restrictive from a scheduling complexity/risk standpoint, thus a test lab will provide you with the confidence to test any changes before executing them. Although it may not be necessary to test every change, certain changes are definitely worth testing in the lab instead of experimenting on your production environment:

- Deploying Fault Tolerance
- Isolating vMotion, management, NFS, and iSCSI traffic, including the configuration of jumbo frames
- Deploying and working with vSphere Distributed Switches

◆ Enabling VMware Enhanced vMotion Compatibility (EVC)

◆ Deploying Distributed Power Management (DPM)

◆ Configuring self-signed certificates for ESXi and vCenter

The list can easily go on and on, especially as the feature set continues to grow. The purpose of the lab is to encourage you to explore options you may want to enable in production but are unsure of what the implications may be. We mentioned earlier a deployment plan, but we want to place emphasis on the rollback plan because it is often overlooked. When it comes to deploying some features, such as vCenter Server Linked Mode, you may find that in the lab it works out perfectly and does everything you want, only to find that implementation in large-scale production rollouts may not act entirely as expected. When that happens, irrespective of what feature set you're deploying, it's always important to know how to roll back and restore your environment without major stress or strain.

Test New Applications and Patches

No administrator ever said, "We deployed a Host Intrusion Prevention System (HIPS) and the latest patches on Tuesday and everything works perfectly." This is the point where your lab steps up to fulfill one of its most important roles. On the surface, you might be thinking this is where you'll test installation of a new application or patch for that application, but depending upon how accurately you build out your lab, it should be so much more. We cannot stress the importance of trying to mirror your lab with production. That will enable you to apply patches to some of the most overlooked yet vitally important infrastructures:

◆ Storage arrays and new patches or releases of code

◆ Fibre Channel or FCoE switch updates

◆ Network switches, OS updates, and patches

◆ Server firmware and ESXi Update and security patches

◆ Fiber Channel, hardware iSCSI, and CNA firmware

We cannot tell you the number of times we've seen systems go down due to very subtle and minor changes that went untested in the lab before being deployed in production, causing major multiday outages. There are numerous benefits gained from being able to test and deploy these patches. Whether they are physical infrastructure or application-level patches, you'll have a point of reference, and after an appropriate bake-in period, you can roll them out into production with confidence.

But what about testing and deploying new applications? Can't we just roll those out into production, because they'll probably work? History has shown that "probably" can often result in a resume-generating event, so you're best to err on the side of caution and test them before deploying. We mentioned HIPS earlier, which makes for a perfect disruptive application if left untested and unchecked. Other such applications may be new management, monitoring, and miscellaneous third-party tools that you should not unleash into your production vCenter without having at least some example of what impact they'll have.

Some tools will interact directly with the VMkernel, execute code on your ESXi Shells, or more. If you're considering implementing any of these, investing time in your lab to determine what they'll do in your environment and whether they'll uninstall correctly, should you choose to remove them, can save you major headaches later. You don't want to be the one to explain to management that the environment went down due to an unchecked and untested application deployed into the production environment.

Re-Create Production Problems

In the production environment, problems continually pop up and need to be solved. Whether a problem is due to something physical in your hardware, virtual in your software, or a mis-configuration, you can leverage your lab as a tool to help troubleshoot and ultimately solve the problem. Often, administrators will take a VM snapshot before making a major change like a patch so they can roll back to that point in time if necessary. Unfortunately, not all environments or applications can sustain a rollback, which may result in data loss. Some require testing differ-ent methods while troubleshooting the problem.

No longer will we be required to spend days on end trying to troubleshoot configuration changes while on the phone with support, only to find in the end a simple modification would have sufficed. Whether taking advantage of the lab in this scenario or operating in produc-tion, we encourage you to clone your virtual machine and convert it to an Open Virtualization Format (OVF) template (see Figure 3.2), which will save you a lot of grief.

FIGURE 3.2
Clone a virtual machine

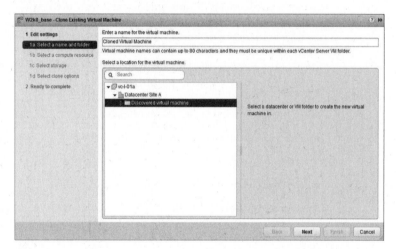

Cloning your virtual machine provides you with a duplicate of the virtual machine with the same configuration and installed software as the original. During the cloning process, you can modify the configuration to change virtual machine name, network settings, and other attributes that may cause a conflict with the original. Cloning can be performed online with-out interrupting the original server and services. During the cloning process, you can make the copy ready to be portable by making the disk thin and leveraging array-based snapshots if available.

Cloning readies you to either bring the virtual machine up to start testing configurations in its slightly modified state or to copy it over into your lab environment to take it through the battery of tests you need to perform. Now that you have your virtual machine cloned, you can convert it to an OVF template to make it even more portable (templates are thin provisioned naturally and provide the ability to create new instances on demand), something you'd be unable to do with the production online instance of the virtual machine. Exporting an OVF encloses the state of the virtual machine or vApp into a self-contained package with the disk files stored in a compressed and sparse format (see Figures 3.3, 3.4, and 3.5).

FIGURE 3.3
The Export OVF
Template option

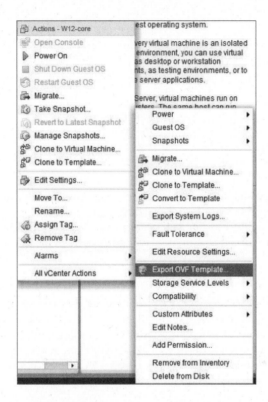

FIGURE 3.4
The Export OVF
Template dialog box

Export OVF Template		?
Name	Export of OVF	
Directory	Choose	
	☐ Overwrite existing files	
Format	Folder of files (OVF)	▼
Annotation		
Advanced	☐ Enable advanced options	
	OK	Cancel

FIGURE 3.5
Export OVF Template
task progress

At this point, whether you've reconfigured the clone with different configuration settings so it doesn't conflict with the original or fully migrated it into your lab environment in order to test it thoroughly, you should be in a position to go through the various iterations of testing and troubleshooting that support may require without the risk of destroying your production instance.

Simulate Performance Problems for Troubleshooting

One of the benefits of mirroring production with your lab is the ability to then re-create the kinds of problems you're having. Representing production-like workloads in the lab also provides you with the opportunity to make drastic changes that may not be possible in production. These changes can help guide you in making decisions that ultimately may modify your production architecture. Here are some examples of changes you might test in the lab:

- Moving an application between storage tiers (SAS, SATA, SSD)

- Increasing an application's vCPU and memory for performance

- Decreasing an application's vCPU and memory under load

- Testing an application under disk load with Thick Eager Zero, Thick Lazy Zero, and thin disks

- Making support-guided advanced configuration changes

There is no one right answer that will solve every performance problem you might experience. This is an ever-evolving study of an application's operation. Even if you throw the best hardware and a solid configuration at a virtual machine, if the application is performing inefficient calls or has memory leaks or any of an infinite number of other systematic issues, you will still have problems., By completing these steps and the iterations of troubleshooting and methodologies, you'll have tangible feedback to help lead to a resolution.

Benchmark New Hardware

For a lot of administrators and architects, this has to be one of the most enjoyable parts: getting new hardware into the lab to test it and establish a baseline before rolling it out into production. Many a hardware vendor uses a test lab as the vehicle for the "bake-off," where they apply an arbitrary set of guidelines to make their product shine best. Irrespective of the interests of the vendors, you can use new hardware in your lab to test your actual business application use cases. Using the SMART methodology, you can apply those principles to help establish a baseline and a series of tangible benefits realized by the new hardware.

As an example, the recent surge of flash-based storage vendors in the industry tend to market their wares as the panacea to all virtualization problems, promising to provide your applications with hundreds of thousands of IOPs. This is great if your problems involve I/O and response time. If not, replacing your existing investment for the latest shiny flash array would be a mistake. If you've already established what your baselines for storage, computing, and networking are, you'll be able to realize whether new hardware will truly improve your environment and user experience without relying on a vendor to tell you so.

At this point you should have a comfortable handle on what decisions would encourage the valid testing of new hardware in the lab, how and why you might go about reproducing production issues, and the benefits of testing. It is time to dive into some specifics for your lab's success.

If you're unable to procure a dedicated lab, consider using another environment as the next best appropriate ground for testing, for instance, a development, QA, or production environment. It is not uncommon to find production environments outnumbered by a ratio of 3:1 or more in terms of mirrored infrastructure. In such environments, change control dictates that changes occur in a structured and orderly fashion, such as Lab ➢ Development & Test ➢ QA ➢ Production, with appropriate cool-down time in between. Cool-down hasn't been called out explicitly, but would be considered part of the test workflow/script in a non-production environment.

Learn about Virtualization

Last but not least, this test lab environment can be the perfect use case for learning about virtualization and working with tools you have not introduced into production yet. Fortunately, you do not need to reinvent the wheel for every opportunity or create your own lab run books to make this possible, especially in areas you're not familiar with. Through the use of two resources—vSphere AutoLab by LabGuides and VMware Hands-On Labs Online—you'll be able to take advantage of this immediately!

The first of these tools is the vSphere AutoLab by LabGuides. The vSphere AutoLab is a lab builder kit designed to produce a nested vSphere lab environment with minimum effort. Prebuilt open-source VMs and the shells of other VMs are provided along with automation for the installation of operating systems and applications into these VMs. The lab was originally created to aid study toward VMware Certified Professional (VCP) certification, but it has many other potential uses. Table 3.1 shows the hardware requirements.

TABLE 3.1: vSphere AutoLab Hardware Requirements

HARDWARE	MINIMUM	USED TO BUILD THE LAB
CPU	Dual core, 6- bit	Core2 Duo
RAM	8 GB	8 GB
Hard disk	60 GB free space	Additional hard disk
Operating system	64-bit	Windows 7 64-bit
Virtualization software	VMware Player	VMware Workstation

The minimum hardware requirements are rather modest, at the same time providing you with the tools to do so much with them. The minimum requirements listed in Table 3.1 and the source material in the *AutoLab 1.1a vSphere Deployment Guide* by Alastair Cooke provide guidance for installation on VMware Workstation, VMware ESXi, VMware Fusion, and VMware Player. It is outside the scope of this book to reproduce that material, which has already been so well documented by the AutoLab team, so if this is an area you're looking to introduce into your environment, a majority of the work is done for you.

This project lives at www.labguides.com and updates occur there. Details and the inside scoop of the vSphere AutoLab project are published at www.professionalvmware.com.

Sometimes time does not permit producing a complicated lab to test a new capability that is not present in your infrastructure at the time. Those who have attended VMware's VMworld Conference in the past can dedicate a portion of their time to exposure of and working with the VMware Hands-On Labs. The wealth of knowledge available in those labs through the availability of the equipment, the labs, and the source material became a primary portion of their virtualization education, as shown in Figure 3.6.

Thankfully, through the introduction of VMware's Hands-On Labs Online, you need not wait until you're at a conference to test out those scenarios! This resource is available and only a browser visit away. Just by visiting http://labs.hol.vmware.com, you'll immediately have access to this wealth of resources. And it truly is "immediately." Merely click the Login link in the top right, click Register?, and enter an email address and contact name and you'll receive an email within seconds to verify your account. Then answer a few arbitrary security questions and your account will be activated and ready for you to start working with the labs!

Once you're in, you can browse through the large list of labs available, look through the lab archives, and even search for a particular lab for something you do not currently run in your environment but may want to consider building your own lab for.

For example, you can click Enroll on the Horizon Workspace – Explore and Deploy lab (see Figure 3.7).

As you can see in Figure 3.8 and Figure 3.9, within seconds, your lab is built and ready for you to start working!

FIGURE 3.6
Introduction to
VMware Hands-On
Labs Online

FIGURE 3.7
Horizon Workspace –
Explore and Deploy

FIGURE 3.8
The Starting Lab
screen

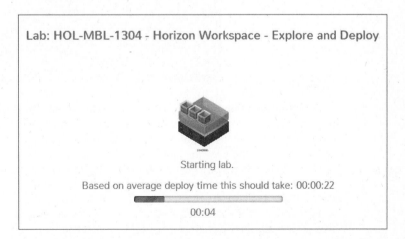

FIGURE 3.9
Your lab is ready for
you to start learning!

But wait; what are you supposed to do now? This is where you truly benefit from the expertise of the VMware Hands-On Labs Online. On the right side of the screen there is a Manual
tab, and contained in that, for each one of the lab environments, are steps to go through for lab
scenarios, as seen in Figure 3.10.

FIGURE 3.10
Using the Lab Manual

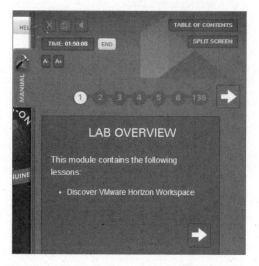

This gives you the ability to go through a series of regular tasks you're likely to use in the
respective applications (whether through discovery, configuration, or deployment) so that you
can get comfortable and familiar with the use of the tools.

In addition to the VMware labs that are available, participants in the VMware Partner
Network have also made investments in creating labs to get familiar with the use of their tools.
The major contributors to the lab space at this time are partners like EMC, NetApp, Cisco, and
Puppet Labs and security partners like CatBird and HyTrust.

With a wealth of access to technical tools, expertise in the form of pre-built labs and lab
scenarios, and a strong partner ecosystem ready to support your application use case, the use

of the VMware Hands-On Labs Online should be a major portion of your personal learning experience portfolio.

It is not a replacement for the desire or need to build a lab environment that mirrors or replicates your production environment, but this resource should be utilized in support of those very same goals.

Strategies for a Successful Test Lab

The test lab understandably is one of the most undervalued and misunderstood resources an organization can employ. The often-asked question of how one would go about defining whether the lab is successful is easily answered by whether it is used or not. Even the most over-resourced labs go unused and lie idle. With the steps discussed earlier, and the criteria for success that lie ahead, your investment will never go wasted, unwanted, or unused.

Build a Realistic Environment

It is important to build your lab with its end state in mind. Part of this end state should mirror as accurately as possible the features of production you'll want to be testing. For example, if your production environment is using the latest Intel processors, deploying the lab with the latest AMD processor won't give you an accurate representation of workload, application, or use case, unless of course you're applying it solely on the Benchmark New Hardware lab use case. Using like hardware in a nonproduction environment also affords the ability to depot the organization's own replacement hardware in the case of an emergency. Essentially, hardware may be "borrowed" from the nonproduction environment to be put into service in the production environment—not just parts either, but entire hosts to immediately increase cluster/infrastructure capacity during unexpected peak times.

At this point you should take an inventory of what your production environment looks like and the use cases you'd like to apply into the lab. The following checklists should help to get you started if you don't have it already on paper.

The first category is hardware:

- Server type
- Type and number of processors
- Amount and speed of RAM
- Storage type(s), capacity, and connectivity options
- Network interface type(s) and transport options
- Network switch for connectivity
- HVAC, BTU, and power needs

In reality, lab or nonproduction environments often get populated with hand-me-down equipment. Do the best with what's available and understand that not all equipment may be viable for a fitting or realistic lab infrastructure. In cases where shared storage isn't going to be a reality, consider using a VMware vSphere Storage Appliance (VSA) (many available, some free) as shared storage to unlock many of the key features of vSphere, or leverage vSphere 5.5's new storage function VMware Virtual SAN (VSAN).

As a plus, find something with native thin provisioning capabilities at the storage/volume layer to get the most efficient use out of the spindles so that raw storage isn't pinned to a LUN until write I/O is actually requested from a VM within. This provides the ability to deploy and overcommit many LUNs of capacity for testing purposes, even though the backing storage may not physically be available.

The next category is software:

◆ Server firmware versions

◆ ESXi and vCenter versions

◆ Storage array OS firmware versions

◆ Network, storage, or CNA card firmware versions

◆ Network or storage switch OS firmware versions

◆ Operating system versions

◆ Application instance versions

◆ Other miscellaneous software

Then there are the following miscellaneous items to capture:

◆ IP address and hostnames

◆ Port configuration and network layout

◆ DNS, time server, syslog, and IP services

◆ License keys for hardware, software

◆ Password and credentials for access and applications

◆ Current configurations (switch, vSphere, server)

Documenting how these tools are used in conjunction with the lab can be infinitely valuable, regardless of your lab environment. It will enable you to deploy and configure the lab in a realistic and production-like fashion and use this collateral to help troubleshoot and solve production problems over the long run. Once you have this information and some planning in hand, the fun begins!

Building the Lab

Whether this is the first lab you've ever built or one in a series of datacenters, a lot can be said for planning and preparation. A well-thought-out lab environment can be built up in a few days, mainly involving racking, stacking, wiring, and cabling, and the remaining time can be spent on configuration. But in the event that everything does not go according to plan, in the following sections we cover some pitfalls to watch out for and hopefully mitigate.

Ensure That You Have Adequate Power and HVAC in Your Lab

We cannot tell you the number of times we were ready to bring a system online in our lab only to find that it needed 220 and we only had 110, or that we only had 15 amps when our demand called for a 30-amp circuit. These problems can be further complicated by the fact that just because you have power doesn't mean you can keep the area cool with your equipment running at full load. If possible, talk with facilities personnel to ensure that you not only have sufficient resources available but that you are also up to code so you don't run the risk of unintentionally bringing something down. Definitely involve the stakeholders early on in the project, including but not limited to budget owner, facilities, electricians, and those involved with security, the network, and storage. Excluding them from the project is a recipe for failure and embarrassment and could ruin credibility/relationships going forward.

Get Your Network Connections Cabled and Run

Some organizations have a catch-all admin who handles making and running the cables for everything including Ethernet, fiber, and beyond. Others outsource the operation to a cabling firm to do all of the heavy lifting. Whether going it alone or working with an outside organization, scheduling and planning has never been so important. We've seen entire projects, whether production or adding an additional connection into the lab, go from being an afternoon of simply plugging in a cable to taking weeks or months to get things properly run and terminated. Figure out just how many network connections will need to be run, terminated, and connected, because adding them after the fact can be quite tedious, arduous, and sometimes downright impossible.

Build Your Software Repository Now

Establish a software repository where you store your ISOs, templates, and other critical files needed for building servers. Having this available will enable you to quickly respond to new requests as they come in versus having to find your original source media, rip it to an ISO, and then transfer it to your cluster. Having your configuration and application software available in a single place can save you a lot of time and hassle. This repository should include what's running in production. Use those templates, those lockdowns, those GPOs, and so on to establish a quality control group for testing. Inconsistencies in the lab will inevitably yield inconsistent results.

Get Your Switch Configurations in Order

Network and storage configurations should always start on a whiteboard, on a spreadsheet, or on paper. In design methodology, this starting point is commonly referred to as the "napkin diagram." After you have a good sense of what you're going to build, you can implement it, and then with minimal effort, you can commit the configuration that is agreed upon. When networking or storage changes are executed by a separate team or even by your own team, knowing what you're going to do and then doing it will save hours or days of troubleshooting.

Get Your IP Space Allocated

The allocation of IP addresses has to be one of the easiest activities. Getting the IP addresses properly configured, routed, addressed by firewalls, and established in any configuration changes is no cakewalk. It is often best to get your hands on a copy of a working switch configuration to validate and make it similar while also identifying what is important and necessary to your success. The transport medium, which vSphere relies upon, is often out of your control, so ensure that you have all of your ducks in a row!

Use Proper Tools for Measurement

In Chapter 2, "Building Your Toolbox," we discussed a number of tools you can use to measure and monitor performance and how to assess your capabilities. To validate the success of your lab environment, some tools are more valuable than others. Unlike in production where you rely upon the macro ecosystem of applications and services to interoperate successfully, the lab is intended to take a microscopic view of the individual use case you're testing. We'll apply some of those principles in the next sections.

How to Build Your Lab

At this point you have a repository of tools at your disposal, and a good sense of why you're building and running your lab and what you plan to do with it. The question now becomes how you go about building the lab. Environments, needs, and demands will vary based upon your environment. In the following sections, we'll work with a sample scenario of a real lab built to demonstrate how to test operational performance.

Test Objective

The goal of this test is to validate the maximum throughput capabilities of vSphere for application access. This provides us with a picture of what the expected ceiling and baseline for our production application access can be, based upon deployed compute, network, and storage solutions.

Lab Summary

For this test, we're creating a VMware ESXi 5.x datacenter consisting of the following items, which closely replicate a microcosm of production:

♦ One 48-port 10 Gigabit Ethernet (10 GbE) networking switch

♦ Two Intel servers with 24 CPUs (4x6) with 96 Gb of memory

♦ One storage controller with 28 500 GB SAS drives

Each of the ESXi servers will have two 10 GbE with one connection dedicated to network access and one connection dedicated to storage access. The storage will be connected by two 10 GbE connections to the switch. The performance workload will be generated by 10 VMs running Microsoft Windows. In addition, the following configurations are made:

♦ An additional switch will be provided for out-of-band management access for compute, storage, and network.

♦ Unless stated otherwise, all configurations will be default.

All of the components are configured using respective vendor best practices for storage, network, and compute (see Tables 3.2-3.4).

Figure 3.11
Infrastructure
diagram

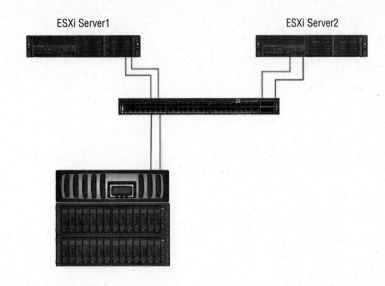

Table 3.2:   ESXi host components

Component	ESXi Host Implementation
Virtual infrastructure	VMware ESXi 5.0, 5.1, 5.5
Server	Intel server
Processors	Four six-core Intel 2.66 GHz
Memory	96 GB
NICs for network and storage	Two 10 GbE controllers
10 GbE switch	10 GbE 48-port

Table 3.3:   Storage components

Component	ESXi Storage Implementation
Storage system	Storage controller
Controller version	Version x.x
Number of drives	28
Size of drives	500 GB
Speed of drives	10K RPM
Type of drives	SAS

TABLE 3.4   Virtual machine configuration

COMPONENT	VIRTUAL MACHINE IMPLEMENTATION
Operating system	Windows Server 2008 R2
Number of virtual processors	1
Memory	4,096 MB
Virtual disk size	100 GB

Provisioning the Lab

For this test we configured a total of five virtual machines on each of the two ESXi hosts. Each of the 10 virtual machines used storage provisioned from the storage controller defined. All of the virtual machine disk files were created on a single VMware datastore created using the 28 500 GB disks allocated on the storage controller. Each of the servers were provisioned with an additional 100 GB disk for the purpose of load testing.

Defining the Workload and Configuration of IOmeter

For this test we used the publicly available IOmeter application discussed in Chapter 2 to generate the load. To test multiple workloads of random and sequential read/writes, the following specifications were defined:

- 4K block size, 75% read, 25% write, 75% sequential, 25% random
- 4K block size, 75% read, 25% write, 100% random
- 64k block size , 90% read, 10% write, 100% random
- 64k block size, 25% read, 75% write, 100% random

If testing VDI workloads, the I/O mix will be inverse, that is, 75%+ write, 25% or less read, except during boot storms.

During the tests, IOmeter was configured with a single worker running on each of the VMs to generate the load. To control the load, we modified the number of outstanding I/O up or down, depending upon the particular use case being tested. Running the IOmeter tests for a consistent period of 15 minutes each, we then collected and recorded the results. With results in hand, the information was calculated, analyzed, and reviewed.

Lab Postmortem

The purpose of this lab was solely to test some scenarios based upon application use cases and report the results. The metrics you define as important beforehand can really help dictate whether a test is successful. Often, people will create a lab scenario with the sole purpose of revealing the outcome they're looking for, tweaking the knobs until the truth is hardly distinguishable from something you might reasonably deploy in production.

The preceding steps help you decide what parameters you want to define in specifying not only what your lab can look like but also what specific and actionable steps you take in producing valid tests. Methodology goes a long way to producing consistent and reproducible results, which will benefit your production environment.

When you're working with a particular vendor's solution, they will often have performance reports that provide a comprehensive framework. Taking advantage of the existing configuration, components, and test cases, you can take a lot off your plate and leverage their efforts so you can focus on your specific business's test lab needs.

Summary

In the end, the test lab is great for not only learning virtualization but also for testing and proving out your production environment and transforming and troubleshooting your most critical applications. Hopefully the strategies here help you produce or improve your existing lab environment to give you confidence and comfort in taking your enterprise to the next steps. While the lab is very beneficial, basic processes are easy to overlook, which can cause unanticipated chaos in the lab, rendering it unusable when needed most. As with any infrastructure, labs require a minimum amount of care and feeding. Neglect leads to the wheels falling off. Consider establishing a formal or informal Lab Manager role within the organization. This is the go-to person for anything pertaining to the lab environment.

Chapter 4

CPU

The allocation of CPU resources is critical to ensuring optimum performance in a virtualized environment. Modern processors are equipped with multiple cores per processor and various technologies to help improve performance for virtualized environments.

In this chapter we look at some of the technologies at work in modern processors and how these technologies are used in virtualized environments based on VMware vSphere 5.5. The first part of this chapter dives into the technical aspects of how CPUs are virtualized, which will provide you with a sound fundamental understanding of what is happening under the hood of virtualization. We also look into one of the most crucial performance components in ESXi, the CPU scheduler, to gain an understanding of how the ESXi CPU scheduler ensures that CPU resources are allocated efficiently and fairly.

In this chapter we look at:

◆ CPU virtualization basics

◆ Hardware protection within the X86 architecture

◆ Hardware- and software-based virtualization

◆ CPU states

◆ The ESXi CPU scheduler

◆ CPU resource management

◆ Virtual machine sizing

◆ Basic CPU performance troubleshooting techniques

Getting to Know the Basics of CPU Virtualization

To gain a better understanding of why performance issues occur in virtualized environments, we need to understand what CPU virtualization is as well as have a basic understanding of how it works. The information contained in this chapter should enable you to size your virtual machines correctly, taking into consideration factors such as the underlying architecture and the type of workloads that your virtual machines will support. In these first sections, we look at the very basics of CPU virtualization.

CPU virtualization enables a virtual machine (VM) to execute the majority of its instructions directly on a physical processor. It enables multiple virtual machines (VMs) running alongside each other to have direct access to a physical processor.

CPU virtualization is made possible by use of a hypervisor, such as VMware ESXi. A hypervisor is also known as a Virtual Machine Manager (VMM) and is essentially a thin layer of software that runs directly on the physical server hardware and is responsible for ensuring the overall system stability. CPU virtualization does not enable multiple VMs to execute on the same processor at the same time, and the VMM is therefore also responsible for ensuring that each VM is scheduled to execute on physical processors fairly.

As you will see later in this chapter, there are situations where the VM needs to execute instructions that could affect other VMs that are running on the same host. In such an event, the VM is not allowed to execute the instruction directly on the physical processor, and the VMM executes the instruction on behalf of the VM in order to make the guest operating system (guest OS) of the VM operate as if it were running on a physical machine.

NOTE   CPU virtualization should not be confused with CPU emulation. With CPU emulation, a software emulator reproduces the behavior of a physical processor type that is not necessarily present in the physical machine. All instructions are run in software by the emulator rather than directly on a physical processor. Although CPU emulation provides portability that allows software that was designed for one platform to run across several platforms, CPU emulation is not best suited for performance-critical environments because it carries some significant performance penalties compared to CPU virtualization.

Understanding CPU Protected Mode in the x86 Architecture

Believe it or not, the x86 architecture, by design, presents some real problems for virtualization. In fact, due to the design of the x86 architecture, it used to be almost impossible to virtualize it. However, through very clever code implemented in software, virtualization of the x86 architecture became possible and VMware is the company that made it happen.

In the following sections, we look at the main obstacle to virtualizing the x86 architecture and how it was overcome. This obstacle is hardware protection that is built into every x86 processor since Intel's 286 and is known as CPU protected mode. We're now going to take you through CPU protected mode and some of the privilege levels in x86-compatible processors as well as how the hypervisor deals with these privilege levels. We also look at the differences between guest application code and guest privileged code as well as determine the privilege levels that each of the two types of code has access to.

REVIEWING THE BACKGROUND OF CPU PROTECTED MODE

CPU protected mode, also called protected virtual address mode, is an operational mode of x86 processors that essentially provides (among other features) hardware-level memory protection. CPU protected mode has been around since the early 1980s when it was first introduced in the Intel 80286 architecture. Before the 80286 architecture, a CPU had only one operational mode, which offered no memory protection with unlimited direct software access to all hardware and memory resources.

In order to comply with a primary design specification of the x86 architecture requiring all new x86 processors to be fully backward compatible with software written for all x86 processors before them, the 80286 processor was made to start or reset in a mode called real mode. Real mode is essentially a mode that turns off the new memory protection features so that it is capable of running operating systems (OSs) written for the 8086 and 80186. When a modern operating system (OS) loads, the processor is switched from real mode into protected mode so that only the kernel of the OS may have unrestricted access to all hardware resources. All other software applications running on the OS has restricted access to hardware resources.

Even today, the newest x86 processors (including x86-64 processors) start in real mode at power-on and can run software written for almost any previous processor (with a few exceptions due to slight instruction set differences).

CPU PROTECTED MODE PRIVILEGE LEVELS

The x86 architecture supports four privilege levels, or *rings*, in which code can run on a processor, with ring 0 being the first level and the most privileged level. Ring 0 is generally used by OS kernels and device drivers. When code is running in ring 0, the processor allows privileged code to have full, unrestricted access to all hardware resources.

The second and third privilege levels are ring 1 and ring 2. They have more restricted access to hardware resources, and although they are not typically used, they can provide address space that some device drivers can use.

The fourth privilege level is known as ring 3, and it's the least privileged level. All user space applications as well as OS code that is determined not to be kernel or driver code will run in ring 3. The code that runs within ring 3 is constrained to run within specific parameters that are set by the privileged code running within ring 0. Most modern OSs make use of ring 0 and ring 3. The four privilege rings are shown in Figure 4.1.

FIGURE 4.1
The x86 architecture has four privilege rings where code can run.

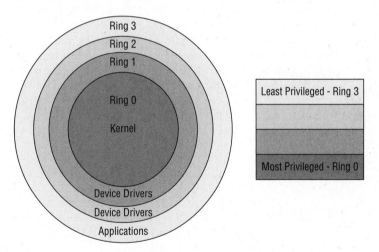

Defining the Types of CPU Virtualization

There are two types of CPU virtualization, namely software-based CPU virtualization and hardware-assisted CPU virtualization. With software-based CPU virtualization, the guest application code within the VM runs directly on the processor, while all guest privileged code is translated by the VMM and the translated code executes on the processor.

With hardware-assisted CPU virtualization, processors with features such as Intel VT and AMD-V provide hardware assistance for CPU virtualization and the binary translation of code within the VMM is therefore not necessary.

In the next two sections, we dive a little further into software-based CPU virtualization as well as hardware-assisted CPU virtualization to help you gain a better understanding of how each of these methods make virtualizing the x86 architecture possible.

Software-Based CPU Virtualization

Software-based CPU virtualization allows the VM's guest application code to run at native speeds directly on the processor in user mode, or ring 3. However, modern OSs are written to expect their kernel and driver code, also known as privileged code, to run on the processor within ring 0. Modern OSs are designed and written to expect their kernels to essentially "own" all of the hardware resources. This is not a problem and works well if the OS is running on a physical machine.

When the OS is running on a VM, it still expects to have its privileged code running within ring 0 and therefore still expects to have full ownership of all of the physical hardware resources.

To manage physical hardware resources as well as all of the VMs running on the host, the VMM also needs to be running within ring 0. This creates a problem if the privileged code for both the VM guest OS and the VMM needs to run within ring 0 at the same time. However, the VM guest OS privileged code cannot be allowed to run in ring 0 alongside that of the VMM. If the VM guest OS privileged code is allowed to run in ring 0 alongside the VMM, the privileged code within the VM guest OS could affect what's happening on other VMs as well as compromise the stability of the VMM itself.

To get around this conflict of interest between the VM guest OS and the VMM, the VMM is the only code that is allowed to run in ring 0. The VM guest OS therefore has its privileged code running in ring 1 if the guest OS is a 32-bit OS. If the guest OS is a 64-bit OS, its privileged code will run within ring 3. This approach requires the VMM to closely monitor the execution of the VM. The VMM will then trap instructions from the VM guest OS privileged code that cannot be virtualized and translate them into new sequences of instructions that have the effect on the virtual hardware that the guest OS intended, as shown in Figure 4.2.

FIGURE 4.2
Software-based CPU virtualization with binary translation by the VMM

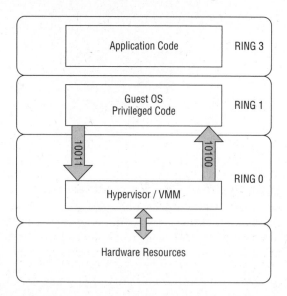

Because the guest OS privileged code has to be trapped and translated before it can execute on the processor, the code normally ends up being slightly larger than the native code and therefore usually executes more slowly. Applications or programs with a significant privileged code component, such as system calls, context switches, traps, and page table updates, can run slower in a virtualized environment, especially when software-based CPU virtualization is in use. However, programs with a small privileged code component may run with speeds that are very close to native.

HARDWARE-ASSISTED CPU VIRTUALIZATION

In 2006, both Intel and AMD launched the first of their processors that included support for hardware-assisted CPU virtualization. Intel's Virtualization Technology (VT) and AMD's AMD-V provide extensions to the x86 architecture, and both offer two modes of execution, known as root mode and guest mode. Each mode of execution provides support for all four privilege rings (ring 0 to 3).

These two modes of execution allow both the VMM and the VM guest OS to use all four privilege rings by running in different modes on the processor. For example, the VMM uses ring 0 and 3 within root mode, while the VM guest OS uses ring 0 and 3 within guest mode. However, the semantics of execution are different in each of these two modes. For example, privileged instructions in guest mode ring 0 will cause the CPU to exit from guest mode and enter root mode, whereas privileged instructions by the VMM in root mode will execute on the processor as specified by the x86 architecture.

Although Intel VT and AMD-V now allow VMs to execute privileged code in guest mode ring 0, some privileged instructions still need to be intercepted and handled by the VMM for correct operation. These privileged instructions are targeted by the CPU hardware and are automatically trapped to the VMM, as shown in Figure 4.3.

FIGURE 4.3

Hardware-assisted CPU virtualization enables two modes of execution, namely root mode and guest mode.

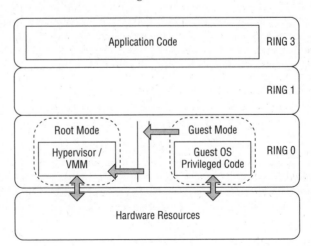

In addition to the two modes of execution, the processor contains a virtual machine control structure (VMCS). The VMCS is used to store the states of both the host (root) and guest. The VMCS is a critical component that allows interaction between the host and guests. When a privileged instruction is trapped to the VMM, the CPU will store the current guest state in the VMCS and then exit guest mode. The processor then loads the host state from the VMCS and enters root mode. Once the CPU is running in root mode, the VMM emulates the instruction that had caused the exit from guest mode and ensures that it has the intended effect on the virtual hardware. Once the VMM has finished processing the instruction, it issues the VMRUN instruction to the processor. The guest state is loaded from the VMCS and the VM continues processing in guest mode.

Because guest mode exits are expensive in terms of CPU time, both Intel and AMD have put in place numerous optimizations to improve performance by trying to avoid unnecessary exits. For example, simple instructions that would require very simple processing to be done by the VMM could actually be processed in guest mode without even exiting to the VMM.

However, in the case where a privileged instruction within guest mode had to be trapped and had therefore caused an exit from guest mode, the VMM would have to fetch and decode the instruction that had caused the exit in order to determine the operation that should be performed. This can also be a costly exercise in terms of CPU time. To save the VMM from having to manually fetch and decode the instruction itself, the CPU hardware can record the information and have the VMM read it out of a register, which greatly improves performance.

Distinguishing between Physical CPUs and Virtual CPUs

It is important to understand the difference between a physical processor (pCPU) and a virtual processor (vCPU). Most modern processor packages have multiple physical processor cores per package. A processor package is defined as single core or group of cores mounted on a single physical CPU socket. In VMware ESXi, each physical processor core is detected as a pCPU in its own right. For example, when installed on a server with one quad-core CPU package, VMware ESXi will report and make available for use four pCPUs. If hyper-threading is available and enabled on an Intel processor, each physical processor core will have two hardware threads. In this case, ESXi will detect each thread as a pCPU in its own right.

NOTE   Depending on the workload, hyper-threading could have a positive or negative impact on performance. We look into the scheduling impact of hyper-threading later on in this chapter in the section "Load Balancing on Hyper-Threading Architecture."

A vCPU is the representation of a pCPU to the guest OS of a VM. Each VM will be configured to have at least one vCPU. Each vCPU is scheduled in turn to execute on any available pCPU by the VMM. The concept of a vCPU essentially provides you as a VMware ESXi administrator with a method of defining how many pCPUs any VM is able to simultaneously access at any given time. In other words, a vCPU cannot be scheduled to run on more than one pCPU at a time.

Understanding vCPU States

In this section we look into the different states that a vCPU can be in. Like a software process, a vCPU may be in one of the following states:

Running State   When a vCPU is in a running state, it has been scheduled to run and is processing instructions on a physical CPU core.

Ready State   When a vCPU is in a ready state, it is ready to be scheduled to run on a physical processor core but is unable to execute on a physical core because one or more physical or logical cores are not available to the respective vCPUs at the time as a result of co-scheduling latency. Time spent in a ready state counts toward the %RDY metric.

Wait_Idle State   The wait_idle state is a special state that the vCPU can enter. The wait_idle state does not depend on a resource and an idle CPU in this state will wake up when interrupted.

Wait State   A CPU is in a wait state when it is experiencing a delay in processing because it is waiting on I/O operations to complete on external system components that are typically slower than the processor, such as memory, disk, or network operations. Because modern processors run at very high speeds, other system components might struggle to keep up with the CPU. In this state the CPU is waiting on information to be delivered from these other components. When a processor is in a wait state, it is deemed a wasted resource because it has the capacity to process large amounts of data but is dependent on other components to deliver sufficient data to process.

Techniques such as CPU cache and instruction pipelines have been designed to try to reduce the time that a CPU will spend in a wait state. Although these techniques help improve performance a great deal, they are unable to completely solve the problem. Typically the wait state applies only to physical CPUs.

Introducing the ESXi CPU Scheduler

At the heart of VMware ESXi is the CPU scheduler. The CPU scheduler is a critical component that ensures the optimal assignment of worlds to pCPUs. In VMware ESXi, a world is an execution context similar to a process or a thread in a conventional OS such as Windows.

The primary objective of the VMware ESXi CPU scheduler is to schedule worlds to be executed on pCPUs in a way that meets strict objectives in terms of performance, throughput, and processor utilization.

As discussed previously, in the section "Defining the Types of CPU Virtualization," the CPU scheduler is also responsible for ensuring that the VM guest OS is "fooled" into believing that it completely owns the shared pCPU resources without compromising the VMs' security or stability.

In the following sections, we look into the CPU scheduler and the technologies it employs that make VMware ESXi the market-leading hypervisor that it is today in terms of performance, stability, and security.

Understanding the Proportional Share-Based Algorithm

VMware ESXi employs a proportional share-based algorithm to determine which VMs should be favored in terms of CPU and memory resources when resources are being contended for by different VMs. Because one of the main responsibilities of the CPU scheduler is to schedule worlds in a way that meets objectives in terms of performance and utilization, it will from time to time have to make difficult calculations. The CPU scheduler will have to calculate the next world to be scheduled, and if the target physical processor is occupied by another world, it needs to calculate whether or not to interrupt the world that is currently running on the processor in order to schedule the selected world on that processor.

To solve this problem, the proportional share-based algorithm enables the ESXi CPU scheduler to make important scheduling calculations by associating each world with a share of the available physical CPU resources. The share entitlements are assigned to each world based on calculations made from the resource settings such as shares, reservations, and limits. The VMware ESXi system administrator configures these settings.

CALCULATING PRIORITY VALUES

Before the CPU scheduler schedules the next world, it calculates and assigns numerical priority values to each world that is ready to be scheduled. In VMware ESXi, a numerically lower priority value is considered a high priority and a high numerical priority number is considered a low priority. For instance, a priority value of 0 would be considered a high priority, while a priority value of 50 would be considered a lower priority.

Unlike Unix, where a process can be assigned a higher priority by the administrator, VMware ESXi dynamically calculates priority values based on the consumption of entitled resources. As an administrator, you have control over entitlements, but consumption depends on many factors, including application workload and system load.

To calculate the priority value of a world, the CPU scheduler looks at the amount of CPU resources that are currently being consumed by the world as a percentage of its CPU resource entitlement. If the world has consumed less than its entitlement, it is considered to be a high priority and will likely be scheduled to run next. In addition, the degree in difference between the entitlements of two worlds also dictates the amount of CPU time that should be allocated to each world.

BENEFITS OF PROPORTIONAL SHARE-BASED SCHEDULING

In an environment where CPU resources are contended for by VMs, the proportional share-based scheduling algorithm allows us to control the amount of CPU time that each VM can consume by assigning share values to VMs, as shown in Figure 4.4.

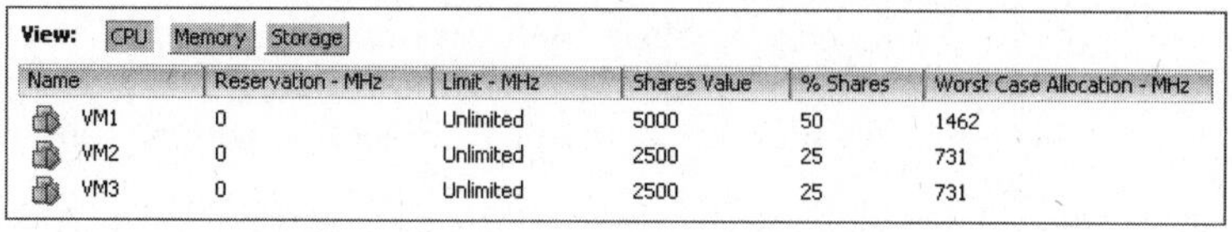

FIGURE 4.4
VMs can have share values assigned to determine the entitlement of CPU time allocated to each VM.

View: CPU Memory Storage					
Name	Reservation - MHz	Limit - MHz	Shares Value	% Shares	Worst Case Allocation - MHz
VM1	0	Unlimited	5000	50	1462
VM2	0	Unlimited	2500	25	731
VM3	0	Unlimited	2500	25	731

In Figure 4.4, we have three VMs on a VMware ESXi 5.5 server, VM1, VM2, and VM3, contending for CPU resources. We require VM1 to have 50 percent of the available physical CPU resources and require that VM2 and VM3 have 25 percent each. To achieve our goal, we have assigned 5,000 shares to VM1, 2,500 shares to VM2, and another 2,500 shares to VM3. As a result, we have issued a combined 10,000 shares between the three VMs. Because VM1 has 5,000 of the 10,000 shares, it will be scheduled to run for 50 percent of the available CPU time, assuming that the only resource management settings changed were the VMs share values and that no reservations or limits are in place. Later on in this chapter, we will look at reservations and limits.

Figure 4.5 and Figure 4.6 show proportional share-based scheduling in action.

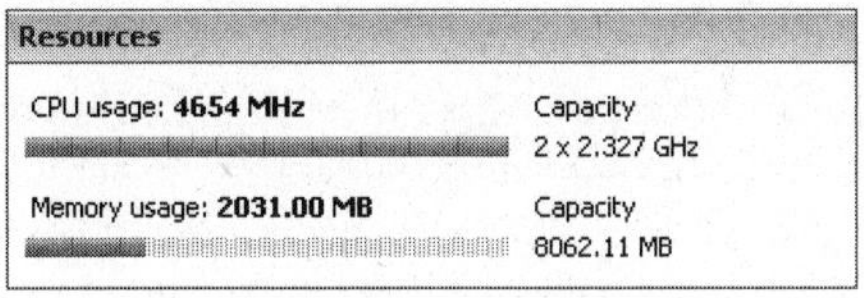

FIGURE 4.5
All physical
processors in the
ESXi host are 100
percent utilized, and
VMs are therefore
contending for
resources.

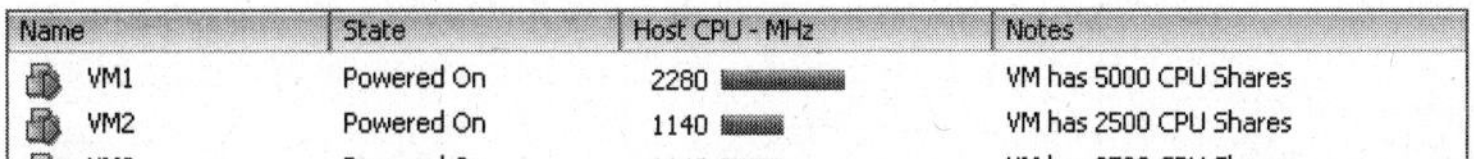

Resources	
CPU usage: **4654 MHz**	Capacity 2 x 2.327 GHz
Memory usage: **2031.00 MB**	Capacity 8062.11 MB

FIGURE 4.6
Proportional share-
based scheduling in
action. VMs are only
scheduled to run
based on their share
values.

Name	State	Host CPU - MHz	Notes
VM1	Powered On	2280	VM has 5000 CPU Shares
VM2	Powered On	1140	VM has 2500 CPU Shares
VM3	Powered On	1140	VM has 2500 CPU Shares

Here we have a VMware ESXi 5.5 host with two physical CPUs, which makes available a total of 4,654 MHz. The VMware ESXi host has only three VMs running on it. Each VM has a single vCPU and has been loaded with identical workloads within the guest OS. Each VM is using 100 percent of its vCPU.

Because there are only two physical CPUs available in the ESXi host and three vCPUs being scheduled at 100 percent each, we have a situation where the VMs are contending for CPU resources. The CPU scheduler now divides the available physical CPU resources between the VMs based on the number of shares that have been allocated to each VM.

NOTE Proportional share-based scheduling is invoked only when physical resources become contended for. When there are sufficient hardware resources available to satisfy demand, VMs will be scheduled according to their requirements, regardless of any share values that have been configured.

NOTE The 10,000 share value is purely an example. If we were to issue 1,000 shares by assigning 500 shares to VM1, 250 shares to VM2, and another 250 shares to VM3, we would end up with the same share percentages.

As you can see from the previous example, proportional share-based scheduling allows us to specify custom share values on individual VMs to suit our requirements.

In addition to assigning share values to individual VMs, shares can also be defined on pools of VMs. These pools are called resource pools and allow administrators to configure resource settings on groups of VMs. Shares assigned to a resource pool entitles the child VMs of the resource pool to some of the ESXi hosts resources and will be distributed between child VMs within the resource pool. Resource pools are covered in more detail later in this chapter.

The proportional share-based algorithm will only be enforced by the CPU scheduler if VMs are contending for physical CPU resources. If there is no resource contention, the VMs will be scheduled to run on the physical CPU as and when they require.

Understanding CPU Co-Scheduling

In multiprocessor systems, such as VMs with multiple CPUs or cores assigned, it is possible to execute a set of threads or processes at the same time to achieve better performance. Because some threads or processes synchronize with each other, it is important that they are scheduled to execute on their respective processors at the same time to avoid an increase of latency in the synchronization of those threads. For this reason, modern OSs require all of their CPUs to progress in a synchronized manner, since they have been programmed to run on physical hardware with exclusive access to all available resources. If the OS detects a skew in synchronization among its CPUs, the OS might malfunction.

In the same way that an OS on a physical machine will be required to maintain synchronous progress on all of its CPUs, an OS running in a VM will also require synchronous progress on all of its vCPUs. A vCPU is considered to make progress if it consumes CPU time or halts.

The ESXi CPU scheduler has the responsibility to ensure that all vCPUs assigned to a VM are scheduled to execute on the physical processors in a synchronized manner so that the guest OS running inside the VM is able to meet this requirement for its threads or processes.

STRICT CO-SCHEDULING

In the early versions of the ESX hypervisor, the CPU scheduler implemented what's known as strict co-scheduling. With strict co-scheduling, the CPU scheduler maintains a cumulative skew on each vCPU of a multiprocessor VM. However, it is a common misconception that the strict co-scheduling always requires all of the vCPUs to be scheduled on physical CPUs at the same time, even if not all of the vCPUs were in use by multi-threaded applications. This is not exactly the case because there is no co-scheduling overhead for idle CPUs. When a single-threaded application runs in a multiprocessor VM, one of the vCPUs will execute on a physical processor and the other vCPUs will be idle. Therefore, only one physical CPU will be required to be available.

Although only one physical CPU needs to be available, there are some major drawbacks in terms of performance when assigning multiple vCPUs to a VM with a single-threaded application, especially in a strict co-scheduling environment. As discussed earlier, a vCPU is considered to make progress if it consumes CPU time. As the single-threaded application executes on one of the vCPUs, that vCPU is progressing while the other vCPUs stay idle. This causes the skew in synchronization between the vCPUs to grow. At some point the skew will grow to exceed a threshold in milliseconds, and as a result, all of the vCPUs of the VM will be co-stopped and will be scheduled again only when there are enough physical CPUs available to schedule all vCPUs simultaneously.

Although this approach ensures that the skew does not grow any further, it might lead to CPU fragmentation. VMs with multiple vCPUs will not be scheduled until enough physical CPUs are available to schedule all vCPUs of multi-vCPU VMs at the same time, causing scheduling delay and lower CPU utilization.

UNDERSTANDING RELAXED CO-SCHEDULING IN VMWARE vSPHERE 5.5

With relaxed co-scheduling in ESXi 5.5, the progress of each vCPU in a VM is tracked individually. The skew is measured as a difference in progress between the slowest vCPU and each of the other vCPUs.

Also, in ESXi 5.5, the co-scheduling enforcement becomes a per-vCPU operation. In previous versions of ESX, the entire VM was stopped when the accumulated skew exceeded the threshold. However, in ESXi 4 and later, including ESXi 5.5, only the vCPUs that advanced too much are individually stopped, allowing the lagging vCPUs to catch up. In addition to stopping vCPUs individually, they can now be started individually

In terms of measuring the progress made by a vCPU, the VMM in ESXi 5.5 considers a vCPU to be making progress only if it consumes CPU time at a guest level or halts. Any time spent by the VMM on behalf of the VM is excluded from the progress calculation. As a result, the VMM might not always be co-scheduled, but this is not a problem because not all operations in the VMM will benefit from being co-scheduled anyway. When an operation in the VMM can benefit from being co-scheduled, the VMM makes explicit co-scheduling requests.

The CPU Scheduler Cell

It is important to design a CPU scheduler that scales well on systems with many physical processors. To help achieve this goal, the CPU scheduler cell structure was implemented in previous versions of VMware ESXi.

The CPU scheduler cell is essentially a group of physical processors that serves as a local scheduling domain. This allows the scheduler to make scheduling decisions that will only involve a single cell of processors that does not impact other processors or cells of processors.

Modern OSs are designed with the scalability of the CPU scheduler in mind. Remember, all OSs have their own CPU schedulers, not only hypervisors. A well-designed scalable CPU scheduler allows the overhead of the CPU scheduler to remain relatively small as the number of processors or the number of processes, or in ESXi terminology, worlds, increases.

DISTRIBUTED LOCKING WITH THE SCHEDULER CELL

The CPU scheduler code in VMware ESXi can concurrently execute on multiple physical processors. It is therefore possible that the CPU scheduler code will have concurrent access to the same data structure that contains the scheduler states. To ensure the integrity of the scheduler states, all accesses to the data structure are serialized by a lock. A simple approach would be to have a global lock, protecting all scheduler states. However this would significantly impact performance because it serializes all concurrent scheduler invocations. Thus, for better performance, a finer-grained locking approach is required.

In earlier versions of VMware ESXi, distributed locking using the scheduler cell is used because this provides finer-grained locking of the scheduler states. Instead of using a global lock to serialize scheduler invocations from all processors, ESXi partitions physical processors on a host into multiple cells where each cell is protected by a separate cell lock. Scheduler invocations from the processors in the same cell would mostly contend for the cell lock.

A VM performs best when all its vCPUs are co-scheduled on distinct processors. All sibling vCPUs might also be required to be co-scheduled to ensure correct operation of the guest OS and its applications. It is also more efficient to restrict the sibling vCPUs to be scheduled only within a cell at any moment. For this reason, the scheduler cell must be large enough to fit all of an entire multiprocessor VM's vCPUs into the cell.

Although the scheduler cell provides a method of protecting the scheduler states while maintaining optimum performance, it could actually cause the same problem that it was designed to solve. The scheduler cell was implemented to enable the CPU scheduler to be more scalable. However, as you will see in the next section, scheduler cells could actually limit scheduler scalability.

ELIMINATION OF THE SCHEDULER CELL IN vSPHERE

As mentioned in the previous section, the scheduler cell was implemented in earlier versions of VMware ESXi in order to make the CPU scheduler more scalable. However, VMware calculated that the scheduler cell could actually limit the scalability of the CPU scheduler.

The width of a VM is defined by the number of vCPUs that it has assigned to it. In VMware vSphere 4, the maximum number of vCPUs that can be assigned to a single VM is 8. In VMware vSphere 5.5, the maximum number of vCPUs that can be assigned to a VM is 64.

The width of a VM directly impacts the size of the scheduler cell. In VMware vSphere 4, the scheduler cell would have had to be increased to 8, and in vSphere 5.5, the size of the scheduler cell would have had to be increased to 64. If we had a host with 64 physical CPUs (or cores), this would mean that all physical CPUs would have formed part of a single scheduler cell, creating a global lock that would serialize all scheduler invocations and effectively render the scheduler cell useless. This would seriously limit the scalability of the ESXi CPU scheduler.

In addition to the size of the scheduler cell, this approach might also limit the amount of cache as well as the memory bandwidth on multi-core processors with shared cache. To illustrate, let's consider the following scenario. Suppose we have a host with two CPU sockets, each containing a quad-core processor. The processors share the same memory subsystem, including memory bandwidth and cache. It is likely that we would end up with two scheduler cells, each corresponding to a physical processor package. If a VM with four vCPUs is scheduled, it might perform better by utilizing cache or memory bandwidth from two sockets rather than one socket. However, under the scheduler cell approach, the rules state that a VM's sibling vCPUs can only be scheduled within a single processor cell. The VM will therefore only be able to use one socket at a time. As a result, the memory subsystem on the host is not fully utilized.

A new approach had to be found to solve this problem, and as a result, the CPU scheduler cell was eliminated as of VMware vSphere 4. Instead, ESXi now implements a per-physical CPU lock that protects the CPU scheduler states associated with the physical CPU. In addition, a separate per-VM lock protects the states associated with a VM.

Understanding CPU Topology-Aware Load Balancing

VMware ESXi has the ability to detect the physical processor topology as well as the relationships among processor sockets, cores, and the logical processors on those cores. The scheduler then makes use of this information to optimize the placement of VM vCPUs.

Load balancing workloads evenly across physical processors is critical to performance. ESXi achieves CPU load balancing by performing a migration of a world from one busy processor to an idle processor. In a multiprocessor system, an imbalance occurs when a number of worlds are ready to run on one processor and no worlds are ready to run on another processor. If such an imbalance is not corrected, the worlds that are ready to run will accrue unnecessary scheduling latency.

There are two policies that can initiate the migration of a world from one processor to another. The first is referred to as a pull migration, where an idle physical CPU initiates the migration. The second policy is referred to as a push migration, where the world becomes ready to be scheduled. These policies enable ESXi to achieve high CPU utilization and low latency scheduling.

Although worlds can be migrated between physical processors, such migrations do come at a cost. The cost is incurred in terms of latency because it's not simply a matter of executing a world's instructions on an alternative processor. When a world runs on a physical processor, it will contain instructions as well as a working set, which is an amount of memory that is actively being accessed for a period of time. When the world migrates away from the source physical CPU, it has to bring this working set into the cache of the destination physical CPU. If the world has been running on a processor for a long time, the amount of memory that will need to be transferred to the destination processors' cache could be quite large and therefore take a long time to transfer. For this reason, the CPU scheduler has to calculate whether a world would benefit from a migration to another CPU by ensuring that a migration occurs only if the world has not consumed enough CPU resources in the past so that the benefit of the migration outweighs the cost.

UNDERSTANDING CPU AFFINITY

VMware has given you as an administrator the ability to restrict the pCPUs that a VM's vCPUs can be scheduled on. This feature is called CPU scheduling affinity.

NOTE CPU affinity only provides a way for you to restrict a VM to be scheduled on a single pCPU or a set of specific pCPUs. CPU affinity does not dedicate the selected pCPUs to a VM, and the ESXi CPU scheduler will still schedule other VMs on the pCPUs selected for affinity on any particular VMs.

We've seen many configurations where administrators have elected to use affinity settings on some VMs, but in a very restrictive way. For instance, we've seen vSMP VMs with two vCPUs that were configured to only run on two pCPUs. Not only does this configuration restrict the VM's vCPUs to only two pCPUs, but in fact the entire VM world is restricted to two pCPUs, including processes required to emulate device operations such keyboard inputs and mouse inputs.

There is a misconception that setting CPU affinity will automatically lead to improved performance for a specific VM. The truth is that it can and in most cases will lead to decreased performance. Workloads with high intra-thread communications could suffer degraded performance when CPU affinity has been set. CPU affinity can lead to improved performance if the application has a larger cache footprint and can benefit from the additional cache offered by aggregating multiple pCPUs.

It is generally recommended to not manually set CPU affinity and to let the ESXi scheduler take care of ensuring that vCPUs are scheduled in the best possible way, based on the underlying architecture. However, if CPU scheduling affinity is to be used in your environment, be sure that you don't limit the VM world to the number of pCPUs based on the number of configured vCPUs for the VM. In other words, always allow the VM to be scheduled on at least one more pCPU than the number of vCPUs configured for the VM.

CPU AFFINITY AND vMOTION

A VM cannot be migrated with vMotion if CPU affinity has been configured on the VM. If a VM is running a DRS cluster, the options for setting CPU affinity on the VM are available only if the cluster's DRS automation level has been set to manual or if the VM's DRS automation level has been set to manual or disabled in the VM overrides settings of a DRS cluster.

INTRODUCING NUMA

Nonuniform memory access, or NUMA, attempts to address the issue of latency in accessing memory from multi-core processors. To date, memory technologies have struggled to keep up with the ever increasing speed of modern processors. As a result, processors are increasingly starved for data while they have to wait for data to be accessed in memory. In an attempt to limit the number of memory accesses from a processor, large amounts of cache memory are installed on modern processors to allow the processor to keep frequently used data in cache on the processor chip rather than having to access the data from memory. Although this helps to reduce the number of memory accesses, as well as to reduce latency, a dramatic increase in the size of modern operating systems and applications has overwhelmed the improvements in cache memory. In addition, new multi-core processors make the problem even worse because multiple cores are now being starved for memory during memory access operations.

NUMA attempts to address this problem by providing each processor with its own separate memory. However, not all data will be confined to a single task or process. Therefore, more than one processor still requires access to the same data. NUMA systems include additional hardware and software to move data between memory banks, which enables multiple processors to access the same data.

In a NUMA system, there are multiple NUMA nodes. Each NUMA node consists of a set of processors and the memory assigned to those processors. When memory is accessed within the same node, the access is local. When memory is accessed in another node, the access is remote. When memory is accessed remotely, a multi-hop operation is required to get to the memory, therefore causing access latency, which degrades performance. In order to optimize performance, the best approach would be to keep memory access local.

Figure 4.7 depicts an overview of the NUMA architecture.

FIGURE 4.7
NUMA architecture

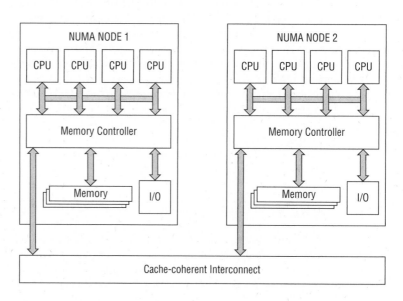

Load Balancing on NUMA Systems

As you saw earlier in this chapter, for optimal performance, the best approach is to keep memory access local to NUMA nodes. However, for ESXi, it is also critical that the CPU load is balanced across NUMA nodes, in order to better utilize available CPU resources, reduce the amount of time VMs have to wait for processors to become available, and improve overall VM performance.

VMware ESXi is capable of load balancing workloads across NUMA nodes by migrating VMs between NUMA nodes.

Verifying NUMA BIOS Settings

It is recommended that you disable node interleaving in the BIOS settings so ESXi can detect the system as a NUMA system. With node interleaving disabled, ESXi will apply NUMA optimizations to the system.

On systems where the BIOS settings for node interleaving are enabled, ESXi will detect the system as a uniform memory accessing (UMA) system and will not apply NUMA optimizations.

Migrating Memory

The NUMA load balancer in VMware ESXi assigns a home NUMA node to each VM. Therefore, the memory for the VM will be allocated from within the home NUMA node. As you saw earlier in this chapter, migrating worlds between physical processors comes at a cost, therefore VMs will rarely be migrated to other physical processors and will rarely be migrated away from a NUMA node. As a result, the memory access for the VM is local in most cases.

There are times that a VM's home node is more heavily utilized than other nodes. In such an event, the VM might be migrated to a less utilized NUMA node, which will improve performance. Once the VM has been migrated to another NUMA node, it will still initially access its memory from the original NUMA node, which of course is remote access, which incurs latency. If the VM is then expected to stay in the new NUMA node, the migration of its memory from the original home NUMA node can happen. Because copying memory has a high overhead, the migration of the memory from the original NUMA node to the new NUMA node will happen gradually.

Load Balancing Wide-VMs on NUMA Systems

As described in the previous section, a NUMA node is made up of a set of processors and the memory assigned to those processors. To reduce latency in memory access times and to improve performance, the ESXi scheduler will always try to schedule all sibling vCPUs of a VM in the same NUMA node. However, there might be a situation where the VM has more vCPUs assigned than the available physical CPU cores in a NUMA node. For instance, a host with two dual-core CPUs will have two NUMA nodes. When a VM with four vCPUs is running on the host, the VM will have two of its vCPUs running on the first NUMA node and the other two vCPUs running on the second NUMA node. This is known as a wide-VM.

To be load balanced on NUMA systems, a wide-VM can be split into smaller NUMA clients that fit within the size of the NUMA node in terms of physical CPU cores. A home node is then assigned to each client. For example, a four-vCPU multiprocessor VM running on a host with two dual-core CPUs has 2 two-vCPU NUMA clients. Thus, the VM has two home nodes because it consists of multiple clients, each client with its own home node.

Figure 4.8 depicts a wide-VM running across two NUMA nodes.

FIGURE 4.8
A wide-VM running across two NUMA nodes

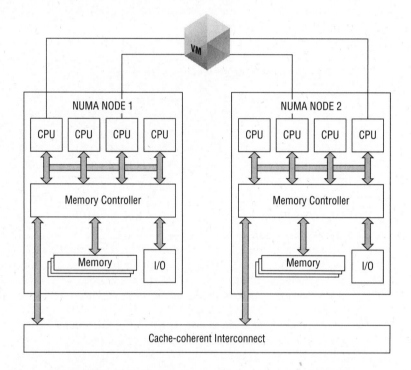

The vCPUs of each NUMA client is scheduled to run within its own home NUMA node. However, because vCPUs in a wide-VM might need to access memory outside their own NUMA node, the memory is interleaved between the home nodes of all the NUMA clients that form part of the VM. This could, however, cause the vCPUs to experience higher average memory access latencies than VMs that fit entirely within a NUMA node. This potential increase in average memory access latencies can be mitigated by appropriately configuring virtual NUMA, a feature that is discussed later on in this chapter.

On systems with hyper-threading enabled, a wide-VM that makes use of full processor cores across NUMA nodes but has less vCPUs configured than the number of logical processors (hardware threads) in each physical NUMA node might benefit from using logical processors with local memory rather than using full cores with remote memory. This can be configured by setting the numa.vcpu.preferHT option to TRUE in the specific VM's advanced configuration.

VM-specific advanced options can be configured in the virtual machine configuration file, although the preferred method is to use the Configuration Parameters dialog in the vSphere Web Client. The Configuration Parameters dialog can be accessed from the VM's settings in the vSphere Web Client, as shown in Figure 4.9.

FIGURE 4.9
Accessing a virtual
machine's advanced
configuration
parameters using the
vSphere Web Client

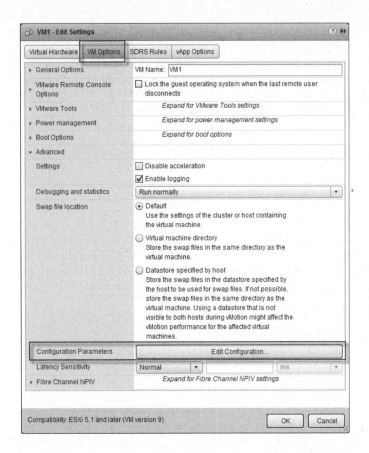

VMware has also given us the option to specify whether or not to prefer using hyper-
threaded logical processors on the same NUMA node over full cores on multiple nodes for all
VMs on a particular host. This option can be set by setting Numa.PreferHT to 1 in the advanced
system settings of each ESXi host. This option is turned off by default. We recommend setting the numa.vcpu.preferHT option on a per-VM basis where required rather than forcing the
behavior on all VMs on a particular host by setting the Numa.PreferHT option. The ESXi host
advanced system settings page is shown in Figure 4.10.

FIGURE 4.10
Setting the Numa.
PreferHT Option
in ESXi advanced
system settings

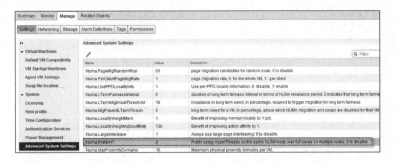

VIRTUAL NUMA

In ESXi 5, virtual NUMA, or vNUMA was introduced. vNUMA exposes the NUMA topology of the ESXi host to the guest OS of the VM. This enables NUMA-aware guest OSs and applications to make the most efficient use of the underlying hardware's NUMA architecture. This can provide significant performance benefits when virtualizing OSs and applications that make use of NUMA optimizations.

When a VM is running on an ESXi 5 host and has been upgraded to virtual hardware version 8 or above, the VM will be able to make use of vNUMA.

When deploying VMs with vNUMA enabled, the sizing of the VMs could also impact performance. Therefore, VMs with vNUMA support should always be sized so that they align with the physical NUMA node sizes. For example, if the ESXi host has a physical CPU with six cores in a single NUMA node, VMs should be sized with multiples of six vCPUs to make efficient use of the underlying NUMA node.

NOTE   vMotion migrations do not alter the vNUMA topology of virtual machines. Therefore, it is important that all hosts within an HA/DRS cluster have a consistent NUMA topology because a vMotion migration of a vNUMA-enabled VM to a host with a different NUMA topology could lead to performance issues.

Enabling vNUMA on a Virtual Machines

vNUMA is enabled on a per-VM basis and is available to VMs with hardware version 8 or above. vNUMA is enabled by default for VMs with more than eight vCPUs.

It is recommended that you use the default vNUMA settings for VMs where the amount of memory is proportionally sized to the number of vCPUs. However, for VMs that consume a disproportionally large amount of memory compared to their configured number of vCPUs, it is possible to manually override the default vNUMA settings by using advanced options.

Table 4.1 shows the advanced options for vNUMA that can be set as part of the advanced configuration for virtual machines.

TABLE 4.1:   Advanced options for vNUMA controls

OPTION	DESCRIPTION	DEFAULT VALUE
cpuid.coresPerSocket	Determines the number of virtual cores per virtual CPU socket. This also determines the size of the vNUMA nodes if a virtual machine has a vNUMA topology. You can set this option if you know the exact vNUMA topology for each physical ESXi host.	1
numa.vcpu.maxPerVirtualNode	If cupid.coresPerSocket is too restrictive, the numa.vcpu.maxPerVirtualNode option may be set directly. However, if this option is set, do not set the cupid.coresPerSocket option.	8

OPTION	DESCRIPTION	DEFAULT VALUE
numa.autosize	Setting this option to TRUE will result in the vNUMA topology having the same number of vCPUs per virtual node as there are pCPU cores on each physical node.	FALSE
numa.autosize.once	With this option set to TRUE, the virtual machine vNUMA topology is set automatically the first time that the VM is powered on. The topology will remain in place for each subsequent power-on operation and will be reevaluated only if the configured number of vCPUs on the VM is modified. Set this option to FALSE if you would like for the vNUMA topology to be reevaluated each time the VM is powered on.	TRUE
numa.vcpu.min	This option specifies the minimum number of vCPUs that are required in order to generate a vNUMA topology for the VM.	9

The settings in Table 4.1 should only be used if and when you are familiar with the physical NUMA topology of your server hardware. If the VM has fewer than nine vCPUs but has a lot of memory, then vNUMA can be enabled using these settings. However, be sure to configure a VM's vNUMA topology so that it fits into the physical NUMA nodes. The cupid.coresPerSocket setting can also be set by adjusting the virtual cores per virtual socket in the VM's CPU settings.

NOTE vNUMA is enabled by default if the VM has more than eight vCPUs and has a virtual hardware version of 8 or above.

CORES PER SOCKET

When VMware initially released a feature in vSphere that is generally referred to as cores per socket, it addressed issues mainly related to software licensing. The feature basically allows you to add multiple vCPU cores to vCPU sockets rather than just having multiple sockets. This allows you to reduce the number of software licenses required when software is licensed per socket while still allowing a VM to have multiple vCPUs.

Although this feature is handy when it comes to software licensing, using it without considering the ESXi hosts' NUMA topology could have a negative performance impact on your VMs. When sizing a vSMP VM with the default configuration of multiple sockets each with a single core, you enable ESXi to automatically select the vNUMA topology for the VM based on the underlying NUMA topology of the ESXi server hardware.

However, when using multiple cores per socket for your VMs, you are essentially defining the vNUMA topology for your VM, and ESXi will honor your selected configuration regardless of whether or not it fits within the NUMA topology of the ESXi server hardware.

If you need to make use of the cores per socket feature, ensure that you mirror the NUMA topology of the underlying hardware.

VMware has carried out a performance study using cores per socket. You can refer to the following location for a detailed description and performance test results of the study:

```
http://blogs.vmware.com/vsphere/2013/10/does-corespersocket-affect
-performance.html
```

LOAD BALANCING ON HYPER-THREADING ARCHITECTURE

Intel's hyper-threading technology has been around for quite some time now. It allows the concurrent execution of instructions from two hardware threads in one processor or core. Although hyper-threading might improve performance on some workloads, the overall performance of both threads is still limited by the computational resources of the single processor core.

The ESXi scheduler will always prefer to schedule worlds on a whole idle core, where both threads are idle. This is because a partial idle core with one thread in use will be slower than a core with both threads in an idle state since two hardware threads compete for a single processor. In addition to a possible performance hit, scheduling a vCPU on a partial core degrades fairness. If two vCPUs have the same resource specification and demand, it is unfair to persistently allow one of the vCPUs to use a whole core and the other vCPU a partial core.

However, if no whole idle core is available, the CPU scheduler will still schedule a vCPU on a partial core, but in order to give a fair account of actual CPU consumption, the CPU scheduler charges only for the CPU time used on that partial core. Accurate accounting of actual consumed CPU enables the scheduler to schedule the vCPU on a whole core if the vCPU has been running on a partial core for a long time, therefore compensating the vCPU for lost time.

By keeping the processor pipeline busier, hyper-threading can provide a performance increase. If the server hardware supports hyper-threading and it has been enabled in the system BIOS, ESXi will automatically make use of it.

On systems with hyper-threading enabled, ESXi displays each CPU thread as a logical CPU core. ESXi will assign sequential CPU numbers to logical cores on the same physical CPU core, with CPUs 0 and 1 on the first core, CPUs 2 and 3 on the second core, and so on.

Because hyper-threading can provide from a slight to a significant performance increase depending on the type of workload, it is recommended that hyper-threading is enabled.

WARNING　Care should be taken when making use of CPU affinity on systems with hyper-threading enabled. For example, a two-vCPU VM with CPU affinity set to pin both of its vCPUs to logical cores that both reside on the same physical CPU core, such as CPUs 0 and 1, could cause poor performance because both vCPUs will be forced to make use of the threads on only one physical CPU core, in effect resulting in each vCPU having access to only half a physical CPU core at any given time.

Multicore-Aware Load Balancing

Modern processors have multiple cores per physical processor. This is also known as the chip multiprocessor (CMP) architecture, where one physical CPU can have many logical CPU cores, each core functioning as a physical CPU in its own right. It is important for the CPU scheduler to be aware of layout processors and their cores. ESXi 5.5 can distinguish between physical processor packages and the cores that reside on those CPU packages.

Due to the various cache implementations in CMP, the ESXi load balancer faces interesting challenges. Some modern processors are equipped with shared L2 or L3 cache, which could be shared by many cores. The last-level cache, or LLC, denotes the cache beyond which access has to go to the memory. In other words, if the requested data is not held in the LLC, the processor will need to access the main memory. A cache-hit occurs when the processor succeeds in accessing data from cache. A cache-miss occurs when the data requested is not held within cache. Because the LLC is still significantly faster than the main memory, it is important to maintain a high cache-hit ratio in the LLC in order to maintain good performance.

As previously mentioned, the ESXi CPU scheduler is able to balance CPU load by migrating worlds from one physical CPU core to another. We also know that costs in terms of latency will be incurred when migrating vCPUs to other processors because the vCPUs will have to warm up the cache in order to successfully migrate to the new processors. The cost of the migration could be relatively small if the cache warm-up can be satisfied by the data held within the LLC. If the LLC is unable to satisfy the cache warm-up, then memory accesses will have to satisfy it, therefore increasing the cost of the migration in terms of latency. In other words, an intra-LLC migration tends to be significantly cheaper than an inter-LLC migration.

As a result, the load-balancing algorithm for the CPU scheduler in ESXi 5.5 has been written to ensure that intra-LLC migrations are always preferred to inter-LLC migrations. The scheduler will always try to migrate a vCPU to a destination physical CPU that shares the LLC with the physical CPU at the origin. However, in the case where a destination processor cannot be located on the local physical CPU socket, the vCPU will be migrated to a remote processor to resolve the load imbalance.

CPU Load-Based Migration Throttling

In ESXi 5.5, vCPU migrations are limited and calculated based on the contribution that the vCPU is making toward the overall load of the current physical CPU. If a vCPU contributes significantly high CPU load to the current physical CPU, the vCPU will not migrate to another physical processor. Instead, a vCPU with a lower contribution is likely to migrate. This prevents too-frequent migrations of vCPUs due to fake imbalances of the physical CPU load.

In an undercommitted environment, it is possible to have only a few processors busy at any given time. This could cause a physical CPU to initiate a pull migration of a vCPU, where an idle physical CPU initiates the migration of the vCPU. Once the vCPU has migrated, it is likely that the original physical CPU would be idle, and as a result it could initiate a pull migration on another vCPU or in fact the same vCPU that was just migrated from it. This could cause a number of unnecessary migrations, which in turn would cause a significant performance impact.

However, in an undercommitted environment, we still require sufficient load balancing to ensure that not all of the vCPUs end up being scheduled on the same physical processors. It is therefore important to note that migrations are throttled only when a vCPU contributes a significantly high portion of the current physical CPU load. The threshold is set high enough to allow migrations that actually improve the load balancing of vCPUs across the overall system.

Virtual SMP Consolidation

ESXi will by default try to schedule all vCPUs of a vSMP virtual machine into as much last-level cache (LLC) as possible in order to increase the cache capacity of the VM. This attempts to reduce the amount of memory accesses the VM has to perform because the processor can store data in the LLC. However, a single VM could end up having all of its vCPUs in separate LLCs.

vSMP consolidation causes sibling vCPUs from a multiprocessor VM to be scheduled within a single LLC. This could be beneficial for certain workloads that could benefit from sharing the cache memory. Identifying such workloads is a challenging task and should be approached on a per-application basis. However, you can statically enable vSMP consolidation.

vSMP consolidation is enabled on a per-VM basis. Note that the vSMP consolidation preference set by you might not always be honored, depending on the availability of physical CPUs sharing the LLC. vSMP consolidation should be enabled only if it is certain that a workload within a VM will benefit from sharing the LLC cache and would not benefit from a larger cache capacity.

Perform the following steps to enable vSMP consolidation for a VM:

1. Right-click the virtual machine and select Edit Settings.

2. Select the Options tab.

3. Under Advanced, click General, and on the right, click the Configuration Parameters button.

4. Click Add Row.

5. Add sched.cpu.vsmpConsolidate and set it to TRUE.

INTER-VM CACHE AFFINITY

When two VMs on the same host communicate frequently, they might benefit from sharing the cache.

The CPU scheduler can transparently detect communications between VMs that are on the same host and attempt to schedule the VMs in the same LLC. This is known as inter-VM cache affinity.

Inter-VM cache affinity applies to uniprocessor VMs as well as multiprocessor VMs. However, depending on the system load, such scheduling is not guaranteed. For example, the CPU scheduler will not migrate all the vCPUs of a VM to a physical processor that is already heavily utilized simply because the VM is in frequent communication with another VM that is already scheduled on the destination physical CPU.

Sizing CPU for Virtual Machines

Virtualization allows organizations to make better use of available server hardware resources by running multiple instances of different operating systems on the same hardware while at the same time completely isolating the operating system instances from one another in VMs. However, because all VMs make use of the same underlying hardware resources, it is important that VMs are sized correctly to ensure optimum performance of each of the VMs.

Some might think that assigning four or more vCPUs to VMs will always help applications perform better than they would with one to two vCPUs. The truth is that when it comes to virtualization, having more assigned resources does not always equal better performance. In fact, as you will see later in this chapter, oversizing VMs can have a negative performance impact on

VMs and applications. Having said that, it goes without saying that failing to assign sufficient resources to a VM might also lead to a negative performance impact.

As you saw earlier in this chapter, not all instructions that a VM's guest operating system will issue can be executed directly from the VM on the CPU. Some privileged, sensitive instructions have to be trapped and handled by the VMM. As a result, there is a slight overhead in CPU virtualization caused by having to handle these sensitive instructions. Thus, configuring a VM with more vCPUs than what its applications are actually able to use (such as running a single-threaded application on a multi-processor VM) might result in increased resource usage, which could lead to a performance impact.

In addition, it should be noted that some applications, even though they have been developed to support multi-threading, might have limits to the number of threads that they support. Deploying such applications on VMs with more vCPUs than what is supported by the application could lead to increased resource consumption and degraded performance. It should also be noted that the guest operating system might migrate the working set of a single-threaded application or process to other vCPUs, which could be scheduled by ESXi to run on another processor, causing the process to lose cache affinity and also possibly leading to degraded performance.

If you're unsure, it is recommended that you create VMs with the minimum number for vCPUs the application to be deployed to the VM supports. Once the application has been deployed, performance tests can be carried out to verify that sufficient CPU resources are available to the application.

Considerations for vSMP

VMs with more than one vCPU assigned are known as vSMP or multi-core VMs. Multi-core VMs enable applications that are able to make use of multiple threads (multi-threaded applications) and processes to be running simultaneously on different physical processors. Although multi-core VMs can greatly improve performance of multi-threaded applications, there are some considerations that should be taken into account when sizing VMs with more than one vCPU.

UNDERSTANDING GUEST OPERATING SYSTEM HALS

Guest operating systems employ their own hardware abstraction layers, or HALs. There are two HALs available to most operating systems, namely the uniprocessor (single-core) HAL and multiprocessor (multi-core) HAL. Although recent versions of Microsoft Windows (such as Windows Vista, Windows 7, Windows 2008, and Windows 2008 R2) have a single HAL that supports systems with uniprocessor and multiprocessor configurations, earlier versions of Windows (such as Windows 2000, Windows Server 2003, and Windows XP) provided a separate HAL for each configuration.

For optimum performance, it is important to ensure that the operating system HAL matches the virtual hardware configuration of the VM. If the VM is configured with a single vCPU, ensure that a uniprocessor HAL is in use by the guest operating system. If a VM is configured with two or more vCPUs, ensure that a multiprocessor HAL is in use by the guest operating system.

Some operating systems, such as Windows Server 2003, will automatically replace a uniprocessor HAL with a multiprocessor HAL if a second vCPU is added to the VM, but this will require a guest operating system reboot. It should be noted that an operating system configured with a uniprocessor HAL that is running on a VM with two or more vCPUs configured will be able to make use of only one vCPU. It is therefore important to ensure that the HAL is changed to a multiprocessor HAL in order to utilize the additional vCPUs.

A VM that has been reconfigured from having two or more vCPUs to having only one vCPU, and that is running a guest operating system prior to Windows Vista or Windows 2008 with a multiprocessor HAL, will not have its HAL replaced automatically by the guest operating system and will continue to operate using a multiprocessor HAL. In this case, it is important that the HAL is changed to a uniprocessor HAL manually by an administrator.

Considerations for NUMA and vNUMA

As we discussed earlier in this chapter, NUMA can greatly improve performance for workloads on an ESXi host. However, the sizing of VMs can have an impact on the effectiveness of NUMA support in ESXi.

The general rule is to always try to size larger VMs to fit within the physical NUMA node boundaries. For example, when a physical server's NUMA nodes is made up of six cores per node, try to size the VM in multiples of six vCPUs.

In certain cases, and depending on their workload type, for smaller VMs (VMs with fewer than eight vCPUs assigned), it might be beneficial to enable vNUMA and split each VM's vCPUs between NUMA nodes in order to make use of the increased memory bandwidth. As discussed earlier, this behavior can be forced by setting the numa.vcpu.maxPerVirtualNode option in each VM's advanced configuration settings.

Hot Plug of CPU Resources

Some operating systems support the addition of vCPUs while the VM is powered on and the operating system is running. This is known as CPU hot plug. This feature is disabled by default and can be enabled on a per-VM basis from the VMs options in the VMware vSphere Web Client.

As mentioned, this feature is disabled by default because there is overhead that is incurred when it's enabled. In order for the guest operating system to accommodate additional CPU resources that can be added at any given moment by an administrator, it will reserve the resources required to support the maximum number of CPUs that can be added. In vSphere 5.15, this number is 64. Although the overhead and the resulting performance impact is not significant, for best performance, it is recommended to enable this feature only if it is required by the VM. CPU hot plug can be enabled under the CPU section of the VM Settings dialog, as depicted by Figure 4.11.

NOTE   It should be noted that with the CPU hot plug feature enabled, vNUMA will be disabled on the VM. vNUMA is not supported on VMs with CPU hot plug enabled.

Understanding CPU Resource Management

Allocating the correct number of vCPUs to virtual machines based on the workload requirements is important to maintain optimum performance of individual virtual machines are well as the overall vSphere environment. However, sizing virtual machines is only one of the many aspects of managing performance. In addition to the number of vCPUs allocated to a virtual machine, VMware vSphere also provides mechanisms that allow administrators to fine-tune the amount of CPU resources that a virtual machine can consume, such as reservations and limits.

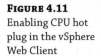

FIGURE 4.11
Enabling CPU hot
plug in the vSphere
Web Client

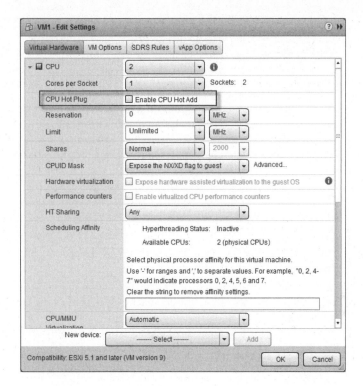

Understanding CPU Reservations

You can configure CPU reservations for virtual machines. A CPU reservation essentially guarantees a specified amount of CPU resources in terms of MHz or GHz to virtual machines. For instance, if you want to ensure that VM1 will always have at least 2 GHz available, you can create a reservation of 2 GHz for the virtual machine.

Reservations can be configured on individual virtual machines or on resource pools. When a reservation is configured on an individual virtual machine, the virtual machine will be allowed to power on only if there is enough unreserved CPU capacity available on the ESXi host to guarantee the specified reservation.

It is important to understand that when an ESXi host becomes constrained for CPU resources, virtual machines will have to contend for *unreserved* CPU resources. When the host is constrained for CPU resources, VMs with reservations will be granted enough CPU resources to satisfy their reservation.

Unlike memory reservations, which we look at in Chapter 5, CPU reservations are not hard reservations. In other words, if a virtual machine VM-A is configured with a 2 GHz reservation and not making use of its full 2 GHz, other virtual machines will be allowed to make use of all the CPU resources, including part of the 2 GHz that has been reserved by VM-A. However, if VM-A is to then demand more CPU time, it will be granted the demanded CPU resources up to its configured reservation, at the expense of other VMs without set reservations.

NOTE VMware ESXi 5.5 also requires access to pCPUs in order to manage VMs and run other host-based services such as the vCenter Agent, HA agents, SSH, and so on. Because some of these services are essential to the stability of the ESXi host and the vSphere environment as a whole, ESXi has to ensure that it always has sufficient CPU resources available to function. Therefore, a minimum reservation of 233 MHz has been configured for ESXi system resources.

CPU reservations on individual VMs can be helpful when it is essential that a virtual machine has at least a set amount of resources available. However, we would use CPU reservations on individual virtual machines with caution and only in circumstances where it's essential to guarantee resources to a particular virtual machine. Also, ensure that the reservation is placed at a level at which the virtual machine is expecting to be running. For instance, if you know a virtual machine will be running between 300 MHz and 600 MHz, a reservation of 500 MHz might be a good size. Placing a much greater reservation on a virtual machine than what the virtual machine requires is a waste of CPU resources that could otherwise have been consumed by other virtual machines.

Understanding CPU Limits

You can limit the amount of CPU resources that is available to virtual machines. CPU limits can be placed on individual virtual machines as well as resource pools. CPU limits are specified in MHz.

With a CPU limit in place, the ESXi scheduler will only schedule the affected virtual machine up to the configured limit. The limit is applied to the virtual machine as a whole and not to individual vCPUs. When the virtual machine demands more CPU resources than the configured limit allows, the virtual machine's vCPUs will be placed in a ready state.

As with reservation and shares, CPU limits can be misunderstood. How is a CPU limit imposed? Does it come into effect only when there is resource contention? Basically, no. Placing a limit on a vCPU will always slow the VM down. By placing a limit on a vCPU, you are telling ESXi not to schedule the vCPU for more than the specified amount of CPU time. For example, 1 MHz is 1 million cycles per second, and 500 MHz is 500 million cycles per second. Placing a 500 MHz limit on a VM will ensure that the VM will not be scheduled for more than 500 million cycles per second, regardless of whether there is CPU resource contention or not.

Configuring CPU Reservations and Limits

CPU reservations and limits on individual virtual machines can be configured under the Resources tab on the VM's settings dialog as depicted in Figure 4.12. CPU reservations and limits are specified in MHz and once set, take effect immediately without a restart of the VM.

Understanding Resource Pools

Resource pools provide you as a vSphere administrator with a logical way of carving your ESXi host's CPU and memory resources into silos of resources to be consumed by VMs that are placed inside the resource pools. Resource pools can be configured with reservations, limits, and shares, and these settings determine the total amount of resources that are available to VMs running within the resource pool. Every stand-alone ESXi host or vSphere DRS cluster has an invisible resource pool. This is the root resource pool, and any additional resource pools that are created are child objects of the root resource pool. When a virtual machine is placed within a resource pool, the virtual machine is a child of that resource pool and is only able to consume resources that have been granted to the resource pool. Multiple VMs can reside in a single resource pool, and VMs that are all children of the same parent resource pool are siblings to each other.

FIGURE 4.12
Configuring CPU reservations and limits

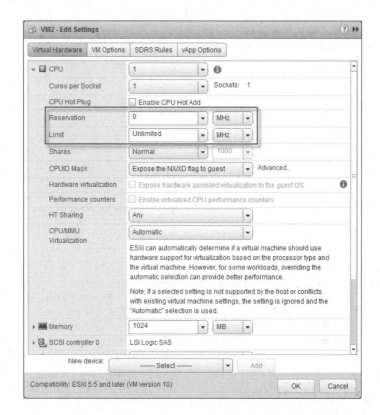

Sibling VMs within a resource pool all have to share the resources that are available to the resource pool. Child VMs can consume only the resources that the parent resource pool are entitled to. If the parent resource pool is configured with a limit of 4 GHz, then all child VMs of the resource pool can consume only 4 GHz in total at any given time.

CPU RESERVATIONS ON RESOURCE POOLS

CPU resources can be reserved at a resource pool level. There are two types of CPU reservations that can be configured on resource pools, namely fixed reservations and expandable reservations.

When a fixed reservation has been configured, the ESXi host will confirm that sufficient unreserved CPU resources are available to the resource pool before allowing a child VM of the resource pool to be powered on. For example, a resource pool has been configured with a fixed reservation of 1 GHz. There are two virtual machines powered on in the resource pool, each with a 400 MHz reservation. Therefore, the used reservation of the resource pool is 800 MHz. An attempt to power on the third virtual machine with a reservation of 400 MHz will fail because the resource pool has insufficient CPU resources configured for the power-on operation to succeed and cannot guarantee that the reservation of the third VM can be met. However, if the third virtual machine has no reservation configured, the power-on operation might succeed because it has no requirement for any of its CPU resources to be guaranteed by the resource pool.

When an expandable reservation has been configured, the ESXi host will allow the resource pool to borrow CPU resources from its parent resource pool (providing the parent resource pool has sufficient CPU resources available) in order to satisfy individual reservations set on child virtual machines.

CPU LIMITS ON RESOURCE POOLS

The amount of CPU resources to be consumed can be limited at a resource pool level. When a limit has been placed on CPU resources within the resource pool settings, the resource pool's child virtual machines' vCPUs will only be scheduled to run on pCPUs as specified by the limit. For example, a resource pool with a limit of 2 GHz contains four powered-on virtual machines. When the combined CPU utilization of all vCPUs of all virtual machines reaches 2 GHz, the vCPUs will not be scheduled above 2 GHz and the CPU-ready metric of each vCPU will increase.

SHARES ON RESOURCE POOLS

CPU shares can be configured at a resource pool level. It is important to understand that a share value assigned at the resource pool level determines the amount of CPU resources that a resource pool is entitled to when the ESXi host is constrained for CPU resources. If a resource pool has sibling objects (such as resource pools or VMs that exist on the same level in the resource pool hierarchy), the share values of each of these sibling objects will determine the amount of CPU resources as a percentage that are available to each object.

For example, say we have an ESXi host with two resource pools configured, namely RP1 and RP2. RP1 has been configured with a custom share value of 1,500 and RP2 has been configured with a custom share value of 500. This means that during times of contention, RP1 will be entitled to 75 percent of the total amount of available CPU resources on the ESXi host and RP2 will only be entitled to 25 percent. Based on this configuration, one would assume that VMs placed within RP1 will always be favored when resources are contended for.

It is, however, not always as straightforward as that. When resources are contended for on an ESXi host, based on the configuration given in the example, we could assume that any child VMs in RP1 will always be favored over child VMs in RP2 because RP1 has been configured to be entitled to 75 percent of CPU resources based on its share value. This is where a very important fact is normally overlooked. When there is resource contention on a host, resources are always first contended for at *a resource pool level* and not at a VM level. That is an important distinction to make because the outcome of the resource entitlement calculation at the resource pool level, which is determined by settings such as shares and reservations, will determine the total amount of resources available to *all* child objects (child VMs as well as child resource pools) of each resource pool. Once the resource pool entitlements have been established, child VMs in each resource pool will have to contend *with each other* for the resources that are available to their *parent resource pool only*.

Using the resource pool configuration given in the example, we can prove to you that during times of resource contention, VMs that are children of RP1 might not necessarily be favored. Say, for example, that RP1 contains 10 VMs, each with a single vCPU. RP2 contains 2 VMs, also with a single vCPU each. Because RP1 has 10 vCPUs to satisfy, RP1's child VMs will each be entitled to 10 percent of RP1's total entitled resources. RP2 only has 2 vCPUs to satisfy, so RP2's child VMs will each be entitled to 50 percent of RP2's total entitled resources.

Based on the example configuration, and bearing in mind that no reservations, limits, or custom shares have been configured for any of the individual VMs, when resources are contended for, each VM in RP1 will be entitled to only 7.5 percent of the total available resources of the ESXi host, while each VM in RP2 will be entitled to 12.5 percent of the total available resources of the ESXi host.

When configuring resource pools, and especially share values on resource pools, ensure that you have calculated what your VMs will be entitled to. The preceding example clearly shows how share settings on resource pools can have unintended effects. Also, never use resource pools as folders to organize the Hosts And Clusters view within vSphere. Placing VMs within nested resource pools could and most probably will have serious performance implications, especially when resources are contended for. Resource pools were designed and are intended to be used to logically create silos of resources, not as folders. It was easy enough for us to demonstrate how unintended negative performance implications can be created by only two sibling resource pools that at first glance looked like a very simple resource pool configuration with a specific goal of favoring the pool with the majority stake in terms of shares. In reality, when we looked deeper into the scenario, the opposite is true.

Troubleshooting CPU Performance Problems

VMware ESXi is the leading bare-metal hypervisor in the industry today. It is light and very secure, has a small footprint on disk, and is finely tuned and capable of delivering outstanding performance. However, each environment in which ESXi can be deployed is unique and differs from other environments in its requirements, combination of hardware resources, size of the deployment, and workload types. VMware has configured ESXi with a set of default options that would best suit most of the possible deployment scenarios in terms of performance, but due to many variables in each environment, performance issues may arise.

In the remaining sections of this chapter, we look at some of the most common CPU performance issues. We look at how to determine the possible cause of such issues and how to resolve them.

Using esxtop to Diagnose CPU Performance Issues

The "top" utility has been around in the Unix/Linux world for many years. It is used by Unix and Linux administrators the world over to gain an insight into the real-time utilization of CPU and memory resources by application processes.

Thankfully, VMware has provided ESXi administrators with a similar tool, esxtop. Although we will be using esxtop in this chapter to help troubleshoot CPU-related performance issues, we will not be covering esxtop in detail. Please refer to Chapter 2, "Building Your Toolbox," for more details on how to use esxtop.

Displaying CPU Performance Metrics in esxtop

You can access esxtop from the ESXi server console or, if SSH is enabled on the ESXi server, over a secure shell using an SSH client such as PuTTY. VMware also provides a utility called resxtop that ships with the vSphere Management assistant. The resxtop utility can be used from the vSphere Management Assistant to remotely access esxtop on ESXi hosts.

Although this chapter is not intended to cover how to use esxtop, it is a good idea to have a quick look at how to navigate to the CPU metrics screen within it.

To access esxtop, log into the ESXi server troubleshooting console, either directly from the server console or via SSH. Once logged in as the root user, type **esxtop** and press return. This will open the esxtop utility.

Now that you have esxtop up and running, you need to switch to the CPU metrics screen by pressing the c key. Once on the CPU metrics screen, esxtop will display CPU metrics for all VMs that are running on the host as well as all system processes that are in use by the ESXi host itself. You can restrict the view to show only VM CPU metrics by pressing V. Note that this is an uppercase V (Shift+V).

By pressing the f key, you can customize the CPU metric view to show only the metrics that you would like to have displayed. For the purposes of troubleshooting CPU-related performance issues, we are most interested in the metrics shown in Table 4.2.

TABLE 4.2:   Esxtop CPU performance metrics

METRIC	DESCRIPTION	POSSIBLE CAUSE	PERFORMANCE THRESHOLD
%RDY	CPU Ready Time A percentage value for the specified monitoring time period. The value returned is the %RDY sum of all vCPUs assigned to the VM.	The ratio between provisioned vCPUs and available pCPUs in the ESXi host is too high, excessive use of vSMP, or CPU resource limits are in place on the VM.	10% per vCPU based on the following guide: Good: 1% to 5% Moderate: 6% to 9% Bad: 10%+
%CSTP	CPU Co-Stop A percentage value for the specified monitoring time period. The value returned is the %CSTP for the sum of all vCPUs that form part of the VM.	Excessive use of vSMP on the VM.	3%
%SYS	CPU time spent by ESXi system services on behalf of the VM.	Possibly caused by high I/O in the VM.	20%

Metric	Description	Possible Cause	Performance Threshold
%MLMTD	Percentage of time that the vCPU was ready to run but was denied CPU time by the CPU scheduler.	The CPU scheduler stopped the vCPU from being scheduled in order to adhere to CPU resource limits set on the VM.	0%
%SWPWT	Time that the VM had to wait for swapped memory paged to be retrieved from disk.	The ESXi host is memory constrained due to memory overcommitment.	5%

NOTE   By default, esxtop metrics are refreshed every 5 seconds. The update interval can be changed to a minimum of 2 seconds by pressing s followed by the number of seconds. The 2 and 8 keys on the number pad can be used to move the highlighted row up or down.

High CPU Ready Time

Usually the very first metric ESXi administrators look at when troubleshooting a poor performance is the CPU Ready Time (%RDY) metric. This metric enables us to see, in real time, just how long a VM's vCPU(s) has to wait to gain access to the pCPUs. A high CPU ready time is not necessarily caused by high pCPU utilization in terms of MHz; it's more likely caused by excessive use or consolidation of vSMP on one or more VMs per host. Another cause could also be the overcommitment of vCPUs in general on the ESXi host.

When troubleshooting VMs with high CPU ready time, it is important to take into consideration that the %RDY metric in esxtop is the sum of all vCPUs that form part of a particular VM. In other words, a VM with two vCPUs assigned may have a maximum %RDY time metric value of 200%. Generally, a %RDY metric for a 2vCPU VM can be 18 to 20 %RDY before a real performance impact will be present on the VM, or roughly 8 to 10 %RDY per vCPU.

The most likely cause of a high %RDY metric is excessive use of vSMP on the VM that is experiencing the issue. On large VMs that have eight or more vCPUs, a high %RDY value might also cause a high %CSTP value because some vCPUs will be make progress faster than their siblings. In this case, the best course of action would be to move the VM to an ESXi host with more pCPUs available or to move some smaller VMs away from the host where the large VM is running.

It could be worth considering removing some vCPUs from larger VMs where possible. Carrying out investigations into the guest operating systems' actual utilization statistics might reveal that all vCPUs aren't heavily utilized. In such cases, it more than likely that a performance improvement will be seen when running the VM with fewer vCPUs because it will help reduce %RDY and %CSTP times, resulting in improved overall performance.

High ESXi Host CPU Utilization

There may be times when administrators find that a few VMs are performing poorly. Further investigation might reveal that the VMs all reside on the same ESXi host and that the ESXi host is showing a relatively high overall CPU utilization figure. Simply because the ESXi host is reporting high CPU utilization does not necessarily mean that the ESXi host is unable to cope with the demand for CPU resources.

We can use esxtop effectively in determining whether or not the cause for the performance issues are due to limited pCPU resources on the ESXi host.

Figure 4.13 depicts a typical esxtop screen, showing vCPU metrics for VMs only.

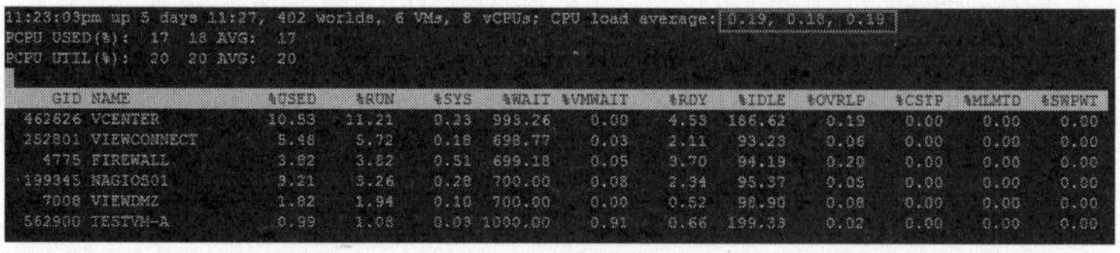

FIGURE 4.13

esxtop showing vCPU metrics for VMs

Whenever investigating the cause for poor performance for VMs all residing on the same ESXi host, the first clue of a possible cause for the poorly performing VMs can be found on the very first line of esxtop, as highlighted in Figure 4.12. If any of the values on the first line indicates 1 or higher, the ESXi host is CPU bound, possibly due to excessive overcommitment of vCPUs (high ratio between deployed vCPUs and pCPUs) or CPU-intensive vSMP VMs. If this is the case, then pressure needs to be taken off the ESXi host by evacuating some VMs from the host, which can be done by powering off VMs or migrating VMs away from the host using vMotion.

Figure 4.14 shows a host that is CPU bound, with the current load average being 112%, whereas historically the host was not CPU bound as indicated by the 84% and 74% values for the last 5 and 15 minutes, respectively

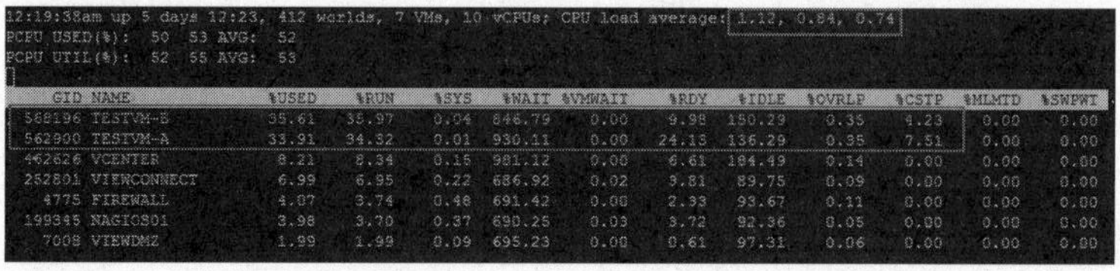

FIGURE 4.14

esxtop showing an ESXi host that is currently CPU bound

As can be seen in Figure 4.13, we have now generated some load on TESTVM-A and TESTVM-B. Both these VMs are vSMP VMs, and they are running on an ESXi host with 2x pCPUs. Also, notice in the top line on esxtop that we have 10x vCPUs running on the host. This gives us a vCPU/pCPU ratio of 5.0. This is an acceptable vCPU/pCPU ratio for ESXi 5. However, notice that because we have generated a CPU load on each of the test VMs of about 40%, the host is struggling to schedule all 10 vCPUs. We can see this by looking at the %RDY figure for both test VMs. Their vCPUs are ready to be scheduled, but they have to wait for pCPUs to become available. Also, looking at the very top line, we can see a value of 1.12, indicating that the host's CPUs are overutilized.

As mentioned earlier in this chapter, the ESXi scheduler will always try to schedule vCPUs in a way that aims to provide entitled pCPU resources to all vCPUs. Because the host is constrained for CPU resources, with relaxed co-scheduling, ESXi is finding gaps in scheduling individual vCPUs to run on pCPUs, even for vSMP VMs. Therefore, at times only one of the vCPUs is running, so the vCPU that is waiting for a pCPU to become available is falling behind its sibling vCPU. To be fair to all vCPUs, ESXi is co-stopping the vCPU that has made the most progress to give the lagging vCPU time to catch up.

All of this leads to performance degradation, and a solution has to be found to relieve some pressure of the ESXi host. The only option we have is to move at least one of the busier VMs to another ESXi host.

High Guest CPU Utilization

High guest CPU utilization is also a common issue and may cause performance problems not only for the VM where the issue if occurring but also, depending on the number of workloads on the ESXi host and available resources, could impact the performance of other VMs.

High guest CPU utilization is normally caused by guest applications; however, guest OS configuration could also result in the guest reporting high utilization. One such cause could be running an incorrect HAL, such as a uniprocessor HAL on a vSMP VM or a multiprocessor HAL on a single vCPU VM.

Where the guest operating system reports high CPU usages, always start by comparing the vCPU utilization figures reported through the vSphere Web Client or esxtop. Large discrepancies between what the guest OS is reporting and what vSphere is reporting could indicate that an incorrect kernel or HAL is being used by the guest operating system.

Summary

In this chapter we looked at the basics of x86 virtualization and the different technologies that are in use to virtualize the x86 CPU. You saw how today's CPU hardware makes virtualization more efficient by offloading some of the tasks that were traditionally performed in software to the CPU hardware.

We also looked at how the VMware ESXi hypervisor manages CPU resources and allows each virtual machine to be granted access to the physical CPUs in a fair and secure manner. We looked at virtual symmetrical processing, relaxed co-scheduling, hyper-threading, and vNUMA. Also covered was how to manage CPU resources with reservations and limits as well as resource pools.

Last, we looked at CPU performance metrics and how to troubleshoot possible CPU-related performance issues.

Chapter 5

Memory

Only a few years ago, memory was a very expensive resource. Back in the early to mid 1990s, 32 MB of memory was pretty hard to come by and would also cost you a small fortune. As technology improved over time, memory became more affordable. Then virtualization came along. Memory once again became one of the most constrained resources in our servers.

Today we pack hundreds of gigabytes of memory into each one of our servers, which enables us to run larger virtual machines and more of those virtual machines on a single x86 server.

Even though our servers now have more memory installed than ever before, memory is still one of the most contended-for resources in our virtualized environments. In this chapter we look at memory considerations for virtualized environments and the technologies that VMware ESXi uses to make the most of this contended resource.

- ◆ In this chapter we look at:
- ◆ ESXi memory management overview
- ◆ Memory reclamation
- ◆ Virtual machine memory allocation management
- ◆ Troubleshooting memory performance issues

Getting to Know ESXi Memory Management

Before diving into memory virtualization and how physical memory is presented to a VM, we need to look into the terminology used to describe different layers, or contexts, of memory. Later on in the chapter, we look at why these layers of memory are required in order for multiple VMs to run on a single ESXi host.

Let's have a look into the three layers of memory that will be covered and mentioned throughout this chapter:

Host Physical Memory Host physical memory is the amount of memory that ESXi detects within a physical host. This is the actual amount of memory that is physically installed within the host. For example, if your server has 128 GB of random access memory (RAM) physically installed, then the amount of physical memory that will be detected by ESXi is 128 GB.

Guest Physical Memory Guest physical memory is the amount of memory that has been allocated by the ESXi administrator to a VM. This is the amount of memory that is visible to the guest OS. The guest OS will see this memory as if it were physical memory. For example, if the ESXi administrator has allocated 512 MB of RAM to the VM, then the guest OS will see 512 MB of memory as if it were physically installed. Remember, the whole idea of a VM is to fool the guest OS into thinking that it owns all of the physical resources. Guest physical memory is mapped by the hypervisor or Virtual Machine Manager (VMM) to host physical memory.

Guest Virtual Memory Guest virtual memory is the memory that the guest OS makes available for use by its applications. It is a virtual memory address space that is mapped by the guest OS to the guest physical memory. This virtual memory address space presented by the guest OS to its applications will exist even in nonvirtualized environments.

Figure 5.1 shows the way the three layers of memory are mapped to one another. It does not, however, account for nor represent Transparent Page Sharing.

FIGURE 5.1
Guest virtual
memory is mapped
to guest physical
memory, which
is mapped by the
VMM to host physi-
cal memory

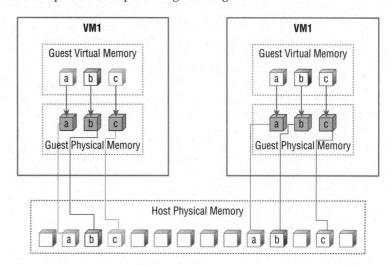

Memory Virtualization

Even in a physical environment without x86 virtualization technologies such as ESXi, a modern OS virtualizes the physical memory that it can see and presents this virtualized memory to its applications. It does so by creating a uniform virtual address space that allows for the OS and hardware to handle the address translation, or mapping, between the virtual memory and physical memory. This approach allows applications to be developed to make use of this virtual memory, which behaves like directly addressable physical memory. Without the use of virtual memory, each application would have to be developed to run in many different types of memory architectures. So, in simple terms, a modern OS acts as a memory abstraction layer to its guest applications.

In a virtualized environment, VMware ESXi creates a contiguous virtual memory address space for each VM that runs on the host. This virtual memory address space is presented upward to the VM as guest physical memory and is also mapped through to the host physical memory. This virtual memory address space literally becomes the memory that the guest OS will recognize as physical memory and has the same properties as the virtual address space that the guest operating system presents to the applications that run on the guest OS. As a result, there are three layers of memory in ESXi: guest virtual memory, guest physical memory, and host physical memory

Creating this contiguous virtual memory address space for each VM and mapping it through to the host physical memory allows the hypervisor to run multiple virtual machines simultaneously while protecting the memory of each virtual machine from being accessed by other VMs or other processes running on the host.

Memory Management in ESXi

An ESXi host creates a virtual memory address space for each VM that runs on it. The virtual memory is mapped downward to the host physical memory and also mapped upward to the guest as guest physical memory. For the overall security and stability of the host and all VMs running on it, each VM cannot simply be allowed to access host physical memory as and when it pleases, so the ESXi host has to manage the allocation of physical memory for each VM.

When a VM first starts up, it does not have any preallocated physical memory and also does not have a standard interface through which it can explicitly allocate host physical memory. Instead, the hypervisor maintains lists of allocated as well as free physical host memory. When the VM starts and first tries to allocate, or "touch," physical memory, it causes what is known as a page fault. A page fault is raised by hardware when a program or application tries to access a memory page that is mapped in the virtual address space but has not yet been loaded into physical memory. In a VM running on VMware ESXi, a page fault will occur when an application running on the guest OS tries to access a memory page that is mapped within the guest virtual memory that has been mapped to guest physical memory but has not yet been assigned in host physical memory. When the page fault occurs, the hypervisor intercepts the memory accesses and allocates free host physical memory to the VM.

NOTE   Before allocating the physical memory to the VM, the hypervisor writes zeroes to the host physical memory to avoid information leaking among different VMs on the host.

Just as the hypervisor maintains a list of "allocated" and "free" host physical memory, the guest OS also maintains a list of "accessed" and "free" guest physical memory. When an OS frees up memory, it actually only adds the freed memory page numbers to a list of "free" memory and does not always modify the actual contents of the physical memory. As a result, when a guest OS frees up memory, only the "free" memory list maintained by the guest OS is updated and the mapped physical host memory is usually not updated at all. Figure 5.2 shows how memory freed by the guest OS is not freed in host physical memory.

FIGURE 5.2
Memory freed by
the guest OS is
not visible to the
hypervisor.

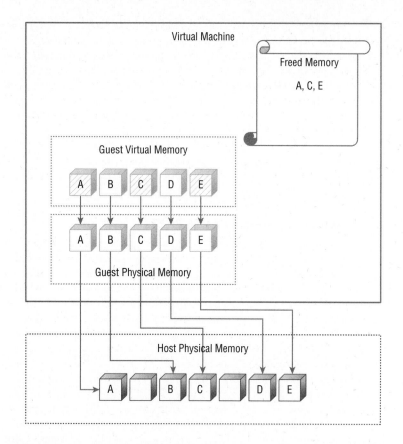

It is easy for the hypervisor to know when to allocate host physical memory to a VM because this action is triggered by a page fault. When the hypervisor has allocated a new piece of memory to a VM, it adds the page numbers of the newly allocated host physical memory to a list of "allocated" memory. This enables the hypervisor to keep track of all the physical host memory pages that have been allocated to VMs.

However, deallocating memory from a VM is not a simple as allocating new memory. As explained earlier, when the guest OS of a VM frees up guest physical memory, it does not always clear the guest physical memory, it only adds the memory page numbers that were freed up to a list of "free" memory. Also, for security reasons, the list of "free" and "allocated" memory maintained by the guest OS is not publicly accessible for the hypervisor to inspect. For this reason, the hypervisor is unable to determine which host physical memory pages that have been mapped to an active VM are actually in use by the guest OS. In other words, once the hypervisor has allocated memory to a VM, it has no way of telling whether the memory in use by that VM has actually been allocated by the guest OS to applications or freed up. Therefore the hypervisor is unable to reclaim host physical memory from a VM when the guest OS of the VM frees up guest physical memory.

Although the hypervisor is unable to reclaim host physical memory from VMs when the guest OS frees up memory, it does not mean that a VM that is repeatedly accessing and freeing memory could fill up the host physical memory. We should remember that the hypervisor does not allocate host physical memory on each and every memory access of a VM. The hypervisor has to allocate a new piece of host physical memory to a VM only when the VM touches the physical memory that has not been touched yet. When a VM's configured guest physical memory has been completely backed up by host physical memory, the hypervisor will not allocate more physical host memory to the VM.

NOTE　The following formula will always hold true in regards to the maximum amount of physical host memory that can be allocated to a VM:

> MAX VM physical host memory usage <= VM's guest memory size + VM overhead memory

Hardware-Assisted MMU Virtualization

As with CPU virtualization, Intel and AMD have developed and integrated technologies into processors to assist hypervisors with virtualization. AMD's Rapid Virtualization Indexing (RVI) and Intel's Extended Page Tables (EPT) are technologies that offer hardware-assisted MMU virtualization by enabling additional page tables that map guest physical memory to host physical memory addresses. This frees ESXi from having to maintain page tables of memory mappings between guest physical pages and host physical pages.

NOTE　For more information on MMU virtualization, refer to the paper "Performance Best Practices for VMware vSphere 5.5," which can be found at the following location:

> www.vmware.com/pdf/Perf_Best_Practices_vSphere5.5.pdf

Reclaiming Memory from VMs

Earlier we looked at how VMware ESXi manages memory between VMs. You saw that once host physical memory has been allocated to a VM, the hypervisor is unable to simply reclaim that memory when the guest OS frees it up. Also, the hypervisor must reserve enough physical host memory to back up all of the guest physical memory assigned to VMs plus the memory overhead per VM. When looking at the requirements, one might think that memory overcommitment cannot be supported. So, why do we have this section about memory reclamation in ESXi then, if it cannot be done? Technically, ESXi can reclaim memory from VMs and it has been able to do so since its first release. Also, because it is able to reclaim memory from VMs, it does support memory overcommitment. This is one of the features that set it apart from all other hypervisors in the market today.

VMware ESXi is the only hypervisor available today that features memory overcommitment. Memory overcommitment is fairly simple to explain and to understand. Memory is overcommitted in ESXi when the total amount of guest physical memory allocated to running VMs is larger than the total amount of host physical memory. ESXi is able to support memory overcommitment because it is able to reclaim memory from VMs using Transparent Page Sharing, ballooning, hypervisor swapping and memory compression, as shown in Figure 5.3.

FIGURE 5.3
Memory overcommitment in ESXi

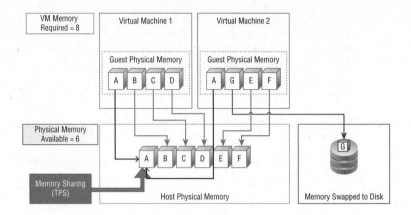

Transparent Page Sharing

Transparent Page Sharing (TPS) is a simple but effective way to reclaim host physical memory (see Figure 5.4). When multiple VMs are running on an ESXi host, chances are they there will be duplicate memory pages in physical host memory. This could be because the VMs are running the same version guest OS or contain similar applications or user data. TPS allows the hypervisor to reclaim redundant copies of host physical memory pages within a single VM or even between VMs that are running on the same ESXi host, while only one copy of the memory page is kept and shared between VMs. Once reclaimed, the redundant memory pages can be allocated to other VMs. As a result, the total VM host memory consumption is reduced and a higher level of memory overcommitment is possible.

FIGURE 5.4
Transparent Page Sharing

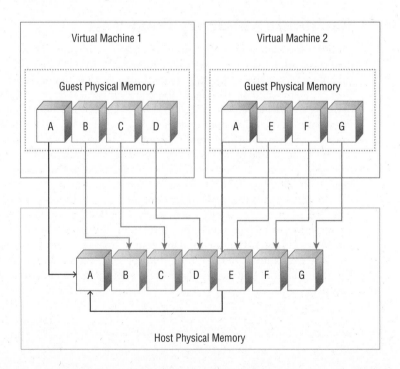

When a VM attempts to change the shared memory page, the hypervisor will create a new copy of the affected memory page. The new copy of the memory page is then mapped to the VM, while the original shared memory page still remains shared between other VMs. TPS generally does not negatively impact the performance of a VM.

Transparent Page Sharing and Large Memory Pages

TPS is used on 4 KB memory pages. Modern operating systems such as Windows Server 2008 R2 and Windows Server 2012 supports large memory pages with a size of 2 MB. As of VMware ESXi 4.1, large memory page support is enabled within ESXi by default, and this remains true today in ESXi 5.5. When a guest operating system makes use of large memory pages that are in turn backed by large physical pages, ESXi will not attempt to share the large memory pages with TPS. This could lead to reduced memory consolidation ratios when the ESXi host is not under memory pressure.

There are two main reasons ESXi will not use TPS on large memory pages. The first reason is overhead. In order to determine if there are duplicate memory pages in host physical memory, the ESXi host scans the contents of all memory pages and does checksum calculations on the memory pages to find pages with matching contents. Doing this checksum calculation on a 4 KB memory page is relatively quick and easy for the ESXi host. However, performing a checksum calculation on 2 MB memory pages is much more taxing and resource intensive. The second reason is that the opportunity and likelihood of finding identical contents in large memory pages of 2 MB in size diminishes quickly compared to the sharing opportunities available with smaller 4 KB pages.

In the event the ESXi host comes under memory pressure, it will start to split 2 MB physical memory pages into 4 KB pages and perform TPS on the 4 KB pages. In other words, TPS will only start sharing large memory pages by breaking them up into smaller 4 KB pages, if and when the host is under memory pressure. The use of small memory pages and AMD Rapid Virtualization Indexing (RVI) and Intel Extended Page Tables (EPT) is mutually exclusive. Disabling large memory pages support will force ESXi to back all memory with 4 KB memory pages and will enable ESXi to use TPS on them. Large memory page support can be disabled on a host-wide basis by setting Mem.AllocGuestLargePage to 0 in the advanced settings of the ESXi host. Disabling large memory pages support on an ESXi host can in some cases lead to an increase in memory consolidation ratios with TPS. However, in doing so, guest operating systems with large memory page support will lose RVI and EPT features and performance benefits that large memory pages have to offer, which could have a negative effect on the VM's performance. We therefore recommend that large memory pages support is left as enabled.

Ballooning

ESXi cannot simply reclaim host physical pages as and when the guest OS of a VM frees up memory. In addition, the guest OS running inside a VM is unaware of the fact that it is actually running on a hypervisor, probably alongside other VMs on the host. The VM will also be unaware of what the host physical memory utilization figures are. When host physical memory is under pressure, the host can use memory ballooning to reclaim some of the physical memory pages that have been allocated to a VM as guest physical memory pages. ESXi is able to do so by using a "balloon" driver that is installed in the guest OS of a VM as part of VMware Tools. The official name of this balloon driver is vmmemctl. It is a virtual device driver that is in direct communication with the hypervisor through a special communication channel or interface. Figure 5.5 shows memory ballooning within the guest operating system.

FIGURE 5.5
Ballooning within
the guest operating
system

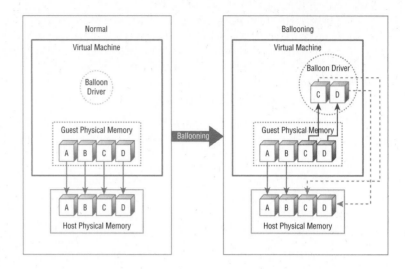

When host physical memory is under pressure and the host needs to reclaim physical memory from VMs, the hypervisor can set a target balloon size that the balloon driver running inside the guest OS of a VM has to try to reach. Once the balloon driver in the guest OS has obtained the target memory size, the balloon driver is inflated by the allocation of "free" guest physical memory pages to it. For example, if the hypervisor is required to reclaim five memory pages from the VM, the hypervisor will set the target balloon size to five pages. The driver obtains this target balloon size of five pages from the hypervisor, and requests from the guest OS, five free guest physical memory pages. Once the guest OS has allocated the five guest physical memory pages to the balloon driver, they are locked. The guest OS will then not be able to swap these memory pages to a page file on disk. The balloon driver informs the hypervisor what the physical guest page numbers are that have been allocated to the balloon driver. The hypervisor can then safely reclaim those five host physical memory pages from the VM and allocate them to other VMs. When the balloon driver is inflated, the amount of host physical memory used by the VM is reduced and the amount of guest physical memory used by the VM is increased.

NOTE Once the host physical memory pressure is relieved, the hypervisor will lower the target balloon size. The balloon driver will hand back the guest physical memory pages to the guest OS. Once the guest OS tries to access those pages again, a page fault will occur and the hypervisor will allocate host physical memory pages to back up the guest physical pages.

This cleaver approach of memory ballooning has some advantages in that it allows the hypervisor to reclaim host physical memory pages that have been mapped to guest physical memory without compromising the integrity of the guest physical memory. It also effectively helps in relieving host physical memory pressure by artificially placing the guest physical memory under pressure, enabling the reclamation of host physical memory. This is also beneficial in the event that the host physical memory as well as the guest physical memory is under pressure because the problem of determining which physical guest pages to reclaim is offloaded from the hypervisor to the guest OS. It essentially becomes the responsibility of the guest OS to determine which pages will have to be freed up and swapped to the guest OS page file on disk before those guest physical memory pages are allocated to the balloon driver. Also, because it is the responsibility of the guest OS to swap guest physical pages to disk, the hypervisor is saved from having to carry out memory swapping at a hypervisor level, which is another memory management technique that we look at later on in this chapter.

There could, however, be an impact on the performance of a VM when memory ballooning is active, depending on whether or not the guest physical memory is already under pressure before the target balloon size is raised. If the guest OS is not actively using all of the guest physical memory that has been allocated, memory ballooning will not generally affect the performance of the VM. However, if the VM is using most or all of its allocated guest physical memory, the guest OS will have to swap some memory pages out to its page file (which normally resides on a slower disk in order to allocate those memory pages to the balloon driver) so that the hypervisor may reclaim the physical host memory pages. So, when troubleshooting a performance issue on a VM, we generally do not want to see high ballooning figures because this might mean an increase in disk storage I/O. Figure 5.6 shows guest operating system memory pages being swapped to disk as a result of memory ballooning.

FIGURE 5.6
Guest operating system paging to disk as a result of ballooning

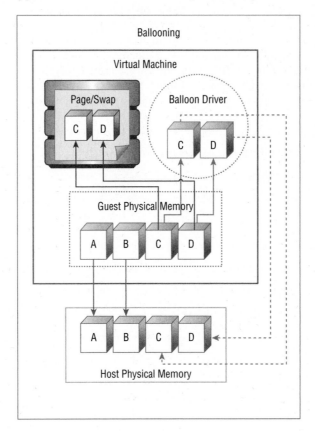

A Note on Guest Operating System Paging

As memory ballooning could cause the guest operating system to swap (or page) reclaimed memory pages to disk, it is important to ensure that the guest operating system has been configured with sufficient swap space that matches the size of the configured memory for the virtual machine. If you are unable to change the swap space of the guest operating system, you can limit the amount of memory that can be reclaimed using memory ballooning. See the section "Configuring Memory Ballooning."

Configuring Memory Ballooning

By default, memory ballooning is enabled on all VMs with VMware tools installed, and the maximum size of the memory balloon driver is set to unlimited. There may be instances where you would like to disable memory ballooning or reduce the maximum size of the balloon driver. As with most things in ESXi, the default behavior of memory ballooning can be altered by an administrator.

Memory ballooning settings are set on a per-VM basis using the sched.mem.maxmemctl advanced option in the settings of any given VM. The sched.mem.maxmemctl advanced option specifies the maximum amount of memory in megabytes that the ESXi is allowed to reclaim from the VM using memory ballooning. As stated, the default value is set to unlimited and is specified as -1 in the configuration. If a limit has been specified by an administrator, and the host is required to reclaim additional memory above the specified limit, the host if forced to start swapping the VM's memory pages to disk using hypervisor swapping. We will cover hypervisor swapping later on in this chapter.

Perform the following steps to configure the balloon size limit on a VM:

1. Log in to the VMware vSphere Web Client.

2. Navigate to the VMs And Templates view.

3. Locate the VM on which to configure memory ballooning.

4. Ensure that the VM is powered off.

5. Right-click on the VM, and click Edit Settings.

6. Click the VM Options tab, and expand the Advanced settings.

7. Next to Configuration Parameters, click the Edit Configuration button.

8. Click the Add Row button.

9. In the Name field, enter **"sched.mem.maxmemctl."**

10. Click on the Value field and enter the desired maximum balloon size in MB. For instance, to specify a maximum balloon size of 128 MB, enter **128**.

11. Click OK to close the advanced settings.

12. Click OK to close the Edit Settings dialog.

Figure 5.7 depicts the advanced settings with memory ballooning configured to a maximum of 128 MB.

FIGURE 5.7

Memory ballooning configured to a maximum of 128 MB in the advanced settings of a virtual machine

Configuration Parameters

Modify or add configuration parameters as needed for experimental features or as instructed by technical support. Entries cannot be removed.

Name	Value
tools.remindInstall	FALSE
migrate.hostlog	./WKSTN03-714ac128.hlog
sched.swap.derivedName	/vmfs/volumes/51e3afc6-deb56fa8-1a3b-00226434
vmware.tools.internalversion	9344
vmware.tools.requiredversion	9344
migrate.hostLogState	none
migrate.migrationId	1382271949654858
toolsInstallManager.lastInstallError	0
toolsInstallManager.updateCounter	2
sched.mem.maxmemctl	128

Add Row

OK   Cancel

With the sched.mem.maxmemctl setting set as 128 in the VM's advanced settings, we would now expect to see a maximum of 128 MB reclaimed from the VM using memory ballooning. Figure 5.8 shows the target and current balloon size for the altered VM.

FIGURE 5.8

VMware vSphere performance graph showing the target and current memory balloon size for the altered VM.

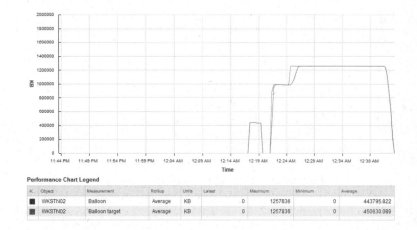

K...	Object	Measurement	Rollup	Units	Latest	Maximum	Minimum	Average
■	WKSTN02	Balloon	Average	KB	0	1257836	0	443795.822
■	WKSTN02	Balloon target	Average	KB	0	1257836	0	450630.089

DISABLING BALLOONING

Memory ballooning can be disabled on a per-VM basis by disabling the balloon driver. However, we strongly suggest that memory ballooning is kept enabled because by disabling it, you are disabling one of the most advanced memory reclamation techniques in vSphere.

Although we don't really want to see high ballooning values in our vSphere environments, especially on our most important VMs, it is an important technology because it helps make memory overcommitment possible. There is a common misconception in the industry that performance could be improved by disabling the balloon driver. However, the opposite is true.

Unlike transparent page sharing, ballooning comes into play only when there is memory contention on the ESXi host. The balloon driver places the VM's guest operating system under memory pressure. This forces the guest operating system to select the memory pages that it deems to be of the least importance in order to swap those pages to disk. With the balloon driver disabled, the VMkernel on the ESXi host will turn to more drastic measures to free up memory, including host swapping (hypervisor swapping) and memory compression.

With hypervisor swapping, the host will start swapping memory pages to disk. The host will not be able to consult the guest operating system on which pages to swap and can therefore swap important memory pages to disk, reducing performance.

Before deciding to disable the balloon driver, it would be best to configure the environment using resource pool settings such as shares or reservations. Using shares can be a very effective way to prioritize VMs. Using shares, the ESXi host can make informed calculations when reclaiming memory using ballooning, starting with the least important VMs first, keeping your mission-critical VMs running at the maximum possible performance.

DISABLING MEMORY BALLOONING

The balloon driver can be disabled on a per-VM basis by setting the balloon target size to 0. This can be achieved by setting sched.mem.maxmemctl to 0 in the VM's configuration file (.vmx)

The balloon driver can also be disabled from the Windows Registry. For more information, please refer to the VMware Knowledge Base article 1002586.

Memory Compression

In ESXi, when the host physical memory is under pressure to the extent that memory ballooning is not a sufficient solution, the host has other options to relieve some pressure from its memory. One option is hypervisor, or host, swapping and the other option is memory compression. As you will see later in this chapter, hypervisor swapping carries a significant penalty in terms of performance, so the hypervisor will calculate whether or not memory compression is a suitable solution prior to resorting to hypervisor swapping.

So first, let's look at memory compression. ESXi is able to compress VM memory on a per-VM basis. Memory compression allows ESXi to compress some memory pages of a VM that would otherwise be paged to disk. The compressed memory pages are then stored in a compression cache in the VM's main memory. ESXi will try to compress memory pages rather than swapping them to disk using hypervisor swapping, simply because it is exponentially quicker to read and decompress the compressed memory pages from cache than to read swapped memory pages from disk.

NOTE   ESXi will attempt to use memory compression only when the host physical memory is under pressure and memory pages have been selected to be swapped out to disk using hypervisor swapping.

Before ESXi can use memory compression on memory pages, it needs to determine if the memory pages that have been selected to be swapped out are suitable for compression or not. If a memory page can be compressed with a compression ratio of 50 percent or more, ESXi will compress the memory page. If the compression ratio of a memory page is less than 50 percent, the page is swapped out to disk using hypervisor swapping.

NOTE   When a memory page is determined to have a compression ratio of less than 50 percent, it is not compressed and is swapped to disk using hypervisor swapping. ESXi will swap only uncompressed memory pages and will never swap compressed memory pages to disk using hypervisor swapping.

The compressed memory pages are stored in a compression cache. Memory compression cache is configured on a per-host basis but is applied on a per-VM basis and by default can be up to 10 percent of the configured VM memory, or in other words, the configured guest physical memory. This does not include any memory overhead. For example, using the default ESXi 5.5 settings, if a VM has been configured with 1024 MB of memory, the compression cache for the VM will be up to a maximum of 102.4 MB (10 percent of 1024 MB) in size and will form part of the configured 1024 MB guest physical memory. Any memory overhead that has been added to the 1024 MB by the hypervisor will be excluded from the cache size calculation.

The memory compression cache size starts off as zero when the host physical memory is undercommitted. As the pressure increases on host physical memory, the compression cache size is grown and memory pages are compressed and placed in the compression cache.

When memory pages are selected to be swapped using hypervisor swapping and ESXi has determined that the pages have a compression ratio that is 50 percent or greater, the pages are compressed to a ratio of 50 percent and placed in the compression cache. For example, let's say that the hypervisor needs to free up 16 KB of memory from a VM. This will require the hypervisor to reclaim four 4 KB pages from the VM. If the pages are found to be suitable for memory compression, each page will be compressed to 2 KB in size and placed in the compression cache of the affected VM. This means that the four memory pages that used to occupy a total of 16 KB in memory now occupy only 8 KB of memory in the compression cache. If the memory pages were found not to be suitable for memory compression, the four 4 KB pages would be swapped to disk as a total of 16 KB, because ESXi does not compress memory pages that are swapped to disk.

CONFIGURING MEMORY COMPRESSION

VMware has configured ESXi with sensible default settings for everything, including memory compression. For best performance, it is recommended to keep the default settings. However, if required, an administrator can change the default settings for the memory compression cache by navigating to the advanced settings of an ESXi host in the vSphere Web Client, as shown in Figure 5.9.

FIGURE 5.9

Memory compression advanced settings in the vSphere Web Client

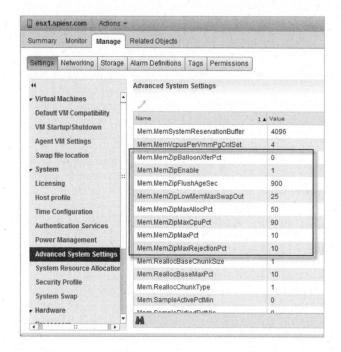

By default, memory compression cache is enabled. Changing the Mem.MemZipEnable setting from 1 to 0 will disable memory compression on the host. With memory compression enabled, there are several other settings relating to memory compression that can be changed. However, as stated before, the defaults should be sufficient for optimal performance when memory is under pressure.

By default, ESXi will allow the compression cache to grow to a maximum of 10 percent of the amount of guest physical memory configured for the VM. The Mem.MemZipMaxPct advanced setting can be used to increase or decrease the maximum size the compression cache is allowed to grow to, as a percentage of the VM's configured memory.

To maintain good VM performance, it is important that the maximum memory compression cache is set correctly. If the value is set too low, some compressed memory pages will have to be decompressed and swapped out and any further swapping actions on those memory pages will hurt VM performance. Also, if the maximum memory compression cache is set too high, it could waste VM memory and could therefore cause host physical memory pressure.

The Mem.MemZipMaxAllocPct advanced setting can be used to configure the maximum size the compression cache is allowed to grow to as a percentage of the allocated virtual machine memory. Remember, when a VM is first powered on, no memory is allocated to the VM unless the VM tries to "touch" a memory page, so the allocated memory size will most probably be smaller than the configured guest physical memory.

Memory compression will have an impact on the ESXi host CPU load because CPU time is required to compress and decompress memory pages to and from the compression cache. By default, if the host consumes more than 90 percent of its total available CPU resources, it will not attempt to compress memory pages that have been queued for hypervisor swapping in the hypervisor swapping path. However, this setting can also be configured by changing the value for the Mem.MemZipMaxCpuPct advanced setting.

NOTE Memory compression is configured on a per-ESXi host basis, not a per-VM basis. When you configure it on an ESXi host, it will apply to all VMs that are running on that host. However, the ESXi host will compress memory on a per-VM basis, based on the Mem.MemZipMaxPct value specified within the host advanced configuration.

Hypervisor Swapping

When host physical memory is under pressure, ESXi will attempt to reclaim memory form VMs using techniques such as Transparent Page Sharing, memory ballooning, and memory compression. When all these techniques fail to reclaim enough host physical memory, the hypervisor will focus on reclaiming memory using hypervisor swapping.

Hypervisor swapping enables the ESXi host to swap [some of the] host physical memory that is backing a VM's guest physical memory, to a physical disk device in order for it to be able to reclaim the host physical memory. By default, the memory is swapped to a swap file that is created on the same datastore as the VM. The swap file has the filename extension .vswp and is created by the hypervisor when the VM starts up. The file is the same size as the configured guest physical memory for that particular VM.

Hypervisor swapping is very much a last resort to reclaiming memory because it could cause some severe VM performance issues. This is because the hypervisor does not know which physical guest pages are the best candidates to be swapped out to disk. The information that is required for the hypervisor to calculate the best pages to swap out to disk is not available. As a result, the hypervisor will select random guest physical pages to swap out to disk, which may cause unintended interactions with the guest OS native memory management policies.

The lack of information relating to guest physical memory pages can also lead to double paging. Double paging occurs when the guest OS attempts to swap a guest physical memory page to its local page file when the hypervisor has already swapped the memory page to disk using hypervisor swapping. This causes the guest physical page to be swapped back into physical memory from disk only to be swapped back out to disk by the guest OS.

The other problem that hypervisor swapping suffers from is high swap-in latency. If the hypervisor has swapped a guest physical page to disk, the guest OS will have no knowledge that the page is not in physical memory anymore and that the page now actually resides on a slower disk. The guest OS may therefore try to access that memory page while under the impression that the page is still in fast physical memory. As a result, the hypervisor is required to swap the page back into physical memory from disk. As disk storage devices are significantly slower than physical memory, the swap-in of the memory page is subjected to swap-in latency, and while the page is swapped in from disk, the VM will be blocked from accessing the page. This can severely affect VM performance.

To reduce swap-in latency, VMware ESXi 5 and later can be configured to swap to Solid State Disk (SSD) drives. SSD read latency is normally around a few microseconds; that is much faster than the conventional spindle disk access latency, which is normally around a few hundred microseconds. In the next section of this chapter, we look at host SSD cache swapping in more detail.

NOTE The architecture of SSD is outside the scope of this book. More information on SSD can be found here:

http://en.wikipedia.org/wiki/Solid-state_drive

Host SSD Cache Swapping

We know that when an ESXi host is under severe memory pressure, the VMkernel in ESXi is able to swap memory pages to disk. Although this feature enables the ESXi host to reclaim some memory pages, this presents us with some problems that will severely impact performance.

Because the swapped pages will now reside on disk, and with the default ESXi virtual machine configuration, these swapped pages will be located in a VSWP (.vswp) file, which resides on the same datastore and within the same folder as the virtual machine. This presents us with a problem that comes in two forms, namely disk I/O latency and SAN fabric I/O latency. Spinning disks, in comparison to RAM, have a much higher I/O latency, so it takes a lot longer in terms of computing time to read or write data from disk than to read or write data from RAM. In a SAN environment, this problem is further magnified by the SAN fabric I/O latency. When swapping, ESXi reads and writes memory pages to disk, and in a SAN environment, that means reading and writing over the SAN network fabric, which in turn incurs even further latency before the I/O actually even reaches the spinning disks.

To address the performance issues presented by hypervisor swapping, ESXi version 5 and later is able swap virtual machine memory pages to SSD drives, which are much faster and provide much lower latency times than spinning disks. The SSD drives can be installed in the SAN and presented to the ESXi hosts are LUNs or can be installed locally in the ESXi hosts themselves. However, with SSD drives located on the SAN, we still have the issue of SAN fabric I/O latency to contend with, so our recommendation would be to install two SSD drives in a RAID-1 configuration in each ESXi host and configure them for use by the SSD cache.

SSD host cache makes use of SSD storage to place files that ESXi uses as a write back cache for virtual machine swap files. The cache is shared by all virtual machines running on the host. Again, note that host cache is simply a write back cache, and therefore regular swap files will still need to be updated. However, with host cache, memory pages are placed and accessed from SSD rather than from the conventional VMFS datastore where the virtual machine's swap files are located, which aids in lowering access times and improves overall virtual machine performance on a host where memory resources are contended for.

SSD HOST CACHE VS. SWAPPING

The host cache feature is not the same as placing regular swap files on an SSD-backed datastore, and host cache is not intended to replace hypervisor swapping and the virtual machine swap files. The hypervisor will still create a swap file for each virtual machine, although the speed of the storage where the regular swap file is located is less important. It is important to keep this in mind because regular swap files will still consume space on the datastore selected for swap files (by default, regular swap files are placed in the same folder as the virtual machine).

CONFIGURING HOST SSD CACHE SWAPPING

An administrator can configure host SSD cache using the VMware vSphere Web Client. SSD cache can be configured on any VMFS datastore that resides on SSD storage. Figure 5.10 depicts an SSD VMFS datastore that is available for use with host SSD cache.

FIGURE 5.10
VMFS SSD-backed datastores available for host SSD cache

Perform the following steps to configure host SSD cache on an SSD VMFS datastore:

1. Launch the vSphere Web Client and authenticate as a user with vSphere Administrator privileges. Once logged into the Web Client, select the Hosts And Clusters view.

2. From the Hosts And Clusters view, select the host that you would like to configure host SSD cache on.

3. With the host selected, click the Manage tab.

4. From the Storage tab, select Host Cache Configuration.

5. As depicted in Figure 5.11, a list of SSD datastores compatible with host SSD cache will be displayed. Select the desired SSD datastore and click the pencil icon on the toolbar just above the datastore list.

6. You may choose to make use of all the available space on the SSD datastore or specify a custom space allocation that host cache can make use of on this datastore.

7. Click OK.

NOTE Although you can configure host cache to make use of all available space on an SSD datastore, in doing so you might trigger disk space usage alarms against the datastore in the vSphere Web Client. It is recommended that a size is selected based on the alarm threshold in order to avoid triggering disk space utilization alarms. An alternative configuration could be to use 100 percent of the SSD and exclude the datastore usage alarm from the datastore backed by the SSD.

Figure 5.11 shows the Host Cache Configuration dialog, configured to allocated 80 GB of disk space on the SSD datastore for use with host cache.

FIGURE 5.11
vSphere host cache configured to use up to 80 GB of SSD storage

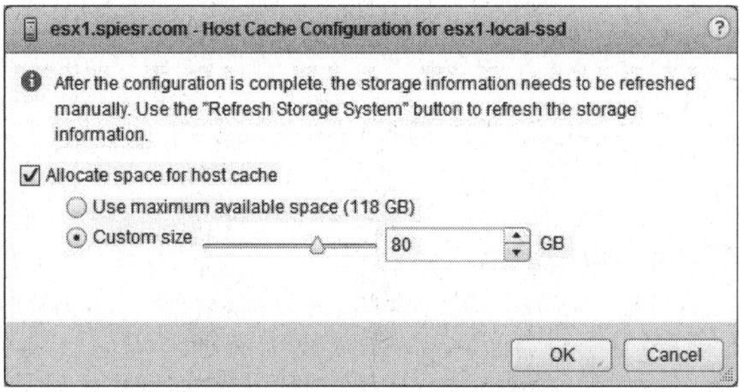

Host Memory Reclamation

We have already looked at techniques that ESXi can employ to reclaim memory from virtual machines. In this section, we look at how ESXi uses thresholds to determine when to start reclaiming memory from VMs and also which technique to make use of.

ESXi has four memory states. These states are determined by the amount of available host physical memory at any given time and are known as High, Soft, Hard, and Low. Each state has an assigned threshold, with High being 6 percent or above, Soft 4 percent, Hard 2 percent and Low 1 percent. These thresholds represent the amount of free host memory. The current memory state can be seen using esxtop, as shown in Figure 5.12.

FIGURE 5.12
VMware ESXi
esxtop showing
the host in a High
memory state

The host memory is in a high state when the combined allocated virtual machine memory for all virtual machines is lower than the total available host memory. Regardless of how overcommitted the host is in memory, in the High state, the host is not under memory pressure and will therefore not attempt to reclaim memory from any virtual machine unless a virtual machine has been configured with a memory limit and is consuming more memory that what is specified by the memory limit.

When the amount of free host memory falls below the 6 percent threshold, toward the 4 percent Soft threshold, the host will start to reclaim memory from virtual machines using memory ballooning. Note that ballooning starts to happen even before the host reaches the Soft state because this gives the balloon driver time to allocate and pin guest memory pages. Because the host is now starting to come under memory pressure, it will aim to reclaim memory fast enough to remain above the Soft state, and the balloon driver is usually able to reclaim memory quick enough for the host to remain above the Soft state.

If memory ballooning is not sufficient and the amount of free memory drops below the Soft state toward the Hard state, the host will start to reclaim memory using memory compression and hypervisor swapping in addition to ballooning. The host should be able to reclaim memory quickly enough to remain above the hard state.

If all of the memory reclamation techniques fail to reclaim sufficient memory and the host memory state drops below the 1 percent Low threshold, the host will continue to reclaim memory from virtual machines with swapping and additionally block access to memory for VMs that consume more memory than their target memory allocations.

NOTE   It is important to note than when host memory is under pressure, memory is reclaimed from VMs based on their share allocations. We will look at memory shares in the section "Proportional Share-Based Algorithm" later in this chapter.

Idle Page Reclamation

When some guest operating systems free memory, they actually only update a memory allocation table with the page number of the memory to be freed, without actually clearing the contents of the memory page. The memory allocation table is not available to the hypervisor, so the hypervisor is unable to reclaim memory pages freed by the guest operating system. In this case, the memory page is allocated to the VM but not actively in use by the guest operating system. This page is now an idle memory page.

VMware ESXi can reclaim this memory page by imposing an idle memory tax on the VM. Idle memory tax is a mechanism tied to the proportional share-based algorithm that enables the hypervisor to reclaim idle memory pages from VMs using the balloon driver (default) or by paging (swapping). This is achieved by assigning a higher cost value to unused allocated shares, effectively charging the virtual machine more for idle memory than for memory that is in use. The "tax" rate increases as the ratio between idle memory and active memory for the virtual machine increases.

By default, the hypervisor polls every 60 seconds for idle memory pages and can reclaim up to 75 percent of idle memory from a VM. The remaining 25 percent of idle memory pages are left for the guest operating system to consume. The default settings for idle memory tax can be changed using the vSphere Web Client, under the advanced host configuration settings. The following three settings affect idle memory tax:

Mem.IdleTax   The percentage of idle memory pages to reclaim. The default value is 75.

Mem.IdleTaxType   The mechanism that should be used to reclaim idle memory pages. This setting can be configured with a value of 0 (flat) or 1 (variable). 0 (flat) configures the host to use swapping. 1 (variable) configures the host to use ballooning. The default setting is 1 (variable) and configures the host to reclaim memory using memory ballooning.

Mem.SamplePeriod   Specifies the time interval in seconds of the virtual machine's execution time, during which memory activity is monitored to estimate working set sizes. The default value is 60 and allows the hypervisor to poll for idle memory pages every 60 seconds.

VMware states that it is not necessary or appropriate to change the default idle memory tax settings but to rather resolve issues where idle memory tax comes into play by right-sizing virtual machines. A virtual machine with a large amount of allocated but idle memory is likely to incur an idle memory tax, and it is therefore important to size VM memory appropriately.

Managing Virtual Machine Memory Allocation

One of the main responsibilities of VMware ESXi is to allocate host physical memory resources to virtual machines fairly, ensuring that memory is allocated to virtual machines in a way that satisfy their entitlements. This is easy for ESXi to achieve when the configured memory for all virtual machines combined is less than the available host physical memory. However, in the event where memory has been overcommitted (more memory configured for virtual machines than what is physically available in the host), there could be situations where ESXi is required to take host physical memory away from one virtual machine in order to give the memory to another virtual machine.

An ESXi host will allocate memory to virtual machines based on the configured memory limit for each virtual machine. The memory limit is generally the configured memory size of the virtual machine, but a lower limit can be placed on memory by adjusting the limit parameter under the resource settings for the virtual machine. In all cases, ESXi will never allocate more memory to a virtual machine than the configured memory for it, even if the value of the memory limit parameter is higher than the configured memory, such as the default limit parameter value, which is unlimited.

When memory is overcommitted, ESXi will allocate an amount of memory that is between the configured reservation and limit. In the case where memory is overcommitted, the amount of memory granted to virtual machines is based on the number of shares allocated to each virtual machine as well as the recent working set size of each virtual machine.

Working Set Size

An ESXi host estimates the working set size for a virtual machine by monitoring memory activity over successive periods of virtual machine execution time. Estimates are smoothed over several time periods using techniques that respond rapidly to increases in working set size and more slowly to decreases in working set size.

This approach ensures that a virtual machine from which idle memory is reclaimed can ramp up quickly to its full share-based allocation when it starts using its memory more actively.

By default, the working set size is determined by monitoring memory activity every 60 seconds. This can be modified by adjusting the Mem.SamplePeriod advanced setting in the vSphere Web Client under the host advanced system settings. If for whatever reason you would like the ESXi host to scan memory pages for changes more or less frequently, the Mem. SamplePeriod setting can be used to adjust the interval. It is recommended to leave advanced settings at their defaults, and the same applies to the Mem.SamplePeriod setting.

NOTE The Mem.SamplePeriod setting is also used to scan memory for active pages. When a memory page has changed within the set sample period, the memory page is considered active and will be included in the active memory metric.

Proportional Share-Based Algorithm

As you saw in Chapter 4, "CPU," ESXi employs a proportional share-based algorithm to provide each virtual machine with its entitled amount of CPU resources. ESXi also employs a similar mechanism to ensure that memory is allocated to virtual machines in such a way that all virtual machines have access to their entitled amount of memory. In an environment where host memory is under pressure, ESXi is able to determine which virtual machines should be favored by using memory shares, reservations, and limits.

MEMORY SHARES

ESXi allocates memory to a virtual machine as and when the virtual machine attempts to touch a memory page for the first time. ESXi will continue to allocate memory to the virtual machine every time the virtual machines tries to touch unallocated memory, up until the point where the virtual machine has reached its maximum configured memory size or the allocated memory for the virtual machine has reached a limit if one has been specified.

When the virtual machine is first created and configured with an amount of memory, a default share value is attached to the virtual machine based on the configured memory of the virtual machine.

Figure 5.13 shows four virtual machines. VM1 and VM2 each has 2,048 MB configured memory, VM3 has 4,096 MB, and VM4 has 8,192 MB. Notice how the amount of shares assigned to each virtual machine relates to its configured memory size.

FIGURE 5.13
Virtual machine
memory shares
are based on its
configured memory.

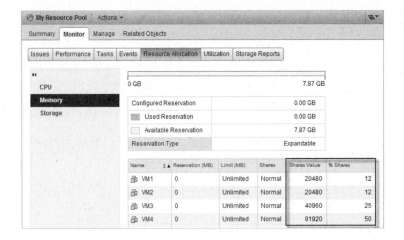

When host memory is under pressure, ESXi makes use of the share values to determine
which virtual machines should be favored. Although the share values are assigned to each
virtual machine individually when the virtual machine is created or when the configured
memory size for a virtual machine is changed by an administrator, the share value can be
changed manually, as seen in Figure 5.14.

FIGURE 5.14
Adjusting memory
share values for
a single virtual
machine

MEMORY RESERVATIONS

Memory reservations allow administrators to effectively guarantee that a given virtual machine will be allocated a set amount of memory. When a virtual machine is configured with a memory reservation, the ESXi host will ensure that the reservation is honored and will not reclaim memory from the virtual machine below the reservation, even if the virtual machine becomes idle. In other words, idle memory tax does not apply to the memory located within the reservation. However, memory allocated beyond the specified reservation can still be reclaimed and, if idle, can be taxed.

VM1 in Figure 5.15 is configured with a reservation of 512 MB and is therefore guaranteed to be allocated at least 512 MB.

FIGURE 5.15

Setting memory reservations for a single virtual machine

NOTE   When a virtual machine has been configured with a memory reservation and the ESXi host cannot satisfy the reservation with available physical memory, the VM will fail to power on and the following message will be displayed in the vSphere Web Client: "The available Memory resources in the parent resource pool are insufficient for the operation."

MEMORY LIMITS

In addition to the configured memory size for a given virtual machine, a limit can be placed by an administrator on a virtual machine by specifying the limit in the virtual machine's settings. When a limit has been configured, ESXi will only allocate memory until the limit has been reached. If the limit is configured while the virtual machine is running and the virtual machine has already been allocated more memory than the limit, ESXi will start to reclaim the memory using ballooning or hypervisor swapping.

The guest operating system will be unaware of the limit placed on its memory resources and will attempt to allocate memory to its applications as if all configured memory is available. This would result in ballooning and hypervisor swapping and would have a negative impact on the virtual machine's performance. The balloon driver will also place the guest memory under pressure and the guest operating system may even be forced to start swapping out guest memory pages to its local disk as well.

We can test the effects that placing a limit on a running virtual machine will have on the balloon driver and hypervisor swapping. Figure 5.16 shows virtual machine memory usage in esxtop. A virtual machine named WKSTN02 has been configured with 2,048 MB of guest physical memory. The virtual machine was powered on and used for a while with this configuration. A memory limit of 512 MB was then configured on the virtual machine.

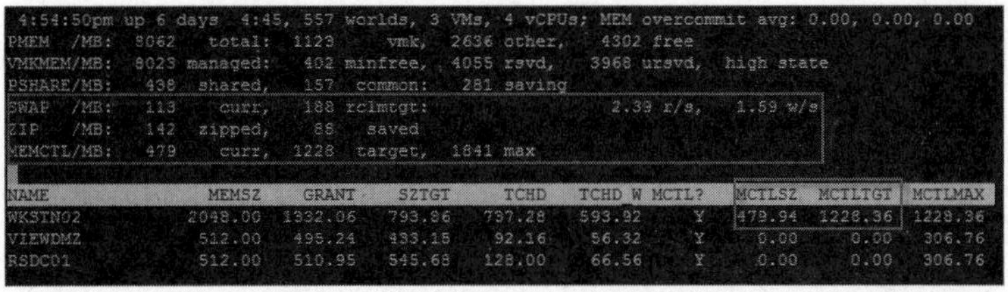

FIGURE 5.16

ESXi reclaiming memory from virtual machine WKSTN02 after a 512 MB limit was configured

Figure 5.16 also shows that the balloon driver inside the guest operating system has been instructed by the hypervisor to reclaim more than 1.2 GB of memory from the VM. This can be seen in esxtop as MCTLTGT, which shows 1,228.36 (MB). The MCTLSZ is the current size of the balloon driver inside the guest operating system, and in Figure 5.16, it is 479.94 MB, working its way up to the target size of 1,228.36 MB. You will also notice that ESXi is swapping and using memory compression to try to reclaim memory to achieve the 512 MB limit.

Figure 5.17 shows the same esxtop screen, but a few minutes later, and you can see that the balloon driver has reached its target size of 1,228.36 MB

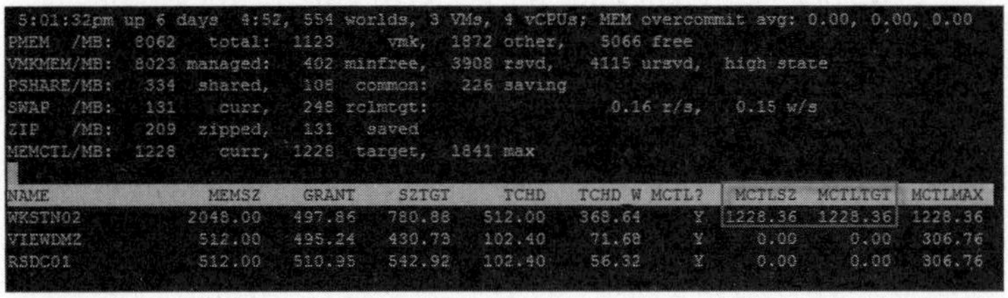

FIGURE 5.17

The balloon driver in WKSTN02 has successfully reached its target of 1,228.36 MB.

CONFIGURED MEMORY VS. MEMORY LIMIT

An ESXi host never allocates more memory to a virtual machine than its specified memory size. For example, a virtual machine can be configured with 2 GB of memory while at the same time the memory limit on the VM is configured as the default limit, which is unlimited. In this case, the ESXi host will allocate only up to 2 GB of memory, regardless of the limit being set to unlimited.

MEMORY AND RESOURCE POOLS

As with CPU resources, memory shares, reservations and limits can be set at a resource pool level as well. When a virtual machine is placed in a resource pool and powered on, the virtual machine will be able to consume only the memory resources that the resource pool has been configured to use as set by its reservations and limits or, if memory is under pressure, the resource pool's share value. Resource pools allow us to create logical pools of memory resources.

WARNING   Never use resource pools as folders to organize the Hosts And Clusters view within vSphere. Placing VMs within nested resource pools could lead to very serious performance implications as well as added complexity during troubleshooting, especially when resources are contended for. Resource pools were designed and are intended to be used to logically create silos of resources, not as folders.

ESXi Root Resource Pool

Every ESXi host has an invisible root resource pool. This root resource pool becomes the parent of all children virtual machines and resource pools created by administrators. When an administrator creates a new resource pool, the new resource pool simply becomes a child of the root resource pool.

Resource Pool Shares

In Chapter 4, we looked at CPU shares on resource pools and how resource pool siblings affect each other in terms of the amount CPU resources that each sibling resource pool is entitled to during times of contention. As with CPU resources, shares can be configured for memory resources as well. A resource pool's configuration options contain share, reservation, and limit settings for both CPU as well as memory resources.

When it comes to shares, the rules that apply to CPU also apply to memory. Resource contention first happens at the *resource pool level*, which determines the amount of memory that each of the sibling resource pools is entitled to. Once this has been determined, the child VMs within each of the sibling resource pools will have to contend with each other for memory resources based on each virtual machine's own share value.

If you would like to have a better understanding of what effects sibling resource pools have on each other, refer back to the section "Shares on Resource Pools" section in Chapter 4.

Resource Pool Memory Reservations

The reservation setting on a resource pool enables us to guarantee a set amount of memory that will be available to the resource pool. More memory can be allocated by ESXi to virtual machines running in the resource pool than what is specified by the resource pool's reservation setting, provided a guarantee of the additional memory is not required by reservations set on individual virtual machines running within the resource pool. In other words, a virtual machine will be allocated more memory than what is specified by the pool's reservation, unless the virtual machine itself has a reservation set that is greater than the unused reservation of the resource pool. Therefore, if sibling virtual machines of a resource pool have set reservations that amount to more memory than the resource pool's memory reservation, not all virtual machines will be allowed to be powered on at the same time unless the Expandable Reservation feature is enabled on the resource pool.

Resource Pool Expandable Reservations

When the Expandable Reservation option is checked in a resource pool's settings, the resource pool will allow virtual machines with reservation settings that are greater than the unused reservations of the resource pool to be powered on. This is achieved by "borrowing" the additional memory required to satisfy the reservation from the resource pool's parent resource pool. If the parent resource pool has available memory, the VMs will power on. If the parent resource pool does not have available memory, the outcome of the VM power-on operation will be dependent on the use of the Expandable Reservation feature on the parent resource pool and whether or not the parent resource pool has enough memory to borrow from.

Resource Pool Memory Limits

Resource pool limits provide a way to limit the amount of memory that can be allocated to all sibling virtual machines of a resource pool. It's important to understand that the limit is placed on allocated memory and not configured memory. For instance, it is possible to have four virtual machines each with 1 GB of configured memory run in a resource pool with a limit configured as 1 GB. Only when the amount of allocated memory for all virtual machines combined in the resource pool reached the limit of 1 GB will ESXi start to reclaim memory using ballooning and swapping.

An example of a specific requirement for placing memory limits could be when a customer has paid for a specific amount of memory resources. A limit can then be placed on a resource pool that contains the customer's or department's virtual machines. This will guarantee that the customer's combined virtual machine memory allocations never exceed the agreed-upon limit.

Unless there is a specific requirement for placing memory limits on virtual machines or resource pools, we recommend that shares and reservations are used for memory resource management instead of memory limits because limits could lead to performance issues that can be difficult to troubleshoot, depending on where in the resource pool hierarchy the memory limits are in place.

Sizing Memory for Virtual Machines

Memory is one of the most contended-for resources in today's virtual environments and to that extent tends to be the gaiting factor in virtual machine consolidation rations. Even if the vSphere environment is brand-new, sizing your virtual machines incorrectly could lead to performance problems later on when the environment becomes more and more memory constrained.

Allocating too little memory to a virtual machine will cause the virtual machine guest operating system to swap to local disk. Not only will this have a negative effect on the virtual machine's performance, but it could also have a negative effect on other virtual machines that reside on the same storage array. For example, if several virtual machines are starved for memory and all of them are running memory-intensive applications and swapping to disk, not only will they be poorly performing, they can also place extra pressure on the storage array, effectively slowing down virtual machines running on other hosts as well due to increased latency caused by an increase in storage I/O contention. This may sound extreme, but we have seen this happen, and vSphere administrators were blaming the storage array for poor VM performance when in fact the problem was caused by guest operating systems of other undersized virtual machines that were swapping to disk.

Allocating too much memory to virtual machines could lead to wasted host memory resources. When several oversized virtual machines are present on a host, the host could become low on available memory because the guest operating systems could be touching new memory pages without reusing idle memory pages. This will cause the host to eventually start reclaiming memory from virtual machines by means of ballooning. Also, as seen earlier in this chapter, virtual machines can be taxed on idle memory, which will also cause unnecessary ballooning to take place.

To maintain optimal performance, it is important to ensure that memory for all virtual machines is sized correctly for their respective application workloads. Before sizing CPU and memory for a new virtual machine, ensure that you are aware of the application requirements and that you size the virtual machine CPU and memory resources accordingly. The application vendor should provide documentation with the recommended sizing guidelines.

In our experience, it is better to stick with the applications' published guidelines to start with than to simply throw large amounts of CPU and memory at an application simply because those resources are available at the time. Just because those resources are available today doesn't mean they won't be contended for in the future. You can always increase the CPU and memory resources for a virtual machine at a later stage if the need arises. On the other hand, sizing virtual machines below the application vendor's published recommended sizing guidelines could lead to the application not performing as expected as well as the application's deployment fall out of vendor support.

Memory Overhead

In order for ESXi to be able to virtualize memory, it has to store some of its own code and data structures that relate to the memory allocated to virtual machines. This information is stored in memory beyond what is allocated to the virtual machine. Accessing memory from within a virtual machine also takes additional time. The extra memory and access time required to virtualize memory is known as memory overhead.

Modern processors have built-in memory controllers and employ hardware mechanisms to internally page memory in page tables. This helps minimize the time overhead involved in virtualizing memory.

The extra space required to virtualize memory is used for the ESXi code itself to run. The VMkernel takes up a small amount of memory for itself on the ESXi host.

To be powered on, each virtual machine requires additional memory above and beyond the memory that is configured for it. This space is reserved for the virtual machine frame buffer and virtualization data structures that relate to the state of the virtual machine, such as the memory page allocation tables. The amount of additional memory required to virtualize a virtual machine is based on the number of vCPUs and the amount of memory configured for the virtual machine.

Table 5.1 shows the memory overhead sizes required for some virtual machine configurations. It shows only a select sample of virtual machine configurations. However, it provides a good overview of how the number of vCPUs and configured memory can increase the required amount of memory for overhead.

TABLE 5.1:   Virtual machine memory overhead

CONFIGURED MEMORY (MB)	1 vCPU	2 vCPU	4 vCPU	8 vCPU
256	20.29	24.28	32.23	48.16
1024	25.90	29.91	37.86	53.82

TABLE 5.1:   Virtual machine memory overhead   *(CONTINUED)*

CONFIGURED MEMORY (MB)	1 vCPU	2 vCPU	4 vCPU	8 vCPU
4096	48.64	52.72	60.67	76.78
16384	139.62	143.98	151.93	168.60

Memory Overcommitment

VMware ESXi is capable of allocating more memory to virtual machines than what is actually physically installed in the host. This is known as memory overcommitment and it's made possible by making use of all of the memory management technologies that we've covered in this chapter thus far.

One advantage that x86 virtualization brings is the ability to run more servers with less hardware. Memory overcommitment also enables us to provision more memory to virtual machines than what we have hardware for.

When properly managed, memory overcommitment is an invaluable tool. We don't have to wait for more memory to be installed in a host in order to deploy a new virtual machine. We can simply create it and ESXi will take care of allocating the memory that the virtual machine guest operating system requests. However, if we abuse the technology, it will lead to performance issues in the future.

With a host where memory has been overcommitted, we have to ensure the following:

◆ Will the running virtual machines require all configured memory to be allocated and in use all at the same time at any point in time?

◆ In the case of a host failure, do we have sufficient memory resources on other hosts in the cluster to take on the additional workloads?

If the answer to the first question is yes, then the ESXi host will have to, at some point, reclaim memory from some of the virtual machines. This is a situation that we should be trying to avoid.

Before starting to reclaim memory, ESXi will attempt to employ Transparent Page Sharing, or TPS. It will try to remove all duplicated memory pages between all virtual machines where possible. This will have no performance impact on virtual machines. However, if TPS fails to reclaim enough memory, the virtual machine guest operating systems will be placed under memory pressure by ballooning, at which point the guest operating system may start swapping. If ballooning is not enough, the hypervisor will start selecting pages to swap to disk. Some of the selected pages might be compressed and the remaining pages will be swapped to disk.

If the answer to the second question is yes, then we really need to start looking at increasing the size of our HA cluster. High availability is beyond the scope of this book, but it is important to note, that in the event of a host failure, extra pressure will be placed on other hosts, which could lead to performance issues.

Troubleshooting Memory Performance Problems

Most performance issues relating to memory can simply be avoided by sizing virtual machines correctly for the workloads they are running and by ensuring that a vSphere host or cluster is not overstretched in terms of memory utilization. Although vSphere does allow the overcommitment of memory, that doesn't mean that we should not be managing capacity. In fact, it is the ability to overcommit on memory that makes managing capacity even more important.

When we place too many virtual machines with large memory requirements on a single ESXi host, performance problems are inevitable. Yes, we can overcommit and allocate 100 percent configured memory for all virtual machines, but if the requirement for allocated memory exceeds the amount of available physical host memory, then ballooning, guest paging, and eventually hypervisor swapping will impact performance.

In the following sections, we look at some techniques to identify potential memory issues by using some of the performance metrics described earlier in this chapter.

Using esxtop to Diagnose Memory Performance Issues

As a vSphere administrator, you have most probably made use of the performance metrics that are made available through the vSphere Web Client. Although the Web Client provides administrators with a graphical interface that is capable of drawing performance metric charts that can be very handy when trying to visualize memory utilization figures, the metrics only update once every 20 seconds. When troubleshooting performance problems, we really want more up-to-date information than what is provided by the Web Client.

This is where esxtop comes in. With esxtop, you are able to see snapshots of performance metrics that update as frequently as every 2 seconds. When monitoring performance metrics using esxtop, it is helpful to understand what some of these performance metrics should look like and what the thresholds are for these metrics.

DISPLAYING MEMORY PERFORMANCE METRICS IN ESXTOP

The esxtop utility can be accessed from the ESXi server console or, if SSH is enabled on the ESXi server, over a secure shell using an SSH client such as PuTTY. VMware also provides a utility called resxtop that ships with the vSphere Management Assistant. The resxtop utility can be used from the vSphere Management Assistant to remotely access esxtop on ESXi hosts.

Although this chapter is not intended to cover how to use esxtop, it is a good idea to have a quick look at how to navigate to the memory metrics screen within esxtop.

To access esxtop, log into the ESXi server troubleshooting console, either directly from the server console or via SSH. Once logged in as the root user, type **esxtop** and press return. Figure 5.18 shows the initial esxtop screen via an SSH session.

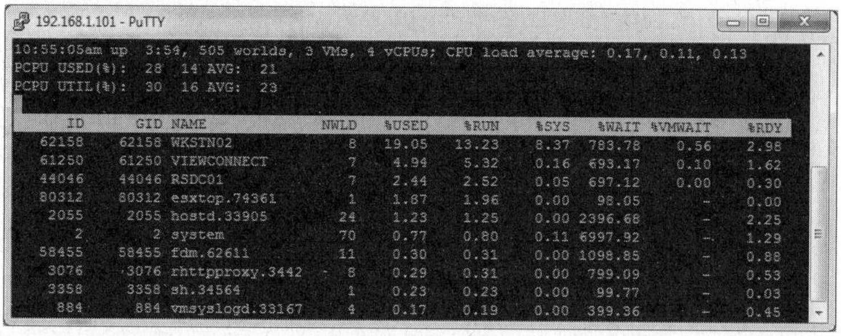

FIGURE 5.18
Initial esxtop screen in an SSH session

Now that you have esxtop up and running, you need to switch to the memory screen by pressing the m key. As seen in Figure 5.19, esxtop now displays memory-related metrics for all virtual machines and services running on the host.

FIGURE 5.19 The esxtop screen displaying memory-related metrics for all virtual machines and services

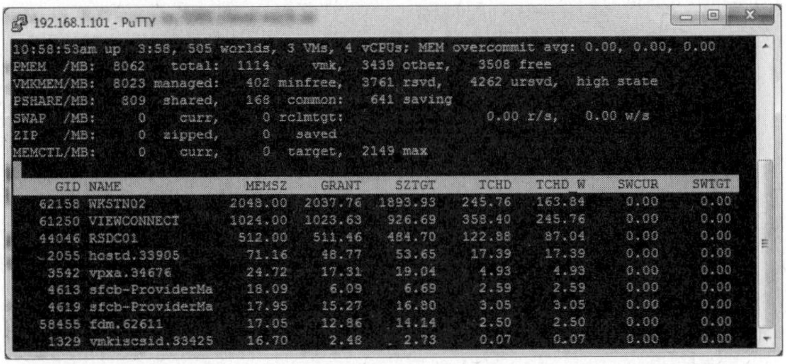

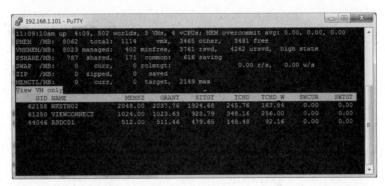

With esxtop displaying memory-related metrics, it would be nice to filter out services running on the ESXi host so that only virtual machines are listed. This is achieved by pressing V (Shift+V). Note that esxtop is case sensitive, so v and V are two separate commands. Figure 5.20 displays the same esxtop memory-related metrics screen but lists only virtual machines.

FIGURE 5.20 The esxtop screen displaying memory-related metrics for virtual machines only

Pressing the f key, enables us to select different memory metric fields to display. A list of available fields is displayed in Figure 5.21.

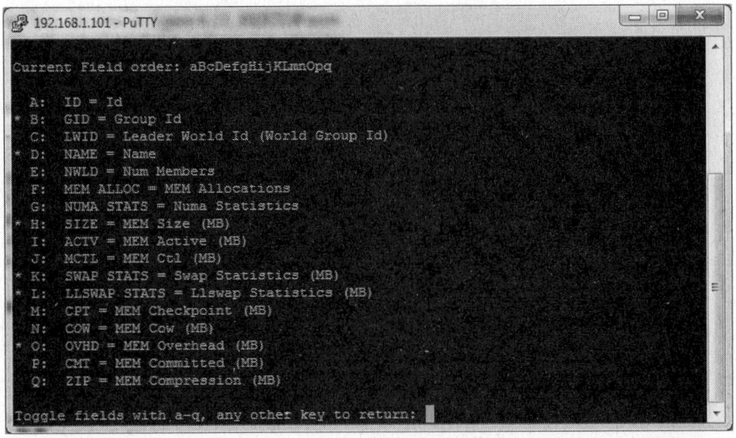

FIGURE 5.21 The esxtop utility displaying the list of available memory metric fields

NOTE By default, esxtop metrics are refreshed every 5 seconds. The update interval can be changed to a minimum of 2 seconds by pressing s followed by the number of seconds. The 2 and 8 keys on the number pad can be used to move the highlighted row up or down.

This book was not intended to cover all performance metrics in detail. However, there are a few metrics in esxtop that are important when it comes to troubleshooting memory performance issues, and we will therefore have a quick look at them.

Table 5.2 shows performance metrics within esxtop to monitor while troubleshooting performance issues and also shows the performance-critical threshold for each metric.

TABLE 5.2   The esxtop memory performance metric thresholds

METRIC	DESCRIPTION	PERFORMANCE THRESHOLD
State	This is the memory state for the host and could be High, Soft, Hard, or Low. A memory state other than High would indicate that the host memory is overcommitted and that the host has less than 6 percent available memory.	Soft
MCTLSZ	This is the current size of the balloon driver. If it's greater than 0, the host memory is either overcommitted or a limit that is smaller than the current allocated memory has been placed on the virtual machine. Either way, the host is trying to reclaim memory from the virtual machine.	1
SWCUR	This metric indicates the current amount of memory swapped to disk using hypervisor swapping. If the number is larger than 0, host physical memory is overcommitted and the host is trying to reclaim memory beyond what is possible simply by means of memory ballooning.	1
SWR/s	The rate at which memory is being actively read from the virtual machine swap file. If this metric is larger than 0, it is possible that frequently accessed memory pages are stored in swap and could indicate that the host physical memory is severely overcommitted.	1
SWW/s	The rate at which memory is being actively written to the virtual machine swap file. If this is larger than 0, the host physical memory is overcommitted.	1
CACHEUSD	The amount of compression cache currently in use by memory compression. A value larger than 0 indicates that the host is compressing memory and host physical memory is overcommitted.	0
ZIP/s	The rate at which the host is compressing memory. If this is larger than 0, the host is actively compressing memory.	0
UNZIP/s	The rate at which the host is uncompressing memory. If this metric is larger than 0, compressed memory is being accessed by the host or virtual machine.	0

High VM Consumed Memory

The Consumed memory metric displays the amount of host physical memory that is consumed by the virtual machine. This includes memory overhead. This figure often confuses administrators because it almost always seems much higher than what the guest operating system is reporting to be in use. In fact, if you have a look at the Active metric, you will probably find that the metric is smaller than the consumed metric as well as what the guest operating system is reporting to be in use.

Consider Figure 5.22. The graph shows the Consumed memory and the Active memory for a single virtual machine.

FIGURE 5.22
Consumed vs.
active memory

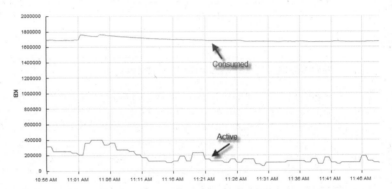

The virtual machine has been configured with 2,048 MB of memory. The Consumed metric is reporting almost 2 GB, but when looking at the Active metric, you can see that the memory that is actually actively being used is much lower, somewhere in the region of 180 MB.

ESXi can reclaim some of the consumed memory using ballooning, and if the active memory is much lower, ballooning can most probably occur without the need for guest or hypervisor swapping. When troubleshooting memory, it is better to look at the Active memory metric, along with metrics for ballooning (vmmctl), swapping, and compression. Simply because a VM has a high amount of consumed memory doesn't mean that performance issues will arise.

When the gap between the consumed metric and the active metric is large, such as what was shown in Figure 5.24, it might be worth doing some in-guest analysis of actual memory utilization. This can be done using the Windows Performance Monitor on Windows VMs or the top command on Linux VMs. Depending on the nature of the application running within the guest OS, it might be worth it to consider reducing the amount of configured memory for the virtual machine if the virtual machine is using much less than what is currently configured.

High Memory Ballooning

One of the most advanced features within an ESXi host is the balloon driver. When ESXi needs to reclaim memory from virtual machines, it will first start to try to reclaim memory using the balloon driver within the VMs' guest OS.

When investigating a performance problem on a particular ESXi host, or even several hosts, keep an eye on the balloon driver size as well as its target size. This should be checked on all virtual machines running on the particular ESXi host. You need to determine why a virtual machine or several virtual machines are ballooning. There could be several reasons memory ballooning has started to occur:

◆ The host memory is overcommitted and the host must reclaim memory from virtual machines in order to allocate the memory to other virtual machines. In this case, it is likely that more than just a single virtual machine is ballooning.

◆ A limit has been placed on the virtual machine memory that is below what is currently allocated to the virtual machine. In this scenario, it is likely that only one virtual machine is ballooning. However, if a memory limit has been placed on a resource pool that contains several virtual machines, it is likely that all or most of the virtual machines within the resource pool could be affected by ballooning.

◆ The virtual machine is oversized and idle and is therefore being taxed by the hypervisor for holding onto idle free memory.

BALLOONING AS A RESULT OF LIMITS

When an ESXi host starts to reclaim memory from a virtual machine simply as a result of a limit placed on the amount of memory and not because the host memory is overcommitted, the host state will not change and will remain High. Simply because memory reclamation is in progress on a single virtual machine doesn't necessarily mean that the memory state of the host will fall below High. Memory reclamation does not affect the host memory state, but the host memory state will determine if the host should be reclaiming memory from virtual machines.

When a virtual machine has high memory ballooning, and yet the ESXi host seems to have sufficient memory available, check to see whether the virtual machine has a memory limit configured. Also, ensure that the virtual machine is not oversized and idle, because that would incur a memory tax that will trigger ballooning inside the guest operating system.

Generally we do not want to see memory ballooning on any virtual machines on a given ESXi host because this could lead to guest or hypervisor swapping. If the Balloon metric in the Web Client or the MCTLSZ or MCTLTGT metrics in esxtop are greater than 0 for any virtual machines, investigate the cause before a performance impact occurs.

Hypervisor Swapping

When ESXi begins to reclaim memory from virtual machines using hypervisor swapping, it is swapping virtual machine guest physical memory pages to disk. If this is already happening on a host, then the host has already tried to reclaim memory using ballooning but failed to reclaim sufficient memory in that way. This means that the host is under considerable memory pressure due to the overcommitment of host physical memory to virtual machines.

Although hypervisor swapping does allow for the allocation of memory to virtual machines beyond what is physically available in the ESXi host, it can lead to serious performance implications. An ESXi host, especially in a production environment, should not be stressed to the point where the hypervisor has to turn to swapping in order to satisfy the memory entitlements of any virtual machine.

To determine whether a host is swapping guest physical memory to disk, you could look at the following metrics:

- Swap In Counters
- Swap Out Counters
- Swap used
- Latency

If any one of these metrics is high, then the host is swapping guest physical memory to disk and you need to determine why it is doing so.

If the host memory state is anything other than High, then the host memory is overcommitted and you need to power off or migrate some virtual machines away from the host to free up some host physical memory.

If the host memory state is indicated as High and the preceding counters are also higher than their thresholds, then you need to investigate to see which virtual machines are being swapped to disk. If all or most of the virtual machines are swapping, it could be possible that a memory limit has been configured on those virtual machines or, more likely, on a resource pool in which those virtual machines reside. If a single virtual machine is swapping, it is likely that a memory limit has been configured on the virtual machine.

As stated earlier in this chapter, hypervisor swapping is one of the more drastic mechanisms that an ESXi host will employ to reclaim memory. It will enable virtual machines to function when the host memory is under pressure, but it will also lead to severe performance degradation. Therefore, when you see a host swapping, you do need to take action.

HYPERVISOR SWAPPING IMPACT ON DATASTORE I/O

If virtual machines with memory-intensive applications are being swapped to disk using hypervisor swapping and SSD host cache is not in use, an increase in disk I/O will be seen on the datastores where the virtual machines reside. This could lead to increased latency for all virtual machines that reside on the datastore, regardless of their host placements. If you experience poor performance or high disk latency times on virtual machines but no swapping is reported on any of the virtual machines on a particular host, it might be worth having a look at the performance metrics of all virtual machines that reside on that datastore because the performance impact could be caused by virtual machines being swapped to disk by another host.

Guest Operating System Swapping

Each guest operating system that is installed on a virtual machine has its own native memory management built in. When a guest operating system is running low on available guest physical memory, the guest operating system could be forced to start swapping its memory pages to disk. On a Windows guest operating system, the swapped memory will be written to a page file on one of the disks, such as C: or D:. On a Linux operating system, there is normally a partition that is formatted specifically for swap space.

ESXi does not provide performance metrics for in-guest swapping because this is a feature native to the guest operating system. However, you can try to use the performance metrics provided by ESXi to determine the memory utilization figures for a particular virtual machine.

If the Active memory performance counter is high and close to the configured guest physical memory for the virtual machine, then it is likely the guest operating system could start swapping.

You can also look at tools within the guest operating system to determine how the operating system is managing its memory. On Windows, the Windows Performances Monitor (perfmon) is a good tool and can indicate the level of swapping inside the guest operating system. Within the Windows Performance Monitor, use the Pages Input / sec counter. In a Linux operating system, you can use the top command from the Linux shell and look at the Swap Used value.

If determined that a guest operating system is swapping, you need to consider whether the virtual machine has been sized correctly, and the most likely cause is due to the fact the virtual machine is configured with too little guest physical memory.

Summary

In this chapter we looked at how ESXi virtualizes memory and how it ensures that all virtual machines are allocated enough memory to satisfy the entitlements of each one. We looked at how memory is allocated to virtual machines only when a virtual machine attempts to touch a memory page for the first time. We also looked at technologies such as Transparent Page Sharing, which is used to minimize the number of duplicated memory pages in host physical memory.

You saw how ESXi is able to overcommit on physical memory and how it can reclaim physical memory that was previously allocated to virtual machines, using techniques such as ballooning, compression, and hypervisor swapping.

Also covered were some of the different performance metrics provided by esxtop and their performance thresholds. In the troubleshooting section, we covered how to look out for and identify potential issues relating to memory performance and utilization.

Chapter 6

Network

Networks can be complicated, but when you introduce a virtual network to the mix, you really have to plan and design it correctly or you'll set yourself up for a multitude of problems once it goes into production use. You hardly ever see the problems when you are installing and configuring; it's typically just after you've gone live with it and suddenly you have to explain an outage that could have been prevented. If you've been in this line of work for long, you have most likely run into this at least once. If not, congratulations. You've done a good job. Thankfully, it normally takes only one occurrence to teach us the value of a solid design. With that in mind, let's look at the design considerations for setting up a virtualized network.

In this chapter we look at:

◆ Designing physical and virtual networks

◆ Choosing a virtual switch

◆ Considerations for host server type

◆ Configuring virtual machine networking for optimum performance

◆ Troubleshooting virtual network issues

Creating a Network Design

You might ask yourself, "Is network design really that important?" Or you might ask, "Do I really need to have a design in place before I create my virtual environment?" The answer to both questions is an emphatic YES! When building out a virtual network, there are several things that have to be considered and designed before you start to lay down the infrastructure. As much as most people may not like to have to sit down and draw out and plan an environment, experience will tell you that if you don't, you'll regret it down the road once you start to actually build the environment and issues start to creep up.

There are two main parts to network design: the physical network and the virtual network. The physical network consists of all of the physical routers and switches that make up your upstream network. The virtual network consists of all of the virtual network components that make up your vSphere environment. This can include standard vSwitches, vSphere Distributed Switches (DVSs), the Cisco Nexus 1000v virtual switch, or the components of the vCloud Network and Security suite.

Designing Your Physical Network

In many larger organizations where there is a dedicated virtualization team and a dedicated networking team, the VMware administrators may not have input into the design of the physical network. It's important to understand the physical network design even if you're a VMware administrator with no networking responsibilities whatsoever. Having a good understanding of the physical network layout will help you better design your virtual networking.

In your network design, ideally you'll want every network path to have redundancy. If your company has embraced virtualization, then you may be targeting as high a percentage of server consolidation as possible. Or you might be virtualizing business-critical applications where application performance and availability are crucial. In either scenario, having a network design that considers both performance and availability is important.

A good network layout typically consists of ESXi hosts connected to multiple uplink switches, and those switches are, in turn, connected to separate uplink switches. Those are usually cross-connected and uplinked to the network core, with the core switches connected in a redundant configuration. This is known as a full mesh design, and it provides redundancy across multiple levels of potential failure.

When designing your physical network, you'll want to make sure you include the following key design considerations:

◆ Ensure that there is sufficient bandwidth to meet your requirements. Understanding your current and expected workloads can help you design the environment based on your overall bandwidth requirements. Sufficient bandwidth is needed for not only virtual machine networking but also management functions, vMotion, and Fault Tolerance as well as any IP-based storage your organization may be using.

◆ Ensure that there are enough physical network uplinks to provide the network isolation and redundancy that your environment requires. Even in situations where 10 Gigabit Ethernet (10 GbE) is used, you'll still want to make sure you've properly isolated traffic for vMotion, virtual machines, and IP-based storage (if required).

◆ As described previously, make sure all physical network uplinks have redundancy not only at the network interface level but also upstream on the switches they are connected to. In a virtual infrastructure, outages are magnified as multiple workloads run on a single ESXi host, so having multiple layers of redundancy can help reduce unexpected outages.

◆ Check for bottlenecks within the network path to make sure there is nothing that may slow down traffic. For example, if you're using jumbo frames, make sure all devices within the path of those frames are configured with the same frame size. Similarly, make sure all cables are rated to work with the speed of your network (particularly with 10 GbE) and all switches and ports are configured with the proper speed, duplex, and flow control settings.

Modern network cards (those released within the last few years) in your ESXi hosts support features that can enhance and improve the performance of network traffic. The following list highlights some of those features, which are recommended when choosing network cards for your ESXi hosts:

TCP Checksum Offload Network cards that support TCP checksum offload can offload the processing of data from the server's CPU onto specially designed hardware on the network card itself. Offloading the processing from the server's CPU can help increase the overall performance of the server. This is sometimes referred to as a TCP offload engine, or TOE for short. Reducing the amount of CPU that must be utilized to handle networking traffic can not only improve performance but also free up resources for virtual machines.

TCP Segmentation Offload   Similar to TCP checksum offload, TCP segmentation offload (TSO) is another technology that allows the network card itself to offload the segmentation of data from the server's physical CPU. This decreases CPU utilization on the server and helps increase performance.

Large Receive Offload   Like the previous two technologies, large receive offload is designed to reduce CPU utilization on the server. It aggregates incoming packets into a large buffer before processing them, which reduces the total number of packets that have to be processed and subsequently reduces CPU utilization.

Jumbo Frames   Jumbo frames are frames that are larger than 1,500 bytes, which is the size of standard frames. Jumbo frames can carry up to 9,000 total bytes, reducing the number of frames that must be processed and increasing performance. The key point to remember with jumbo frames is that they must be enabled end to end to be effective. If any device within the path of the frames is not configured for jumbo frames, you could experience performance issues and lose any potential benefit.

Though there is some debate as to the usefulness of jumbo frames, VMware has found that enabling jumbo frames on the vMotion network can reduce issues with migrating certain workloads. As part of VMware's testing, vMotion migrations were performed on Microsoft Exchange Server 2010 virtual machines that were participating in a database availability group (DAG). DAGs rely on Windows Failover Clustering technology, so they are particularly sensitive to even brief network outages, as are typical during a vMotion migration. When enabling jumbo frames on the vMotion network, VMware found that there were no unintended database failovers, as there can be without jumbo frames. Though this is a specific use case, it highlights one of the potential benefits of enabling jumbo frames in your environment.

More information on this testing can be found at the following location:

```
www.vmware.com/files/pdf/using-vmware-HA-DRS-and-vmotion-with-exchange-2010-dags
.pdf
```

NetQueue   NetQueue is a technology that can improve performance of 10 GbE networks in virtualized environments. It allows a network adapter to use multiple receive queues and utilize multiple processor cores, increasing the performance of the server.

Choosing a Virtual Switch

VMware vSphere supports a variety of virtual switches, including the vNetwork Standard vSwitch, the vSphere Distributed Switch (dvSwitch or VDS), and the Cisco Nexus 1000V. The type of vSwitch you should use depends heavily on the needs and requirements of your deployment, so as with many things in IT, there is no right or wrong answer. For example, a smaller deployment may only need to use the standard vSwitch, but if the deployment requires greater scalability, functionality, or support for vCloud Director, you'll likely want to look into the dvSwitch options.

NOTE   Your choice of vSwitch may come down to the version of vSphere that you're licensed to use. Currently only the highest-tier license in vSphere, Enterprise Plus, supports the use of the vSphere Distributed Switch. Typically only larger environments are licensed with Enterprise Plus due to the cost, so smaller environments may not have access to the dvSwitch.

Considering the Standard vSwitch

The standard vSwitch is the original virtual switch that has been a part of the platform for many years. Unless you are new to managing vSphere, you are likely familiar with this vSwitch, and the good news is that it has not changed significantly in the latest version of vSphere. This vSwitch is best suited for small deployments with smaller numbers of hosts. You can deploy it in larger environments if you choose to, but keep in mind that there is more administrative overhead with the standard vSwitch because you have to manually configure the parameters of the vSwitch on every host to match or you could end up with network problems with your virtual machines. For larger deployments it is often best to use the dvSwitch, which can be centrally managed so settings are more consistent across your hosts. Most of the networking enhancements that VMware is adding to the vSphere platform are going to be found in the dvSwitch, so using the dvSwitch helps future-proof your deployment.

If your requirements dictate that you must use the standard vSwitch, making sure the deployment and configuration of each vSwitch on each host is consistent is important. Luckily you have several options available to you here even if you have to use the standard vSwitch:

◆   ESXi hosts support scripted installations, unattended installations of ESXi that pull a common configuration from an installation script. Using a scripted install can help keep hosts consistent by using a common set of configuration details, reducing the possibility of human error. You can read much more about scripted installations of ESXi at http:// kb.vmware.com/kb/2004582.

If you are not comfortable with performing a scripted installation of your ESXi hosts, you can still use scripting to ensure consistency in the creation of your vSwitch. vSphere supports the use of Microsoft PowerShell and VMware provides PowerCLI, a PowerShell interface specifically created to manage and automate a vSphere environment. Using PowerCLI, an administrator can write a script that will create all standard vSwitches on an ESXi host in a consistent manner. PowerCLI and supporting documentation can be downloaded at www.vmware.com/ support/developer/PowerCLI/.

If scripting with PowerShell isn't your thing, you can still use additional vSphere management tools to create standardized vSwitch configurations. Both the vSphere Command Line Interface (vCLI) and the vSphere Management Assistant virtual appliance support using commands to create a vSwitch rather than using the vSphere Web Client. Either of these methods can be used to execute scripts to create your vSwitches to ensure consistency.

Why are we spending time talking about consistency in vSwitch configuration in a book about performance? Simply put, inconsistencies in vSwitch configuration can lead to unexpected performance problems in your environment. Even small differences in configuration between ESXi hosts can cause unexpected results. Different settings can lead to inconsistent performance between hosts or, possibly worse, the inability to use certain features like vMotion. Inconsistent vSwitch settings between ESXi hosts can make troubleshooting performance problems much more difficult or extend the time it takes to resolve issues. If you are constrained to use the standard vSwitch in your environment, strongly consider using automation tools to help maintain consistency.

Considering the vSphere Distributed Switch

The VMware dvSwitch was first introduced in vSphere 4 as a way to provide a centralized virtual switch solution for larger virtual infrastructures. The dvSwitch can be used in any size environment, but it makes sense to use it in a medium- or large-sized environment with many hosts and virtual machines. This feature is also only available in the highest license level of vSphere, known as Enterprise Plus, so it is more commonly found in larger organizations that can afford it. The configuration is stored inside vCenter and is configured in one place, so when you assign a host to the dvSwitch, all of the settings are applied and you reduce the risk of inconsistencies between the hosts (such as mistyping the name of a port group). If you do have a networking or configuration error, it can be diagnosed and resolved from a central management location and automatically applied to all of your ESXi hosts.

For example, let's say you've created a new virtual local area network (VLAN) that will be used only for connecting ESXi hosts to network storage. With a standard vSwitch, you would need to connect to each host to create the port group with the correct VLAN tag (or use the automation methods described earlier). With the dvSwitch, that port group and VLAN tag are created one time and are automatically available on all hosts at the same time.

NOTE More information about the features that are available when using the vSphere Distributed Switch are available at the following location:

www.vmware.com/products/datacenter-virtualization/vsphere/distributed-switch.html

In addition to its ease of use, there are three features that make the dvSwitch a compelling choice for a virtual switch in your environment:

◆ Link Layer Discovery Protocol (LLDP)

◆ NetFlow

◆ Network I/O Control (NOIC)

Link Layer Discovery Protocol

vSphere has supported Cisco Discovery Protocol (CDP) for many years. CDP allows you to stream physical switch details from your Cisco switches back to your ESXi hosts as well as advertise virtual infrastructure details to upstream Cisco switches. If you did not use Cisco networking equipment, unfortunately this feature was not available to you. vSphere now supports a feature called Link Layer Discovery Protocol (LLDP), which is a vendor-neutral switch discovery protocol that allows you to get the same information from other switch manufacturers' switches in the vSphere GUI. Unlike CDP, which is available on both the standard vSwitch and the dvSwitch, LLDP is available only on the dvSwitch. It provides the following information:

◆ Chassis ID (MAC address)

◆ Port ID of the uplink port

- Time to live (TTL)

- Time-out

- System name and description

- VLAN ID

- Maximum transmission unit (MTU)

- Peer device capabilities

  - Router

  - Transparent bridge

  - Source route bridge

  - Network switch

  - Host

  - Internet Group Multicast Protocol (IGMP)

  - Repeater

NETFLOW SUPPORT

NetFlow is a protocol that is used to collect network traffic and then send it to another device for analysis. Network traffic can be traffic between virtual machines on the same ESXi hosts, traffic between virtual machines across different ESXi hosts, and even traffic between a virtual machine and a physical machine. The protocol was originally developed by Cisco and has become an industry standard for collecting network traffic for analysis.

YOU CAN'T GET SOMETHING FOR NOTHING

As with many things, you can't simply monitor everything without impacting available resources. Monitoring multiple traffic flows, or monitoring flows that have extremely high rates of network traffic, can lead to higher CPU utilization on your host. Configure NetFlow only for the traffic streams you really need to monitor.

For more information on enabling NetFlow, go to www.vmware.com/resources/techresources/1014.

NETWORK I/O CONTROL

In a virtual infrastructure, with different types of virtual machines running on the same ESXi host, it's common to have network traffic with different patterns merged together on the same physical networking hardware. This can cause problems because all the different traffic types can affect performance and the predictability of the network due to lack of isolation, scheduling, and arbitration. As the acceptance of virtualization has grown and organizations have begun to deploy more virtual machines, administrators are starting to see virtual machines compete for the same network resources. This can be especially problematic in public and private clouds where the need to maintain service levels for different groups of virtual machines (potentially owned by different customers) is much higher. A single virtual machine can end up monopolizing the network and reducing the performance of other virtual machines on the same ESXi host. This is commonly referred to as the "noisy neighbor" problem.

Network I/O Control, or NIOC, can be used to prioritize different traffic flowing through the same network pipe. NIOC is an important technology that can be used to help ensure that applications that have low latency and/or high bandwidth requirements get prioritized access to the network to meet these requirements. By prioritizing traffic and limiting the amount of traffic a single virtual machine (or group of virtual machines) can consume, NIOC can help to reduce or solve the problem of noisy neighbor virtual machines.

When you enable Network I/O Control, dvSwitch traffic is divided into the following predefined network resource pools:

- VM Fault Tolerance traffic

- iSCSI traffic

- Management Network traffic

- NFS traffic

- VM traffic

- vMotion traffic

- vSphere replication traffic

- User defined (can be based on the user's specific requirements)

Network I/O Control allows administrators to control network traffic by utilizing the following key features:

Shares   Similar to defining shares that can be used to control CPU and memory (discussed in more detail in Chapter 4, "CPU" and Chapter 5, "Memory" administrators can define shares that are used to determine relative priority of network traffic. When multiple virtual machines all access network resources at the same time, shares can be used to determine which virtual machines get priority access to those network resources.

Limits   Limits are used to determine the maximum amount of network resources particular virtual machines can consume. Limits are useful when lower-priority workloads are mixed with business-critical workloads, helping to ensure that lower-tier workloads can't consume a large portion of the available network resources. Limits can be dangerous, however, so they should be used only in specific scenarios where they are required. If you plan to use limits, make sure to perform testing to make sure you understand the impact of setting them.

Network I/O Control is a key feature for any organization looking to deploy a public or private cloud. It can act as a safety net to help keep all of your applications performing well and to enforce fairness in access to network resources. There are very few reasons not to enable this feature in your virtual infrastructure, even if you do not currently have network resource contention.

Considering the Cisco Nexus 1000V dvSwitch

The Cisco Nexus 1000V is available through VMware by way of Cisco and brings more to the table than the standard vSwitch and dvSwitch. In order to take advantage of the features and functionality of the 1000V, your infrastructure should utilize other Cisco networking hardware. The Nexus 1000V is indeed a real switch, in the sense that it runs a real Cisco operating system (NX-OS) and operates just like a normal switch. This allows your network team to manage the switch as they do physical Cisco switches.

NOTE The decision whether to use the Nexus 1000V virtual switch comes down to how you choose to manage networking in your vSphere environment. The 1000V offers numerous management advantages over the dvSwitch that make it an attractive option for organizations that already rely on Cisco networking.

You can find more information on the Cisco Nexus 1000V at the following two locations, from VMware and Cisco:

www.cisco.com/en/US/products/ps9902/index.html
www.vmware.com/products/cisco-nexus-1000V/overview.html

Which Virtual Switch Do I Choose?

At this point we've reviewed, at a high level, both the standard vSwitch and the dvSwitch. Which switch is right for you and your environment?

Though this decision should come down to the requirements of your particular environment, the reality is that the license you own dictates which of the switches are available for use in the infrastructure. If your organization owns the Enterprise Plus license for vSphere, we strongly recommend using the dvSwitch to ensure the best performance.

The following list offers some key considerations for why choosing the dvSwitch can help deliver the best networking performance for your vSphere environment:

◆ When VMware adds new networking features to the vSphere platform, those features primarily end up only in the dvSwitch. Using the dvSwitch essentially future-proofs your environment for any new features that may be released in future versions of vSphere.

◆ NIOC is available in the dvSwitch. As you continue to virtualize workloads, especially business-critical workloads, NIOC will likely become an increasingly important technology. This can be especially true when using converged network infrastructure where fewer network cards overall are shared between multiple functions.

◆ The dvSwitch offers a load-balancing policy, called Load-Based Teaming (LBT), that can more efficiently load balance network traffic across physical NICs. Load-Based Teaming is described in much greater detail later in the chapter.

◆ In addition to load-balancing policies, the dvSwitch has numerous management features like NetFlow and LLDP that make it more attractive when virtualizing business-critical applications.

Selecting Host Hardware

The type of ESXi host that you choose can have a large impact on your overall network design. In fact, network design should be a key input when choosing the type of host you use for ESXi. Different host vendors and different host footprints will offer varying amounts of networking capabilities, so choosing the right kind of host to meet your performance and availability requirements is important.

Host Server Type

With nearly any technology you are likely to have people split on which is the "best" of a set of options. Servers are no different, with folks frequently debating whether traditional rack mount servers or blade servers are "better" for supporting virtual infrastructures. The fact remains that the type of server you choose to deploy will have an impact on your vSphere network configuration. While we won't cover all specific models of servers, we will talk about server types and provide some specific examples. We'll use Hewlett Packard (HP) servers as example servers, but the concepts apply to servers from other manufacturers as well.

BLADE SERVERS

Blades have become a popular choice for vSphere deployments because of their small rack footprint and the processing power you can get out of them. With current processors and memory sizes growing, you can configure blade servers to be very dense (support many virtual machines per blade) if you choose to. For example, HP's BL460 G8 was, at the time of this writing, shipping as two socket blade servers running up to eight core processors, and you can add up to 512 GB of RAM. In a chassis that can hold 16 blades, you can do the math and see that you can get a very large number of virtual machines and only consume a small amount of space in a server rack. If you plan to deploy a server solution that is that dense, you'll need to make sure your SAN and network connections can handle that much load. With SAN fiber adapters at 8 GbE and NICs now coming as 10 GbE, you have plenty of bandwidth and those issues are less of a problem.

NOTE   You even have the option to use something such as InfiniBand and integrate with a virtual I/O solution such as Xsigo, which allows you to aggregate several 10 GbE connections together, and the same with SAN connections. Not all organizations need that much bandwidth, so 8 Gb fiber or 10 Gb Ethernet ports are typically enough even for very demanding workloads.

Blade enclosures utilize blade switches that are in the back of the enclosure regardless of the manufacturer. That is one of the positive features, so say the manufacturers, because the entire environment is in one package (the enclosure). Keeping all network traffic within the enclosure can improve performance because the traffic does not need to be sent to an external switch, reducing overall latency. That can help speed up network-intensive operations such as vMotion between hosts or if vSphere Fault Tolerance is in use. It does add a layer of complexity when you have blades in a larger environment and you have several of the enclosures, since each one adds at least two Ethernet switches to be managed. The HP enclosure has eight bays in the back of the chassis, with the top two being used for Ethernet switch modules. The next two are often used for fiber SAN switches, and if necessary, the next set can be either Ethernet or fiber depending on your needs for additional network or storage connections. Different server blade vendors may offer different options, so this is only meant to be an example.

Regardless of the blade server vendor that you use, make sure you have sufficient network uplinks to provide the necessary redundancy and performance that your organization needs. Understanding your workload is critical here since blades are often limited in the expansion ports that are available. For example, if you understand your workload and can see that your virtual machines are more likely to be constrained by network bandwidth than they are by storage bandwidth, it may make sense to populate your blades with more Ethernet ports than uplinks dedicated to storage (either fiber or Ethernet). Similarly, if you have virtual machines that rely heavily on communicating with other virtual machines within the same vSphere environment, consider keeping those virtual machines on blade servers within the same chassis to take advantage of the faster chassis-based networking. Remember that network traffic between blades in the same chassis stays within the enclosure (provided that traffic is within the same VLAN) and is likely to have lower latency and faster performance.

When deploying blade servers that are extremely dense, or those that support many virtual machines, you need to stop and consider one note of caution: how dense is too dense? This question is entirely up to the organization deploying the environment, and different organizations will feel differently about the risk that this presents. It's a question about risk versus reward when considering very dense environments. If you have 50 or more virtual machines on a given host and that host experiences a hardware or software failure, that's generally considered to be a pretty large outage for almost any organization. vSphere has technologies like High Availability and Fault Tolerance to limit the impact of failures, but a failure will still result in downtime for most (or all) of the virtual machines on the host. ESXi is a stable and mature platform, so the risk of a software-based failure is lower than in previous versions, but the risk of hardware failure is real and the impact could be significant.

RACK MOUNT SERVERS

Rack mount servers are very common in today's datacenters, and most readers are likely to be familiar with them. They certainly have their advantages over blade servers due to their size and the number of configuration options available. You can often get more processors and memory in rack mount servers than you can with most blade servers, and you have more flexibility with their network connections than you do with blade servers. Rack mount servers with many CPU cores and many GB of RAM can allow you to deploy large numbers of virtual machines and achieve virtual machine density similar to what you get with blade servers. Once again, consider how dense you are comfortable with making your ESXi host and make sure to prepare for the loss of a host due to a hardware or software failure.

In many cases, rack mount servers can be a better fit because of their flexibility in adding additional networking components. If you want to set up a set of hosts that have internal-facing virtual machines as well as external-facing (or public) virtual machines, you can often do this more cheaply with rack mount servers than you can with a blade solution. Rack mount servers typically have far more expansion ports available than blade servers, allowing you to install additional network cards to meet your networking isolation or performance requirements.

Rack mount servers often make it easier to provide the necessary levels of redundancy and performance to meet the demands of today's vSphere environments. It is common today to find network cards that have four individual ports on them, and when they are combined with the ports available on the server itself, you can provide isolation for nearly every networking function. You can isolate traffic for vSphere Fault Tolerance, vMotion, and the various kinds of virtual machine traffic your environment may require.

Network Adapters

The type of network adapters you deploy, and their speed, will dictate how they should ultimately be configured on your ESXi hosts. A best practice for ESXi hosts is to split virtual machine and VMkernel traffic, and really they suggest you separate some of the types of VMkernel traffic from each other. For best performance, you should isolate vMotion traffic from other VMkernel traffic types, especially if you're utilizing Multi-NIC vMotion (covered later in this chapter). Aside from the security concerns with co-locating vMotion traffic with other traffic types (since a virtual machine's memory is transferred over the vMotion network in an unencrypted state), utilizing Multi-NIC vMotion can consume a large amount of bandwidth. By keeping those interfaces isolated from other traffic types, you reduce the chance of an impact on performance during vMotion operations.

The same is true for the networking for Fault Tolerance. vSphere Fault Tolerance requires a low-latency network connection with sufficient bandwidth to mirror all virtual machine operations between two ESXi hosts in order to keep protected virtual machines in sync. Combining Fault Tolerance traffic with other traffic types can increase latency and potentially cause a skew in synchronization between the virtual machines, possibly resulting in a lapse in protection.

Similarly, IP storage traffic (iSCSI and NFS) should be completely isolated from other traffic types. Storage performance, discussed in Chapter 7, is one of the leading causes of performance issues in vSphere environments, and improperly configured storage networking can be a common culprit. Many storage vendors do not even support combining VMkernel interfaces used for IP storage traffic with any other types of virtual networking. Keeping your IP storage networking isolated from virtual machine networking a good practice for avoiding storage performance issues.

DOES IN-GUEST iSCSI REQUIRE DEDICATED NETWORK CARDS?

What about in-guest iSCSI, which is connecting to iSCSI-based storage from inside a virtual machine instead of at the ESXi layer? Does that need to be isolated on its own set of network interfaces, or can it share the network interfaces that ESXi uses to connect to iSCSI storage?

In general, if you have enough network uplinks available, it is best to use dedicated uplinks just for in-guest iSCSI traffic. Though it may seem like it is the same traffic and so it can share the uplinks ESXi is using for iSCSI traffic, in reality they should be separate if possible to maximize performance. We've seen environments where in-guest iSCSI traffic and either ESXi-based iSCSI traffic or regular virtual machine traffic is combined on the same physical uplinks, and during periods of heavy network utilization (such as nightly backup windows), many virtual machines saw significant performance degradation.

Unless you don't have enough physical network interfaces available, you should dedicate uplinks for in-guest iSCSI traffic instead of trying to use the same physical network cards as ESXi-based iSCSI traffic. You'll have better performance, it'll be easier to manage, and you can more easily configure multipathing software without changing settings that might conflict with what is required for connecting an ESXi host to iSCSI storage.

Whenever possible, try to avoid using in-guest iSCSI as a means of connecting virtual machines to iSCSI storage. Doing this utilizes the ESXi host networking stack and not the storage stack, meaning that the guest OS must process the storage traffic. It also means that any multipathing software must be configured inside the guest instead of at the ESXi host level, making setup a challenge and possibly introducing unexpected results. The ESXi host will see the traffic as standard network traffic and you will not be able to take advantage of other storage-integrated VMware products like vCenter Site Recovery Manager and Storage I/O Control (and to a degree Network I/O Control). In previous versions of vSphere, using in-guest iSCSI was a way to circumvent the limitations on the sizes of VM virtual disks (VMDKs) and VMFS volumes, but as of vSphere 5.5, the maximum size of a single virtual disk has been raised to 62 TB. This should eliminate the need to use in-guest iSCSI for all but the most specific use cases.

With blade servers you often don't have as many options for adding additional network cards for redundancy. With 10 GbE interfaces, it is typically not necessary to have physically separated and isolated network cards for each traffic type. Instead, using logical separation technologies such as VLANs is sufficient because 10 GbE is enough bandwidth to share between multiple functions. If you don't have 10 GbE, then you really need to strongly consider splitting these up into their own set of interfaces.

Designing for Performance

So far we've covered some concepts of network design, reviewed the various types of virtual switches available, and covered the different host types to choose from. With that out of the way, it's time to get to the reason we're all here: how do we get the best possible network performance for our virtualized workloads?

The truth is, for a large majority of workloads, the network is not the limiting factor when it comes to performance. Many performance-intensive applications today will heavily tax the CPU, memory, and storage infrastructure but not the network. That doesn't mean, however, that you can just throw some network cards together in a load-balanced pair and call it a day (especially when IP-based storage is in use in your infrastructure). As more workloads are added to your vSphere environment, network utilization can slowly creep up until it becomes a bottleneck for your environment.

In the following sections, we'll cover technologies and configurations that can improve performance at the ESXi host level as well as those that can improve performance at the virtual machine level.

ESXi Host-Level Performance

Delivering good network performance starts at the ESXi host level. Choosing the right host with the appropriate number of NICs to ensure redundancy and performance is the first step, as discussed previously. There is no right or wrong on how many NICs to use so long as you are ensuring redundancy for every function, as each organization's requirements are different. As we've said, though, simply allocating NICs to your ESXi hosts is only one part of the story.

vSwitch Load Balancing

As we discussed earlier in the chapter, new enhancements and features in the networking stack are almost exclusively placed in the vSphere Distributed Switch and not the standard vSwitch. It is for that reason we recommend using the dvSwitch in all cases unless your vSphere licensing does not allow you to use it.

One of the most important of these features in terms of performance is an additional load-balancing policy that is found only in the dvSwitch. Load-balancing policies determine how the ESXi host will handle balancing out the load between all of the physical NICs in the dvSwitch. Table 6.1 lists each of the load-balancing policies and briefly describes how they work.

TABLE 6.1: Load-balancing policies in the vSphere Distributed Switch

LOAD-BALANCING POLICY	DESCRIPTION
Route based on originating virtual port	The dvSwitch chooses an uplink based on the virtual port where the traffic entered the switch. This port remains the same until the virtual machine is powered off, a physical NIC experiences a failure, or a vMotion occurs.
Route based on source MAC hash	The dvSwitch chooses an uplink based on a hash of the source Ethernet. As with above, the virtual machine is tied to this physical uplink until the virtual machine is powered off, the physical NIC experiences a failure, or a vMotion occurs.
Route based on IP hash	The dvSwitch chooses an uplink based on a hash of the source and destination IP address of each packet.
Route based on physical NIC load	The dvSwitch chooses an uplink based on the virtual port where the traffic entered the switch. Uplink mappings can be reassigned automatically based on load. This load-balancing policy is available only on the dvSwitch.

The first two policies, route based on originating virtual port and route based on source MAC hash, essentially work exactly the same. They work in a round-robin fashion, meaning that there is no advanced intelligence as to how virtual machine NICs are assigned to physical NICs on the ESXi host. The placement happens when the virtual machine is powered on, and the NIC assignment does not change unless the VM is powered off, the network card experiences a failure, or a vMotion occurs. Since the round-robin method of placement offers no visibility into how busy the virtual machine's NIC actually is, both of these policies could easily place heavily utilized virtual NICs all on the same physical NIC while other physical NICs sit underutilized. With both of these policies, the network traffic from a single virtual network card will only ever traverse a single physical NIC.

The next policy, route based on IP hash, takes a hash of both the source and destination IP addresses to distribute load across the physical NICs in the dvSwitch. This policy is different from the first two in that it can spread the network traffic of a single virtual machine across multiple physical NICs at the same time. Seems like we've found the winner, right? Not so fast—as always, the devil is in the details. This configuration requires that EtherChannel is used on the physical switches that the ESXi hosts connect to, potentially increasing the complexity of the solution. Also, and more important, since the hash is based on both the source and the destination IP address, traffic is only load balanced across multiple physical NICs if the virtual machine is communicating with multiple IP addresses. If the virtual machine is only communicating with another single IP address (such as during a file transfer operation), the traffic will traverse only a single physical NIC. If, for example, a virtual machine is being backed up via an in-guest backup agent and is sending massive amounts of data over the LAN to a backup server, all of that traffic will traverse only a single physical NIC because the VM is communicating with only one server. And just like the first two load-balancing policies, the IP hash load-balancing policy applies no intelligence to placement of traffic on physical NICs. If another virtual machine is assigned to a physical NIC and is consuming a large portion of the available bandwidth, the IP hash load-balancing policy is unaware of that load and could possibly assign additional virtual machines to that same saturated NIC.

The load-balancing policy with actual intelligence built in is the route based on physical NIC load, also known as Load-Based Teaming (LBT). This policy assigns virtual machines to physical NICs the same way the route based on originating virtual port ID policy does, assigning based on round-robin when the VMs are powered on. However, this policy evaluates the load on the physical NICs and can dynamically reassign virtual machines to other physical NICs to reduce the network utilization and improve overall performance. In this way it is similar to vSphere Distributed Resource Scheduler (DRS), which dynamically performs vMotion of virtual machines to balance out the load (though these two technologies are not actually integrated). LBT also does not require potentially complex networking configurations like EtherChannel.

The LBT policy does not reassign virtual machines to physical NICs unless the network utilization passes a defined threshold. A virtual NIC will be assigned to a different physical NIC only if mean send and receive utilization on a physical NIC exceeds 75 percent of the total capacity over a period of 30 seconds. LBT will only move virtual NICs between physical NICs once every 30 seconds, helping to prevent virtual NICs from flip-flopping between physical NICs. Though this 30-second delay may allow a VM to briefly saturate a network uplink, it may not be enough time to violate any service-level agreements (SLAs). As always, make sure your design, including features like LBT, meets your business and technical requirements.

LOAD-BASED TEAMING PERFORMANCE TESTING

VMware has done performance testing on LBT to show how it responds to increased network utilization. Though this is a somewhat older test (released when the feature was first introduced in vSphere 4.1), it is still relevant to show how the feature works and the potential performance benefits.

You can read more information about the performance study at the following location:

```
http://blogs.vmware.com/performance/2010/12/vmware-load-based-teaming-
lbt-performance.html
```

LBT can be enabled either on an individual distributed port group or on multiple distributed port groups at once. Since you typically want to enable this feature on all of your distributed port groups, it is easier to use the method of configuring it once across multiple distributed port groups.

To enable LBT on multiple distributed port groups at once, follow this simple procedure:

1. Launch the vSphere Web Client and connect to your vCenter Server.

2. From the Home view, select Networking to access your dvSwitch(es). Find the correct dvSwitch, right-click it, and select Manage Distributed Port Groups.

3. On the Select Port Group Policies page, select the check box labeled Teaming And Failover, then click Next.

4. Select the distributed port groups on which you'd like to enable LBT. To select more than one at a time, hold down the Ctrl key while selecting each one. Once you've selected the appropriate distributed port groups, click Next.

5. From the Load Balancing drop-down list, change the option to Route Based On Physical NIC Load, as shown in Figure 6.1, and click Next.

FIGURE 6.1

Enable Route based on physical NIC load policy

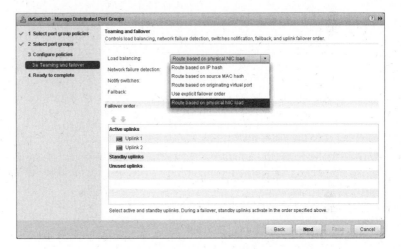

6. Click Finish to apply the LBT policy to the selected distributed port groups.

7. Repeat this process for all appropriate distributed port groups on each of your dvSwitches.

If you're using the dvSwitch (and by now we hope we've convinced you to use it), you should strongly consider the use of the LBT policy for your load-balancing policy. It is the only policy capable of examining actual network utilization and reassigning virtual machines to other physical NICs to help improve performance.

CPU Utilization

We know what you're thinking: "I already read the CPU chapter so why are you talking about CPU again?" This chapter is focused on networking, so should you really have to worry about CPU utilization again?

The reality is that as network throughput increases, the CPU resources required to process the higher throughput also increase. As you consume more and more network resources, the ESXi host must devote more CPU resources to process all of the data. If you have virtual machines on the same ESXi host that are consuming high levels of CPU resources, there will be contention for CPU resources and performance can suffer. Virtual machines may not be able to achieve high levels of network throughput if either the ESXi host CPU cores or the virtual machine's vCPUs are heavily utilized.

Unfortunately, you can't simply allow vSphere DRS to load balance virtual machines that are consuming high levels of network resources. At this time, DRS does not take network utilization into consideration when making migration recommendations. That means it's up to you to properly monitor and manage the environment to make sure there are sufficient CPU resources available for virtual machines with high network throughput needs.

The most direct way to deal with this problem is to add additional ESXi hosts into the cluster. More hosts will allow DRS to distribute the load of virtual machines more evenly to help balance out CPU utilization. It will also allow you to add additional vCPUs to virtual machines with heavy networking demands. Adding hosts, of course, is often easier said than done because budgets are not endless. If you cannot add hosts, consider using DRS anti-affinity rules to separate high CPU or high network resource consumers from each other on different ESXi hosts. Leveraging Enhanced vMotion Compatibility, a vSphere cluster feature that allows dissimilar CPUs to remain compatible with vMotion, can help make it easier to add new hosts if necessary.

Staying on top of CPU resource usage in your environment can help to improve overall network utilization for virtual machines with high network throughput requirements. Using monitoring software such as VMware vCenter Operations Manager can also be an effective way of watching to make sure sufficient CPU resources are available.

Network I/O Control

Network utilization, like storage utilization, is not strictly limited to the amount of resources assigned. For example, if a virtual machine is provisioned with two vCPUs and 8 GB of RAM, it will never be able to consume more than two physical cores' worth of processing power and 8 GB of RAM, even though the host itself may have far more resources actually available. Even if the VM consumes all of its assigned CPU and memory resources, it may not affect any other virtual machines, depending on how many other VMs are deployed on the host. In other words, the VM can't consume any more than the two vCPUs and 8 GB of RAM that are assigned.

That same virtual machine, however, could consume enough network bandwidth to start impacting the performance of other virtual machines on the host. A single virtual machine is capable of consuming all network resources available on the host in certain scenarios. You assign a virtual network card to a virtual machine, not a specific amount of bandwidth. If that virtual machine can send enough data to saturate a physical NIC, then by default, there is nothing stopping that virtual machine from doing so. This is where Network I/O Control comes in.

As discussed earlier, NIOC can assign priority to network traffic and automatically limit the bandwidth consumed by virtual machines. It can also manage a share-based priority system to determine, in the case of network contention, which virtual machines or system services (like vMotion) get priority access to the physical NICs. NIOC can solve the problem of a single virtual machine saturating a network link and causing performance degradation for other virtual machines.

When using NIOC, it is best to use shares instead of limits for controlling network traffic. Just as with limits in other areas of vSphere, a limit is essentially a ceiling on the maximum amount of a resource that can be consumed. Limits can be limiting (no pun intended) because they will be imposed even if there are more resources available and can limit oversubscription, reducing some of the efficiency that virtualization can bring. For example, if you use NIOC to limit a particular function (say, virtual machine traffic) to 1 GbE, the virtual machines will not be able to consume more than 1 GbE even if there is more bandwidth available on the host that is not being utilized.

Shares more fairly distribute access to resources while still prioritizing which traffic types get access to them when network bandwidth increases. NIOC shares work just like shares used to control access to compute resources like CPU and memory. That is, they are assigned directly to the physical resource (in this case, the physical network cards) and are used to determine which resources get priority access to network bandwidth when a physical NIC becomes saturated. By default, there are share values of Low, Medium, and High, but custom share levels can also be defined (and can be useful when there are a large number of user-defined network resource pools).

NIOC is also capable of assigning 802.1p tags for quality of service (QoS) on network traffic. Using QoS allows you to prioritize network traffic and pass that information along to the rest of the network, enforcing the priority outside of the vSphere environment. This is another key feature that is often required for virtualizing business-critical applications.

Combining NIOC with the Load-Based Teaming load-balancing policy (discussed earlier) can help better utilize your available networking. LBT can help properly load balance network traffic across multiple physical NICs, preventing a single virtual machine from saturating a single uplink while additional uplinks are available and underutilized. NIOC will work in conjunction with LBT to prevent virtual machines (or other traffic types) from monopolizing the available network resources and enforce fairness among the different traffic types. Combining these two features is highly recommended and a great way to maximize network performance without allowing one traffic type to saturate all of the available bandwidth.

By default, there are several network resource pools that are created automatically when NIOC is enabled (described earlier). In addition, you can create user-defined network resource pools to control specific virtual machine network traffic. These user-defined network resource pools can then be assigned to port groups in your environment to allow for granular control over virtual machine network traffic. There is no right or wrong number of network resource pools or relative share levels to assign to them. However, when creating additional network resource pools and assigning share values, make sure to consider which virtual machines truly need priority access to network resources.

To enable NIOC, follow this simple procedure:

1. Launch the vSphere Web Client and connect to vCenter Server.

2. From the Home view, select Networking to access your dvSwitch(es). Find the correct dvSwitch and select it.

3. After selecting the appropriate dvSwitch, click the Manage tab. Then select Settings, and select Properties from the menu on the left.

4. On the Properties page, click the Edit button.

5. From the Network I/O Control drop-down menu, select Enable to enable NIOC.

6. Repeat this process for all appropriate dvSwitches in your environment where NIOC needs to be enabled.

As you can see, enabling NIOC is simple to do, and it can help provide predictable and solid network performance in your environment. In many cases the default values for NIOC are acceptable to control access to network resources. There are very few reasons, if any at all, not to enable NIOC.

Multi-NIC vMotion

You might not immediately think of vMotion when thinking about performance optimizations of ESXi hosts. After all, vMotion is primarily a management feature that allows you to migrate virtual machines between ESXi hosts without downtime. So why talk about it here?

The ability to perform vMotion migrations quickly and without impact to virtual machines is important for maintaining good performance in large vSphere environments. Traditionally, vMotion operations all occurred over a single 1 GbE or 10 GbE NIC, limiting the number of simultaneous migrations you could perform at once. Combine that with the growth of today's "monster VMs" that have more and more memory and you can start to see that vMotion operations might end up taking a long time. Consider a scenario where utilization has spiked on several virtual machines running on the same ESXi host and there is contention for CPU or memory resources. vSphere DRS can (and should) kick in and perform vMotion migrations to balance out the load. The longer a vMotion migration takes to complete, the longer it can take DRS to properly balance out workloads across ESXi hosts to improve performance. In that scenario, performance can be impacted until DRS can complete all necessary vMotion migrations. Now do you see why vMotion performance can directly impact virtual machine performance?

To accommodate today's larger workloads, VMware introduced Multi-NIC vMotion in vSphere 5. Multi-NIC vMotion allows you to bind more than one physical NIC to vMotion operations, allowing migrations to utilize more than one NIC at a time. Even when a single virtual machine is being migrated, vMotion can still leverage more than one NIC to significantly speed up the process.

Multi-NIC vMotion is also extremely helpful when administrators need to perform maintenance on a host. Evacuating all virtual machines from a host over a single vMotion interface can take a long time, especially if there are many virtual machines or virtual machines with large amounts of memory configured. Utilizing Multi-NIC vMotion, an administrator can more quickly evacuate an ESXi host and perform whatever maintenance needs to be done to get the host back online and operational.

Multi-NIC vMotion by itself won't help improve performance on your virtual machines or ESXi hosts. It can, however, provide the means for DRS to more quickly balance out workloads to restore optimal performance. If you have enough NICs available in your ESXi hosts, we strongly recommend using Multi-NIC vMotion.

NOTE   VMware has created an excellent Knowledge Base article that describes the steps required to enable Multi-NIC vMotion. The article also provides videos to show the step-by-step process required to enable Multi-NIC vMotion on a standard vSwitch as well as a vSphere Distributed Switch.

You can access the knowledge base at the following location: `http://kb.vmware.com/kb/2007467`.

DirectPath I/O and Single Root I/O Virtualization

It's possible to follow all the guidance and best practices for maximizing network performance in your virtual machines and still fall short. Some applications have very high bandwidth and/or very low latency requirements that cannot be met be using the virtual network cards provided by vSphere. That is where both DirectPath I/O and Single Root I/O Virtualization (SR-IOV) can help. Both technologies allow a virtual machine to directly access a piece of physical hardware (in this case a physical NIC), eliminating any emulation or paravirtualization of virtual hardware devices.

Both DirectPath I/O and SR-IOV can provide better performance by reducing CPU utilization in virtual machines that have high network throughput requirements. In particular, virtual machines that have very high packet rates can likely benefit the most from the reduction in CPU utilization. Additionally, since these technologies directly present the physical hardware to the virtual machine, the VM can take advantage of hardware features on the card that might not be available in a virtualized NIC.

While these technologies can provide performance improvements for virtual machines, they are not without their limitations. DirectPath I/O, for example, only supports presenting the physical hardware to a single virtual machine. SR-IOV allows that single physical device to be shared among multiple virtual machines on the same ESXi host, making it a somewhat more attractive option. The following list provides additional limitations and requirements of DirectPath I/O and SR-IOV:

◆ Both DirectPath I/O and SR-IOV require either Intel VT-d or AMD-Vi technologies in the processor. Older hardware may not support these technologies.

◆ Common virtualization features that administrators have relied upon in the vSphere platform are not supported when using both of these features. This includes vMotion, virtual machine snapshots, memory overcommitment, Fault Tolerance, High Availability, and Network I/O Control.

◆ In situations where CPU utilization is not high or very low latency networking is not required, the paravirtualized virtual network card VMXNET 3 can provide equal network performance with much less complexity than either DirectPath I/O or SR-IOV.

◆ DirectPath I/O requires a memory reservation equal in size to the virtual machine's configured memory to ensure that the ESXi host won't need to swap out memory to disk in the event of memory pressure.

Though DirectPath I/O and SR-IOV are not ideal for all virtual machines, there are certainly use cases where they can improve performance. Applications that require very low latency, such as those that rely heavily on synchronous replication technologies or near immediate response time, may be able to benefit from using these technologies.

Virtual Machine Performance

Once you've configured your ESXi hosts, virtual switches, and physical networking to achieve good performance, it's time to move on to the virtual machines themselves. There are several areas that you can focus on to help improve networking performance at the virtual machine level just like at the ESXi host level.

PARAVIRTUALIZED NIC DRIVERS

VMware includes several paravirtualized network card devices that can be used in your virtual machines. The original paravirtualized NIC was the VMXNET, available all the way back in the earliest versions of ESX Server. Since then, VMware has released the VMXNET 2 (sometimes referred to as Enhanced VMXNET) as well as the latest version, the VMXNET 3. Paravirtualized devices are virtualization aware and are designed to perform better than emulated devices (such as the E1000 device). Since these are virtualization-specific devices, which require their own specialized drivers, they cannot function unless you install VMware Tools in your virtual machine.

In general, if your operating system supports it, there is no reason not to use the VMXNET 3 device in all of your virtual machines. The VMXNET 3 device offers the best network performance of all of the virtual network cards and does so at a lower overall CPU cost. In addition, the VMXNET 3 device offers advanced features typically found only in physical NICs. Some of these features are listed here:

Jumbo Frames Provided jumbo frames are configured end to end in the networking path, virtual machines that use the VMXNET 3 device can utilize larger frames to increase performance. Configuring jumbo frames inside a virtual machine can be especially useful in situations where in-guest iSCSI is required. In the latest versions of vSphere, jumbo frames are also supported on the E1000, E1000e, and VMXNET2 devices.

Receive Side Scaling (RSS) RSS allows the VMXNET 3 device to spread the processing of network traffic across multiple virtual CPUs. When the load is spread out, efficiency is increased and performance can be improved. If RSS is disabled (or not supported) in a multiple-vCPU virtual machine, a single vCPU can act as a bottleneck for network performance. RSS is supported only in modern operating systems, such as Windows Server 2008 R2 and Linux 2.6.37 and higher.

SplitRX Mode   SplitRX mode is a feature in ESXi that uses multiple CPUs to process packets that are received in a single network queue. This mode can help improve performance for virtual machines on the same ESXi host that are all receiving multicast traffic. SplitRX mode is enabled automatically when using the VMXNET 3 device if it is detected that a single network queue on a physical NIC is being heavily utilized and it is processing data for more than eight virtual machines.

These features, such as RSS and jumbo frames, can help improve performance and should be considered in your environment. Certain performance features, such as TCP Segmentation Offload (TSO), are enabled by default. Others, like RSS, are disabled by default and have to be manually enabled in the properties of the virtual NIC.

The VMXNET 3 device is only supported in virtual machine version 7 (and later) and in modern operating systems. To use VMXNET 3, you need to be running one of the following operating systems:

◆ 32- and 64-bit versions of Microsoft Windows 7 and XP and Windows Server 2003, 2003 R2, 2008, 2008 R2, and 2012

◆ 32- and 64-bit versions of Red Hat Enterprise Linux 5.0 and later

◆ 32- and 64-bit versions of SuSE Linux Enterprise Server 10 and later

◆ 32- and 64-bit versions of Asianux 3 and later

◆ 32- and 64-bit versions of Debian 4

◆ 32- and 64-bit versions of Ubuntu 7.04 and later

◆ 32- and 64-bit versions of Sun Solaris 10 and later

VMXNET 3 PERFORMANCE STUDY

In 2009 VMware released a performance evaluation of the VMXNET 3 device. The study covers the features of the VMXNET 3 device and the performance it was able to achieve in a series of benchmark tests. Though the test itself is several years old, it's still useful to show the performance capabilities of the VMXNET 3 device.

You can access the performance evaluation at www.vmware.com/resources/techresources/10065.

CO-LOCATING NETWORK DEPENDENT VIRTUAL MACHINES

When virtual machines communicate with other devices (be they physical servers or other virtual machines), they transmit network traffic just like a physical server. The traffic leaves the virtual machine and goes up through the ESXi networking stack and out to the physical network infrastructure. The traffic flow of a virtual machine communicating with another virtual machine on a separate ESXi host is illustrated in Figure 6.2; it would be similar for a virtual machine communicating with another physical server or other device on the network.

FIGURE 6.2
Traffic flow between
two virtual
machines on two
separate ESXi hosts

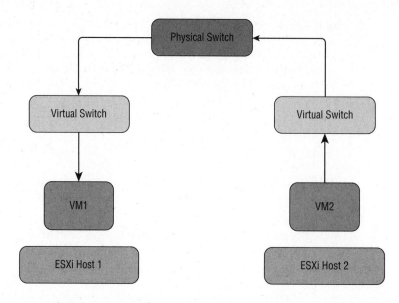

The exception to this rule is when virtual machines on the same ESXi host and connected to the same vSwitch (and on the same VLAN) communicate with each other. In that case, traffic never actually leaves the ESXi host and can be transmitted as fast as the ESXi host's resources allow. The traffic flow of two virtual machines on the same vSwitch communicating with each other is illustrated in Figure 6.3.

FIGURE 6.3
Traffic flow between
two virtual
machines on the
same ESXi host

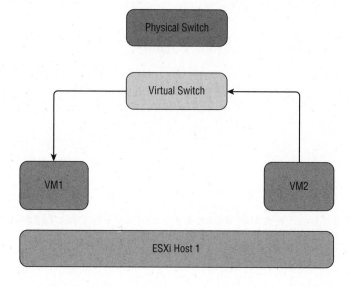

By eliminating the requirement to send network packets out to the physical switching infrastructure, you can improve performance and reduce network latency. Network traffic between virtual machines on the same host is also often as fast as or even faster than the available physical switching infrastructure because it is limited only by the resources on the host.

So how can you take advantage of this? The first step is to understand your workloads and their requirements. For example, do you have a web server that needs to be in constant communication with a database backend? Keeping those two servers on the same ESXi host can help improve response time on the web server and improve the experience for end users. To prevent DRS from migrating the virtual machines onto separate ESXi hosts, you can utilize DRS affinity rules. Affinity rules allow you to create groups of virtual machines that should always run together on the same ESXi host. Creating "keep virtual machines together" rules in DRS will force those virtual machines to always live on the same ESXi host and will help to keep network performance high.

You might say, "Well what if the host fails? Won't both virtual machines be affected in that scenario?" That's absolutely true, and again it comes down to truly knowing your workloads. If there is truly a dependency between the two (or more) virtual machines such that one cannot operate without the other(s), then it doesn't matter whether one goes down or they all go down at the same time, it will result in an outage for the application and end user. Technologies such as load balancing and database replication can allow you to keep multiple copies of each application tier together on separate ESXi hosts for increased redundancy. Work with the vendor of the software you're using to determine if it can support or leverage these kinds of technologies to maintain redundancy.

By understanding your workloads before bringing them into your vSphere environment, you can better control how they behave and ultimately provide them with better performance. Don't try to virtualize these applications in a vacuum; instead, work with application owners, database administrators, and others to find out all of the requirements for the application so you can better plan and design to achieve the best possible performance.

Latency Sensitivity

Certain applications are very intolerant of even the smallest amount of latency. By default, ESXi's configuration settings are tuned to provide solid performance for almost all applications and so adjusting advanced settings is often not required. For latency-sensitive applications, however, some advanced tuning may be necessary.

VMware has introduced a new setting, configurable in the options of the virtual machine, called Latency Sensitivity. When you enable this setting for your virtual machine, ESXi automatically makes adjustments to the virtual machine's CPU priority as well as interrupts coalescing, helping to improve performance of the CPU and the network.

WARNING As with any advanced setting, the Latency Sensitivity setting should not be applied to your virtual machines without proper testing. Always test this setting in a lab or development environment before making this change to a production virtual machine. Also, do not simply apply this setting to all virtual machines in the (incorrect) hope that it will improve performance across the board. You will likely end up hurting performance more than helping it.

Remember, ESXi's default configuration settings are adequate for nearly all workloads. Use this setting only if your application is truly latency sensitive.

To enable Latency Sensitivity, follow this procedure:

1. Launch the vSphere Web Client and connect to vCenter Server. Note that this setting is available only in the vSphere Web Client and not in the older vSphere Client.

2. From the Home view, select either the Hosts And Clusters view or the VMs And Templates view.

3. Find the virtual machine you wish to modify, right-click on it, and select Edit Settings.

4. Select the VM Options tab, and expand the advanced settings.

5. Select the drop-down box next to Latency Sensitivity, as shown in Figure 6.4, and select the appropriate option based on your application's latency requirements.

FIGURE 6.4
Change the Latency Sensitivity option in the vSphere Web Client

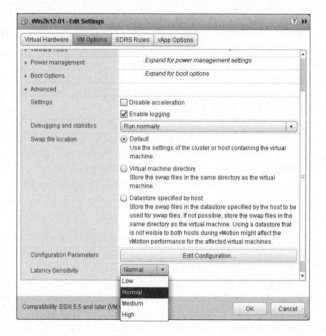

Once this setting has been changed, ESXi will take steps to improve performance for latency sensitive applications. This change can be made on the fly without shutting down the virtual machine.

NOTE If your application requires very low latency operations, there may be other settings or configurations you can try. For more information, VMware created a document called *Best Practices for Performance Tuning of Latency-Sensitive Workloads in vSphere VMs*.

You can access this study at www.vmware.com/resources/techresources/10220.

1. Poirot, series 9
39065126860228   Due: 10/7/2015, 23:59

2. How to catch a Russian spy : the true story of an
American civilian turned double agent
39065145860225   Due: 10/21/2015, 23:59

3. VMware private cloud computing with vCloud
Director
39065132003169   Due: 10/21/2015, 23:59

4. VMware vSphere performance : designing CPU,
memory, storage, and networking for performance-
intensive workloads
39065141493682   Due: 10/21/2015, 23:59

Total 4 item(s).

To check your card and renew items
go to www.calgarylibrary.ca
or call 262-2928

Troubleshooting Networking Issues

Problems with networking are not often at the top of the list of vSphere-related issues when it comes to performance. In many cases you'll explore storage, memory, or CPU before looking at networking these days as 10 GbE networking becomes more common and the network becomes less of a bottleneck. With that said, that doesn't mean you'll never run into a performance problem that is related to networking. Today many applications rely on replication schemes that generate constant network activity, and keeping the applications in sync is crucial for performance and uptime. In the following sections, we'll explore some steps you can take to troubleshoot issues related to networking performance.

Slow Virtual Machine Networking Performance

If the network performance of a virtual machine has slowed down, there could be many reasons that are not directly related to the network. For example, the virtual machine could be trying to read or write data to IP-based storage that is overloaded and not able to service requests fast enough. In that case, the problem is not likely to be caused by the network; rather, the network is more of a victim. A key to properly troubleshooting networking performance problems is to have a good understanding of the workload profile of the virtual machine, how the application(s) work, and what other systems are involved.

Virtual Machine to Physical NIC Mapping

If you're dealing with a virtual machine that is experiencing a networking performance problem, one of the easiest things to check is to see if there is contention for physical resources. In other words, you should check to see if the poorly performing virtual machine is using the same physical NIC as other virtual machines that are also heavy consumers of network resources. Whether the jump in network utilization is brief, such as during a backup window, or sustained can determine whether or not you try to take action.

To quickly determine which physical NIC your virtual machines are using, use the following procedure:

1. Determine which ESXi host is running the virtual machine(s) that are experiencing performance problems.

2. Connect to the appropriate ESXi host and launch either `esxtop` or `resxtop` (depending on which is appropriate in your environment).

3. Type **n** to access the networking view.

4. The USED-BY column lists the names of the virtual machines on the host, and the TEAM-PNIC column indicates which physical NIC the virtual machine is using (as shown in Figure 6.5).

As you can see in Figure 6.5, the virtual machines NJMGMT01 and W12-CN1 are both using vmnic2 and are both trying to utilize the network. In this example, W12-CN1 is sending and receiving a large number of packets, leaving little available bandwidth for NJMGMT01. Look at the columns labeled PKTRX/s, or packets received per second, and MbRX/s, or megabits received per second. In this example, the MbRX/s column shows that W12-CN1 on vmnic2 is utilizing over 900 Mb/s, almost saturating an entire 1 GbE network uplink. This may be a good indication that W12-CN1 is impacting the networking performance of NJMGMT01, and possibly other virtual machines on the host.

FIGURE 6.5
Using esxtop to view the mapping of virtual machines to physical NICs

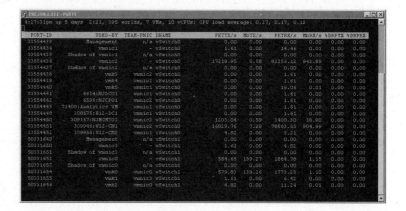

USE TECHNOLOGIES IN vSPHERE TO HELP PREVENT THESE SCENARIOS

The scenario illustrated in Figure 6.5 is a good example of where two previously discussed technologies—the Load-Based Teaming load-balancing policy in the vSphere Distributed Switch and Network I/O Control—could help automatically resolve this issue. The LBT policy would have automatically migrated either W12-CN1 or NJMGMT01 to a different vmnic to balance out the networking utilization.

Similarly, Network I/O Control would apply fairness in access to network resources and not let a single virtual machine monopolize a physical NIC. Since Network I/O Control can be configured with user-defined resource pools, you could also configure it so that certain VMs get priority over others during periods of network contention. That can be important if you have business-critical workloads sharing the same ESXi hosts with less critical workloads. In those circumstances, you'll frequently want to let the business-critical workload have priority access to the network over other, less critical virtual machines.

HEAVILY UTILIZED PHYSICAL NICS

When it comes to poor networking performance on virtual machines, it is not always two virtual machines competing for resources that create the problem. In some cases, there is simply too much network traffic on the physical NICs to accommodate all of the required network traffic for virtual machines.

Figure 6.6 highlights a scenario in which there are only two physical NICs attached to a vSwitch (vSwitch0) that is being shared with both virtual machines and management traffic. In this case, there is simply too much network traffic being transmitted over vmnic0 and vmnic1 (looking at the MbTX/s and PKTRX/s columns), leaving very little available bandwidth for virtual machines. Unfortunately, in this configuration Load-Based Teaming won't help because both physical NICs are saturated, so there is no easy way to balance out the load.

FIGURE 6.6

Using esxtop to show an example of both physical NICs in a vSwitch being heavily utilized, leaving very little available bandwidth for virtual machines

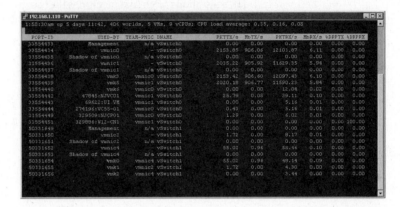

If you find that this is happening to you, these are some suggestions you can follow to try to eliminate the issue:

◆ Utilize Network I/O Control to enforce fairness in access to the network resources. Implement user-defined resource pools to prioritize traffic based on the type of workloads running in your environment.

◆ Make sure to separate virtual machine traffic from other traffic like vMotion, Fault Tolerance, or IP-based storage; put the other traffic on separate physical NICs. Operations like vMotion, especially Multi-NIC vMotion, can consume a large amount of network bandwidth.

◆ Add additional ESXi hosts into the cluster. Having more hosts in the cluster provides more opportunities to separate "noisy neighbor" virtual machines from each other and run them on separate physical hosts.

◆ Add additional physical network cards to your ESXi host(s). If you've exhausted other options, adding additional NICs may be the only way to provide enough network bandwidth.

CHECK FOR HIGH CPU UTILIZATION

Heavy network utilization can cause demand for CPU resources to manage all of the traffic. This is especially true with 10 Gigabit Ethernet, where high network utilization can cause a large demand for CPU resources. When you're dealing with virtual machines that are experiencing network slowness, it's possible that high CPU utilization is at least partly to blame.

If you're dealing with a situation where network performance is slow and you determine that ESXi host CPU utilization is high, you can try the following tasks to help resolve the issue:

◆ Perform vMotion migrations of virtual machines that are heavily consuming CPU resources to other, less utilized hosts. Reducing the CPU utilization on the ESXi host will free up CPU resources to manage the network traffic.

◆ Use DRS anti-affinity rules to keep virtual machines that are heavy consumers of CPU and/or network resources separated from each other on different ESXi hosts.

◆ Add additional vCPUs to the virtual machine to handle the increased network traffic. This is useful only if there are spare CPU resources available on the ESXi host itself. Adding additional vCPUs when the host does not have spare vCPU resources to provide can end up actually hurting performance.

◆ If there are no other ESXi hosts where the virtual machines can be migrated, it may be time to look into adding additional hosts into your environment. Adding hosts will allow you to better balance out the virtual machine load.

CHECK FOR IMPROPERLY CONFIGURED PHYSICAL NETWORKING

Stop us if you've heard this one: An end user reports that it takes a long time to copy files to/ from their virtual machine. The virtualization team wants to blame it on the network. The storage team wants to blame it on the network. Everyone wants to blame it on the network. And the networking team? They are convinced it's not their problem.

As networking and storage become more deeply entrenched in the virtual infrastructure (or "software defined" as is the common term today), teams will have to work more closely together to resolve these kinds of problems. And while networking teams may want to immediately push back and say, "Oh, that's the vSphere environment, so we don't have any control over that," the reality is that it is entirely possible for small misconfigurations on the physical network to have a large impact on the virtual infrastructure.

Duplex mismatch is a common cause for these kinds of problems that, despite all the advances that have been made in networking, can still occur today. Duplex mismatch is a situation where the physical switch ports are configured with a specific speed and duplex (1000 megabits and half-duplex, for example) and the physical NICs on the server are configured with a different speed and duplex (such as 1000 megabits and full-duplex). This mismatch in configuration can result in a drop in overall network performance. Similarly, if the physical switch ports are configured for autonegotiation, where the switch port senses the speed depending on what device is plugged in, and the physical NICs are configured with a specific speed and duplex setting, a similar drop in performance can occur. This mismatch in configuration can lead to a large drop in overall network performance and have a very noticeable impact in your vSphere environment.

"IT'S ALWAYS DUPLEX MISMATCH"

Author Matt Liebowitz recounts: I remember working with a customer a few years ago who was dealing with an issue of slow file copies between a virtual machine and a physical storage device. It was taking them a very long time to copy files from a virtual machine over to a network attached storage (NAS) appliance. Because this NAS was used frequently for backups and other important data, the problem quickly became an important issue that needed to be addressed.

With everyone pointing fingers, someone threw out the idea to check for duplex mismatch. My immediate reaction was, "It's never duplex mismatch. Duplex mismatch is the cause of the problem about as frequently as 'update the firmware' is the solution to other hardware-related problems." I laughed at that moment, but I wasn't laughing when the networking team determined it was in fact duplex mismatch about 10 minutes later. Once the mismatch was resolved, file transfer speeds returned to expected levels.

Throughout my career I've seen duplex mismatch so frequently that I've completely changed my standard answer from "It's never duplex mismatch" to "It's always duplex mismatch" and that's one of the first things I check. Oh, and I admit that "update the firmware" does resolve problems sometimes too.

You should check with your switch vendor to determine the proper setting for your particular configuration. In many cases using autoconfiguration is sufficient (and required) to achieve the best performance. In other cases specifying the speed and duplex are required.

Work with your networking team to verify the setting on the physical switches. To check or change the duplex settings on your ESXi hosts, use the following procedure:

1. Launch the vSphere Web Client and connect to vCenter Server.

2. From the Home view, select the Hosts And Clusters view and then select the ESXi host in question.

3. Select the Manage option, and choose the Networking tab.

4. Select Physical Adapters from the menu on the left-hand side of the screen. This screen will show you the duplex setting (referred to as Configuration Speed) of your vmnics.

5. If you need to change the setting, select the vmnic you wish to modify and select Edit Adapter Settings (the icon that looks like a pencil).

6. In the box labeled Configured Speed, Duplex, select the appropriate configuration value (as shown in Figure 6.7) and then click OK to make the change.

FIGURE 6.7
Change the duplex
settings on a
physical NIC on an
ESXi host

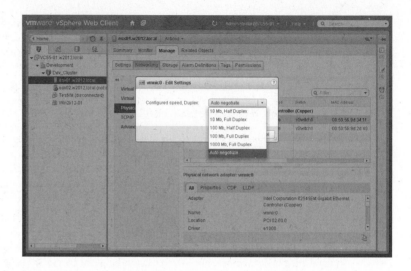

7. Repeat steps 1 through 6 for all physical NICs on which you need to make the change.

If you suspect that duplex settings might be configured correctly for some hosts (or even for some NICs within the same host) but not others, you can run a very simple test to determine if that is the case. Simply run a tool like IOmeter or Iperf to generate network utilization, and while that test is running, perform a vMotion migration of that virtual machine to a different host. If you notice a significant change in performance, either faster or slower, then there is likely a problem with either that particular host or the physical switch(es) that it is connected to. Since vMotion migrations can be done live without any downtime, they are a great way to quickly determine if some ESXi hosts perform better than others. If you find one (or more) hosts where network performance is significantly reduced, don't be afraid to look for duplex mismatch.

WARNING Don't assume that there is no possibility of duplex mismatch just because users of other virtual machines aren't reporting slowness. Virtual machines that aren't heavy consumers of network resources can live happily with mismatched duplex settings without ever really exhibiting symptoms. Only when you encounter a virtual machine with high network resource requirements does the problem become visible. Remember, despite how far networking equipment has come, the problem can still be duplex mismatch!

IMPROPERLY CONFIGURED TRAFFIC SHAPING

Just as with limits on CPU and memory (described in earlier chapters), vSphere provides you with the ability to limit network bandwidth using a feature called traffic shaping. Traffic shaping controls the average bandwidth, peak bandwidth, and burst size for a given virtual switch or port group. All virtual machines attached to that port group or virtual switch will share the available bandwidth and not be able to exceed the values you configure.

As with other limits that can be configured in vSphere, while they sound good on paper, if they are misconfigured they can cause serious performance problems. Let's say an administrator doesn't carefully read the screen when configuring traffic shaping and mistakenly enters a value in megabits per second instead of the expected kilobits per second. For example, an administrator might want to limit bandwidth to 500 megabits, or half of their 1 GbE network, for a particular set of virtual machines on a port group. If the administrator enters in a value of 500, they'll actually be entering 500 kilobits per second and not megabits per second. Doing that would likely result in a configuration that is far slower than expected. Instead, the administrator would need to enter in 512,000 kilobits per second to achieve the desired goal. As you can see, it's very simple to make a mistake when configuring traffic shaping parameters.

To check the traffic shaping configuration on your virtual switch, use the following procedure. Note that this procedure assumes you are using a vSphere Distributed Switch:

1. Launch the vSphere Web Client and connect to vCenter Server.

2. From the Home view, select the Networking view to bring up the distributed switches in your environment.

3. Right-click on the distributed port group in question and select Edit Settings.

4. Select Traffic Shaping from the menu on the left-hand side to bring up the traffic shaping settings, as shown in Figure 6.8.

FIGURE 6.8
Changing the traffic shaping settings on a dvPort of a vSphere Distributed Switch

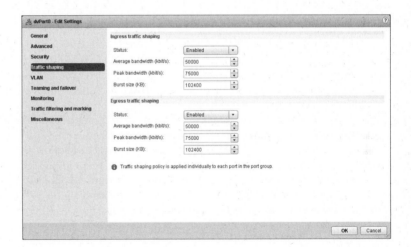

NOTE Traffic shaping is yet another reason to use the vSphere Distributed Switch instead of the standard vSwitch. The dvSwitch offers the ability to configure traffic shaping at either the ingress or egress (inbound or outbound) level; that is, when network traffic is entering the virtual switch as well as when it's leaving the virtual switch.

The standard vSwitch only offers the ability to configure egress traffic, or outbound traffic. Figure 6.9 shows the traffic shaping settings for a standard vSwitch.

FIGURE 6.9
Changing the traffic
shaping settings on
a standard vSwitch

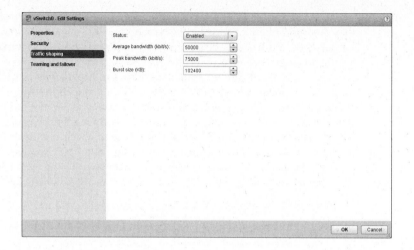

Though traffic shaping can help you granularly control the amount of network traffic you allow in or out of a specific vSwitch or port group, configuring limits can introduce risk into the environment. Instead, it often makes sense to leverage Network I/O Control instead of traffic shaping to provide a more granular level of control over access to network resources.

DROPPED NETWORK PACKETS

Last, but certainly not least, is checking your ESXi host(s) for dropped network packets. Dropped packets are network packets that failed to reach their destination (for a variety of reasons), be it from the virtual machine to another system or vice versa. If you are experiencing dropped packets, it is likely that your virtual machine is suffering network performance problems (or worse).

Packets from a virtual machine have to pass through several different systems before arriving at their destination. Each of these systems, whether they are physical switches, NICs, or the device driver in the guest OS itself, has its own queue to allow it to buffer packets prior to passing them along. If there is very high networking demand, these queues can fill up and not allow any additional traffic to pass through. When queues fill up, packets are dropped.

The virtual switches and virtual NICs inside ESXi are no different than their physical counterparts. Each has its own queues and when those queues fill up, they are forced to drop the packets. Packet loss over an extended period can lead to serious performance problems, or if the applications heavily depend on the network (such as those that use data replication schemes), the application itself can fail.

There are two kinds of dropped packets: dropped transmit packets and dropped receive packets. In either case the end result, from the virtual machine's perspective, is failed network communication. Dropped receive packets can be caused by high CPU utilization in the virtual machine (or CPU resources being exhausted on the ESXi host). If the CPU on the virtual machine is fully consumed but there are additional CPU resources available on the ESXi host, adding more virtual CPUs to the VM can often help resolve dropped packets (since high CPU is often caused by high network utilization). Improper configuration of the virtual NIC could also lead to dropped receive packets, so make sure you fully understand what you're doing if you modify advanced virtual NIC settings. Similarly, tuning those advanced settings (such as enabling features like Receive Side Scaling) can help reduce packet loss.

With dropped transmit packets, there are other solutions that you can try to alleviate the problem. In this scenario, the queues on the virtual switch could be filling up and causing the dropped packets. If that is the case, adding additional physical NICs to the virtual switch could help add additional network capacity. If possible, move virtual machines to a different virtual switch (which will have its own set of network queues) to help alleviate the problem, though that is not always feasible depending on your configuration. If the vSwitch itself is not the problem, you should move up the stack and investigate if the queues on the physical switches are filling up and causing the dropped packets and then add or upgrade hardware to resolve the issue. Once outside the vSphere environment, you may need to work with your networking team to troubleshoot the issue.

You can view the number of dropped transmit or receive packets at either the individual virtual machine level or at the ESXi host level. Looking in both places can be useful to determine if the problem is limited to a single virtual machine, as may be the case with a virtual machine that has a heavily constrained CPU or incorrectly configured virtual NIC, or if it's a more widespread problem affecting multiple virtual machines.

To check for packet loss on either the ESXi host or an individual virtual machine, use the following procedure:

1. Launch the vSphere Web Client and connect to vCenter Server.

2. From the Home view, select the either the Hosts And Clusters view or the VMs And Templates view, depending on whether you want to view packet loss on an ESXi host or individual virtual machine.

3. Select the ESXi host or virtual machine from the list.

4. Select the Monitor tab, and then click the Performance tab to bring up performance metrics for the selected object.

5. Select Advanced to view advanced performance metrics.

6. In the View drop-down box, change the view to Network.

7. Select the Chart Options link at the top of the screen. Packet loss counters are not displayed by default so they must be added to the current view.

8. Select the check box next to the counters Receive packets dropped and Transmit packets dropped, as shown in Figure 6.10, and click Ok to display the new graph.

FIGURE 6.10
Adding Receive
packets dropped
and Transmit pack-
ets dropped to the
vSphere Web Client
performance view

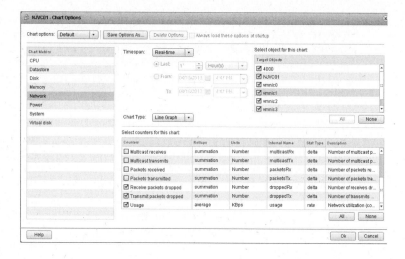

Once you've added the counters to the graph, you can view if your virtual machines are experiencing any dropped packets and, if so, how many. In Figure 6.11, we can see that the virtual machine NJVC01 is experiencing dropped receive packets and should be investigated to see if there is high CPU utilization in the guest or a misconfiguration in the virtual NIC driver or elsewhere in the virtual networking configuration.

FIGURE 6.11
Viewing packet
loss on a virtual
machine in the
vSphere Web Client

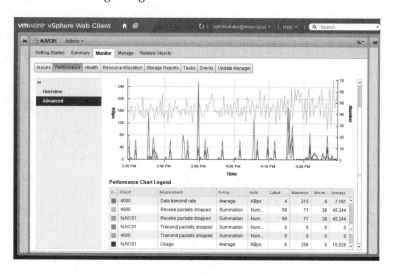

Just as with duplex mismatch situations, you will likely need to involve the networking team at your organization to properly analyze these situations. Dropped network packets could be a result of problems at the physical networking layer, so don't be afraid to involve the proper teams to get to the bottom of the situation quickly.

Summary

As resources in your virtual infrastructure go, networking and network bandwidth are not typically going to be the limiting factors in determining performance. That doesn't mean, however, that networking can be disregarded and not properly designed. If you don't plan for and design a proper network infrastructure for your vSphere environment, you're likely to suffer the consequences.

Your physical network is just as important as your virtual network. Make sure you have sufficient bandwidth to meet the requirements of your vSphere environment. That includes having enough physical network cards to provide network isolation for specific functions as well as redundancy. The switching infrastructure used to support the vSphere environment should also have redundancy, eliminating any single points of failure. Additionally, utilizing features like TCP checksum offload, large receive offload, and jumbo frames can help improve network performance for your ESXi hosts.

When designing networking at the vSphere level, the type of vSwitch you choose can impact performance. The vSphere Distributed Switch offers many key features, such as Network I/O Control and Load-Based Teaming as well as simplified management, that make it the ideal switch choice if your environment has the proper vSphere license.

Choosing the right hardware for your ESXi hosts also has a large impact on network performance. Blade servers, for example, typically have fewer expansion ports available, which can present design challenges for environments that need to support multiple networks or functions (such as Fault Tolerance, vMotion, and IP-based storage). Rack mount servers frequently have more expansion ports available and can be a better choice if many physical network cards are required. As with many things in IT, there is no right or wrong answer and it comes down to your organization's requirements.

Utilizing advanced networking features in vSphere can help in delivering solid network performance. The dvSwitch load-balancing policy Load-Based Teaming can help properly balance out network traffic across multiple physical NICs, preventing a single physical NIC from becoming saturated while other NICs in the dvSwitch are not. Load-Based Teaming with Network I/O Control together make a potent team for helping to deliver good performance while enforcing fairness in access to network resources. It is recommended to use these two features together where possible. Multi-NIC vMotion is another feature that can help aid in performance by increasing the speed with which vMotion operations occur. Faster vMotion operations mean quicker balancing of resources across ESXi hosts, helping to ease performance bottlenecks.

Virtual machines should also be configured with network performance in mind. Unless it is not supported by your guest OS, using the paravirtualized VMXNET 3 network card in all of your virtual machines can help improve network performance and reduce CPU utilization. The VMXNET 3 network card also supports advanced networking features like jumbo frames and receive side scaling to further improve performance. Additionally, it is crucial to know your workloads because running virtual machines that frequently communicate over the network onto the same ESXi host can improve overall network performance. If those virtual machines are on the same VLAN, co-locating them on the same ESXi host means network traffic does not have to traverse the physical LAN.

Finally, it's not all happy times in network-land because sometimes networking performance problems occur within vSphere environments. Virtual machines that heavily utilize the network can end up running on the same physical NIC as other virtual machines that also heavily utilize the network, forcing them to compete for resources. Technologies like NIOC and LBT can help to eliminate that problem. High CPU utilization can also slow down network performance, as CPU resources are required to process networking (especially with 10 GbE networks). Improperly configured features like traffic shaping, or configured limits in NIO C, can also have a dramatic impact on virtual machine performance.

By building your vSphere environment with an eye toward network performance, you can help eliminate common bottlenecks and improve performance. A well-tuned and properly performing network infrastructure will help make your vSphere environment run much better. And don't forget—sometimes the problem is still duplex mismatch!

Chapter 7

Storage

A funny thing happened on the way to the virtualized data center. When enterprise virtualization using VMware ESX 1.x and 2.x first emerged, the vast majority of virtualized workloads were limited by the amount of physical CPUs or RAM in the ESX host and largely ran on local storage in the host. Later on, processor vendors Intel and AMD released multi-core CPUs that provided significantly more processing capacity in a smaller form factor. Around the same time, the price of RAM started dropping dramatically, allowing companies to purchase servers with more RAM than ever before. Once servers had plenty of RAM and CPU to satisfy the performance demands of virtualized workloads, the storage layer became much more important. With more and more virtual machines being deployed and organizations looking to take advantage of advanced vSphere features that require shared storage, properly sizing and designing storage became critical to a well-functioning vSphere environment.

What has caused this change? In a lot of ways, storage has become a victim of the success of virtualization in general. Organizations that had success with virtualizing test and development workloads then looked toward virtualizing production. That success led application owners and IT leaders to virtualize business-critical applications, which often have higher workload demands. Along the way other technologies like Virtual Desktop Infrastructure (VDI) have become more popular, placing an increasing burden on the backend storage to deliver good performance. With all of these workloads virtualized, storage performance in a vSphere environment has never been more important.

In this chapter we look at:

◆ Choosing your storage platform

◆ Designing physical storage

◆ Designing vSphere storage

◆ Designing for performance

◆ Troubleshooting storage performance issues

Choosing Your Storage Platform

Choosing a storage platform is an important factor when considering overall performance for your vSphere environment. The platform you choose will likely dictate not only the protocol you use but also the features that are provided by the storage. Unfortunately, most of the time you cannot simply pick the fastest performing storage without factoring in other considerations like protocol, connectivity, existing infrastructure, or costs (just to name a few).

STORAGE HAS NEVER BEEN MORE IMPORTANT

Over the years we've worked with numerous customers to troubleshoot performance problems in vSphere environments. Over the last several years we've found that storage has been the limiting factor when diagnosing and troubleshooting virtual machine performance problems in almost all circumstances.

Of the four major resources in a virtual infrastructure (CPU, memory, storage, and network), storage is often the most important in delivering solid performance to virtual machines. In fact, that's why you'll see that this chapter is larger than any other in the book.

In the following sections we'll cover the main types of storage that are supported by vSphere. In doing so, we will remain vendor agnostic; that is, specific vendor solutions will not be covered here. Today there are simply too many different storage vendors with competing products and feature sets. It would be nearly impossible to try to cover the features available in all of them. Instead, we will simply cover the most common types of storage used in vSphere and why you may consider choosing each one. As with many things, the specific requirements of your organization determine which solution is best for your environment.

STORAGE IS A HOTLY DEBATED SUBJECT

The type of storage used for vSphere is a hotly debated topic, and the debate can often turn into an argument rivaling those about religion. Folks may feel strongly about one storage vendor, protocol, or topology and believe that it is the best choice for all scenarios.

In reality, there is no right or wrong choice when it comes to storage. Each organization has different requirements that drive the decision of which type of storage to use. Don't get caught up in the debate about what or who is best. Simply choose what is best for your organization based on your requirements.

Storage Area Networks

A storage area network, or SAN, is a dedicated network that provides access to block-level storage devices. Often when people refer to a SAN, they typically mean the storage array, but that is technically incorrect. The SAN is the network that allows connectivity to the storage array (and other block-level devices like tape libraries). To keep things simple, however, we'll use the term SAN to mean storage array throughout this chapter.

The SAN itself is similar to a regular network in that it connects devices so they can talk to one another. When using a SAN, servers connect via either fibre channel (FC) or an Ethernet switching infrastructure to storage devices, making them appear to the operating system (OS) to be local devices.

SANs provide a central point on which to manage the storage in your environment. When using a SAN, local storage (or hard drives installed in physical servers) becomes less important and is often only used to install the operating system itself while the storage array is used to store applications and data. You can also boot your servers from the SAN so that you don't require any physical hard drives in the servers, thus making it quicker and easier to replace a faulty server.

TIP Booting from a SAN takes an additional toll on the array because booting a server can generate a lot of I/O. Some storage arrays also have limitations on the number of volumes that can be created or connections they can manage, so having a large number of servers that boot from SAN is not always ideal.

Aside from easier management, SANs also often provide greater performance than local storage in a server. SANs are much larger and can support larger numbers of disks as well as advanced features like auto-tiering systems and caching mechanisms that can greatly improve performance. And, most relevant to vSphere, using some form of shared storage is required in order to access most of the enterprise features of the platform, including vMotion, Distributed Resource Scheduler (DRS), and High Availability (HA).

THE CHANGING FACE OF LOCAL STORAGE

A newer model of presenting storage to virtual (and physical) environments is starting to become popular. Instead of leveraging SANs for shared storage, local storage inside each host server is bundled together and managed as a single entity, providing functionality similar to that of a SAN with only stand-alone servers. Software manages the features and functionality available in the storage, making it what is known commonly as software-defined storage. The combining of compute, storage, and networking into a single unit is often referred to as hyperconvergence.

VMware supports this model by introducing VMware Virtual SAN, or VSAN, which will be covered later in this chapter. There are also numerous third-party vendors offering similar solutions that leverage local storage instead of SANs.

Remember, there is no right or wrong solution when it comes to presenting storage to your virtual infrastructure. Understand your organization's requirements and choose the best solution to meet your needs.

SANs are accessed over protocols created specifically for storage traffic. The choice in protocol can be driven by the storage vendor, your existing infrastructure, or performance requirements.

FIBRE CHANNEL

Fibre channel (FC) is a fast, low-latency and lossless network technology used for storage. It uses Fibre Channel Protocol (FCP) as its transport protocol, which allows it to encapsulate SCSI commands over the FC network and allows the hosts to communicate to the storage.

Dedicated switching infrastructure is required to connect the server to a fibre channel SAN. The specialized cables and infrastructure allow FC to operate at fast speeds, ranging from 2 gigabit up to 16 gigabit and beyond. Each ESXi host also requires host bus adapters (HBAs) to connect to FC switches, which consumes PCI slots in your server. Though that may not be a problem for larger rack-mount servers, blade servers may be limited in the number of slots available for HBAs and additional network cards.

FC has been around the longest and is likely to be very common in existing environments. It offers very low latency and high throughput connectivity to the backend storage, making it ideal for business-critical applications that require top performance.

FIBRE CHANNEL OVER ETHERNET PROTOCOL

Fibre Channel over Ethernet, or FCoE, is a newer storage networking protocol that can be used to establish connectivity to SANs. FCoE uses standard Ethernet networks to connect to back-end storage. By using standard Ethernet networks, FCoE can be easier to deploy since it does not require utilizing as many FC switches as a full FC implementation. Another benefit is that although FCoE runs over the Ethernet network, it does not leverage TCP/IP. This reduces the overall latency of FCoE and makes it comparable to standard FC.

Despite the fact that the traffic uses standard Ethernet networks and switches, FCoE can be managed with the same tools used to manage FC deployments. This can help simplify storage administration by presenting a common set of administration tools for both FC and FCoE deployments.

FCoE offers a lot of the same benefits as FC, including low-latency connectivity, but in a simplified manner by using existing Ethernet networks. For organizations that leverage 10 GbE Ethernet networks, FCoE can be a good complement to existing FC deployments.

iSCSI

The third block storage protocol available in vSphere is Internet Small Computer System Interface, or iSCSI. Like FCoE, iSCSI communicates over standard Ethernet networks and does not require dedicated HBAs (though iSCSI HBAs are available and can provide additional capabilities like booting from SAN or offloading processing to dedicated hardware). When iSCSI was first introduced, it was mainly used in small/medium businesses due to its lower cost and its ability to leverage existing network infrastructure. Today, however, many top-end storage companies offer SANs that can use iSCSI connectivity, and iSCSI has a foothold in enterprise datacenters.

Network File System

Storage for ESXi hosts is not limited to just block-level storage. ESXi also supports connecting to Network File System (NFS) shares to store virtual machines (and other files like ISO images). These shares are presented over the standard Ethernet network (similar to iSCSI) and do not require any specialized hardware HBAs in ESXi hosts. NFS storage can be presented from a variety of sources, from enterprise-class storage arrays all the way down to stand-alone servers.

NFS Isn't Just for Files

NFS support has been available in ESXi for many years and through numerous product versions (back to the days when only the full ESX hypervisor was available). Many administrators have considered it a "second-class citizen" of sorts in that they would not use it for any production virtual machines.

Raise your hand if you've said something similar to this in the past: "I'll use NFS shares for ISO files and templates, but I only use FC or iSCSI for virtual machines." If you're raising your hand, don't be ashamed because you're in good company (though you might look a little weird raising your hand while reading a book). That mentality persists even today, despite the fact that NFS is supported by major storage vendors and offers performance comparable to the performance of other Ethernet-based storage, like iSCSI.

Don't be afraid to use NFS for more than just ISO files. Not only does NFS offer solid performance, it is adored by many vSphere administrators because of how simple it is to configure and manage.

Even though NFS is a file-level protocol (and not a block-level protocol like FC or iSCSI), the virtual machine still sees block-level storage. From the perspective of the virtual machine, the storage presented is SCSI and it will have one or more virtual SCSI controllers to access the virtual machine disk files (unless you present virtual IDE or virtual SATA storage in vSphere 5.5 or higher).

Verify Application Support before Using NFS

Despite the fact that, from the virtual machine's perspective, the storage presented to it is block-level storage, not all applications will support this configuration. Microsoft Exchange Server in particular has never supported NFS for storing mailbox databases or transport queues, and that is true in virtual environments as well.

Microsoft has an explicit support statement saying that NFS is not supported even if the hypervisor presents that storage to the guest as block storage (as is the case with ESXi). Always check with software vendors to make sure your particular storage configuration is supported—NFS or otherwise.

You can read Microsoft's specific support statement for NFS when virtualizing Exchange Server at the following location:

```
http://technet.microsoft.com/en-us/library/jj619301(v=exchg.150).aspx
```

Virtual SAN

Virtual SAN, or VSAN, is a new feature in vSphere 5.5 that lets you take the local storage in a group of ESXi hosts and aggregate it together to present a shared datastore to your ESXi hosts. VSAN allows you to use important vSphere features such as vMotion, HA, and DRS without requiring a dedicated SAN or NFS share stored on another device. In essence, the local storage in your ESXi hosts becomes the shared storage that enables you to use those features.

VSAN can be considered a scale-out architecture in that if additional storage is required, you can simply add more storage to your ESXi hosts. Similarly, if you need additional ESXi hosts to satisfy compute requirements, the storage in those ESXi hosts can become part of VSAN to increase overall storage capacity. The ability to simply add more compute nodes (ESXi hosts) into your environment in order to expand your VSAN storage makes this an attractive technology to consider as an alternative to a traditional storage array.

VSAN Is Not VSA

You might be wondering if VSAN is an extension of the vSphere Storage Appliance (VSA) that has been available in vSphere for a few versions. Though they are similar in concept, they are quite different in functionality. The largest difference is likely to be in scalability of the technologies. VSA is intended for small businesses or remote office locations where providing a SAN is not cost effective (or possible). It can scale to only three nodes and can support only up to 16 terabytes (TB) of storage.

You can find a more detailed comparison of VSA and VSAN at the following location:

```
http://blogs.vmware.com/vsphere/2013/08/comparing-vmware-vsa-vmware-
virtual-san.html
```

Designing Physical Storage

Storage has become a crucial part of any virtual infrastructure today. It has become one of the largest contributors to overall virtual machine performance and also enables access to most of vSphere's advanced features (such as vMotion, High Availability, and others). Years ago there were just a handful of enterprise storage vendors, but today there are numerous startups and newcomers to the industry offering unique storage solutions designed to meet performance and availability requirements. Never before have there been so many different options available to help design storage for your vSphere environment.

The setup and design of your physical storage solution has a lot to do with how well your virtual environment will perform. The type of storage, the number of spindles and RAID configuration, networking (for IP-based storage), and many other aspects all play a role in the ultimate overall performance of your environment/solution.

In the following sections, we'll cover the important factors to consider when designing shared storage for your vSphere environment.

Determine Your Requirements

The best way to start designing your physical storage to meet your performance requirements is, not surprisingly, to determine what your requirements are in the first place! Most organizations are not able to purchase storage that far exceeds their requirements, so determining your performance requirements will help you procure the correct hardware and configure it properly.

We won't attempt to cover the entire process of gathering requirements here. Instead, we'll focus on a few key ways to gather the requirements you'll need to properly size your physical storage for your vSphere environment.

Assess Performance and Capacity

Many of you are likely to be familiar with capacity planning and capacity assessments if you've been working with virtualization for a few years. Capacity assessments have been used for many years to aid in large-scale physical-to-virtual (P2V) migrations and are still used today for this purpose. We covered some recommended tools you can use to perform capacity assessments back in Chapter 2, "Building Your Toolbox," but here's a short refresher.

A capacity assessment is a process in which tools are used to monitor the utilization of servers, physical or virtual, over a set period of time (typically 30 days). After the assessment has completed, the data is analyzed to determine the actual utilization of the servers and is used to help figure out sizing requirements.

Why bring this up in the context of storage performance? Understanding your actual I/O requirements for existing servers (whether they are physical or virtual) is key to making sure your physical storage is capable of meeting those requirements. CPU and memory can often be reduced during capacity assessments because physical servers are frequently overprovisioned and not using anywhere near their available resources. Storage utilization, on the other hand, is unlikely to change once the server is virtualized. If the server was generating a certain amount of I/O when it was physical, it is unlikely to suddenly need more or less I/O just because it has been virtualized. When you have the data in hand for your servers/applications, there will be fewer surprises once the systems have been virtualized.

There are two popular tools that are used for capacity assessments, and luckily both are free. VMware offers a tool called Capacity Planner and Microsoft offers Assessment and Planning Toolkit (often referred to as MAP). Both work in a similar way: they allow you to choose a set of servers to monitor and then performance metrics are gathered over a period of time automatically. Once the collection period is over, each tool can provide a number of reports to both show the utilization on the servers over time and recommend sizing. Having the tool run for an appropriate amount of time is useful to show trending and to capture the utilization through an entire month's business cycle.

Though both Capacity Planner and MAP are free products, only MAP is a truly free product for everyone. Capacity Planner is free as well, but it is only available to VMware and its certified partners. If you are not working with a VMware partner, you can typically reach out to your account representative at VMware to discuss gaining access to Capacity Planner for an assessment, especially if it is likely to lead to the purchase of additional vSphere licenses!

More Information on Capacity Planning

This section is by no means meant to be an instruction manual for how to perform capacity assessments with either MAP or Capacity Planner. You can learn more about MAP at the following location:

`http://technet.microsoft.com/en-us/library/bb977556.aspx`

You can learn more about VMware Capacity Planner here:

`http://www.vmware.com/products/capacity-planner/`

What if your servers are already virtualized? Perhaps you're looking to purchase a new storage array and want to make sure it can meet the demands of your current workloads. In that case, you can use Capacity Planner or MAP to monitor the utilization just as if the server was physical. If you have access to another great tool, VMware vCenter Operations Manager, you have access to a treasure trove of excellent capacity information. vCenter Operations Manager leverages custom algorithms to help with capacity planning, allowing it to predict the resource demands of the server in the future based on the way it has performed in the past. This data can be very valuable and can also be used to determine the storage requirements for the virtual machine(s).

WORK WITH YOUR SOFTWARE VENDOR

What if the server/application that you're virtualizing isn't already deployed in your environment? What if it's a brand new product in your infrastructure or a new version you're planning for? In that case, work with the software vendor and ask them to provide the storage performance requirements they need to support the application. Some products, such as Microsoft Exchange Server, have very well-known I/O profiles and can easily be sized based on simple environmental criteria.

Some vendors provide minimum storage performance requirements that must be met to even have a supported configuration. Make sure the vendor knows that the application will be run in a virtual machine and ask for any additional guidance, because often the vendor requirements assume the application will be run on a physical server.

GO BEYOND THE NUMBERS

One of our favorite things to say when talking about performance requirements of any kind is this: "Numbers without context are meaningless." Often vendors will provide performance requirements like "The application requires 1,000 IOPS (input/output operations per second)" or "The application requires at least five disk spindles." Those numbers are meaningless without context.

After all, what does 1,000 IOPS really mean? Are those IOPS reads or writes? Random or sequential? What about the block size? What speed should those five disk spindles be and how should they be laid out? The point is that taking a requirement like IOPS by itself doesn't tell you enough to properly size the physical storage to meet that requirement.

Make sure you get all of the details when vendors list their requirements. Don't let them off easy with blanket high-level requirements that do not have any meaning out of context.

WORK WITH APPLICATION OWNERS

Not all applications are off-the-shelf products offered by a company with a support team behind it. Oftentimes applications are developed in-house to meet the specific needs of a business. When dealing with these kinds of applications, it is often best to combine a capacity assessment and a conversation with the application owner(s). Sit down with the folks who own, maintain, and develop the application to determine the way the application works and what it demands in terms of storage I/O and capacity. If the application relies on a database backend where most of the storage I/O is handled, make sure to involve the database administrators as well.

BRING IT ALL TOGETHER

When possible, you should determine your actual requirements based on real data measured on production servers (if available) combined with insights from the product vendor and/or the application owners. Bringing all of this data together will help you determine exactly what is needed to meet the storage requirements (and typically CPU and memory requirements too).

It's important that realistic requirements are determined and agreed upon. If an application owner or vendor tries to say that they need more storage I/O than the application is currently using, you could end up oversizing your storage and spending more money or complicating your setup. The best way to combat unrealistic expectations is by presenting the application owner with the real data gathered on the current production servers. If that is not possible, start small and move to faster storage if necessary. The solution should be easily scalable so that if needs or requirements change, your storage solution can also change and adapt to meet those demands. That's one of the great things about Storage vMotion—it does not require an application outage and can be used on the fly to address performance problems.

By combining any storage requirements provided by a vendor/application owner with those gathered through automated capacity assessment tools, you can get a clear picture of the total storage performance requirements for your environment. That data should be used to purchase the right amount and type of storage for your vSphere environment.

RAID Levels

It seems like just a few years ago, a discussion about RAID (Redundant Array of Inexpensive Disks or Redundant Array of Independent Disks, depending on the age of the person you're asking) would be fairly straightforward. There were a few configurations available, and you chose the one that worked best based on your requirements and how many disks you had available. The world of storage has changed a lot in the last few years, and things have become much less straightforward. With that said, a discussion of RAID concepts is still important because choosing the right RAID configuration can have an impact on storage performance in your vSphere environment.

Simply put, RAID is a technology that allows you to combine multiple physical hard drives and present them as one or more logical drives. RAID is used primarily to introduce redundancy at the disk level (with different RAID configurations offering varying levels of protection) as well as to improve performance. It also decouples the physical disk drives from logical drives, allowing you to carve up the available storage to meet your requirements. RAID is used to protect disks when storage is local to the server as well as when disks are part of a SAN. There are many different configurations possible with RAID, and each has its own performance characteristics and levels of redundancy. We will review the more common RAID configurations, with the understanding that different storage vendors offer different configurations that may not be included here. Always work with your storage vendor to get an understanding of your RAID options and to figure out what works best for your particular array.

DISK PERFORMANCE

Before we go too deep into the different types of RAID, it's important to note that the largest contributing factor to your storage performance is the type of disks used in your storage array. Each RAID type has a different performance profile, but the actual performance you can get out of each configuration comes down to the type of disks you're using.

Hard drives are available in a variety of interfaces and rotational speeds, each with its own performance capabilities. In general, drive performance is measured in I/O operations per second, or IOPS. Table 7.1 lists the IOPS values you can expect to get out of different disk types.

TABLE 7.1:   Average IOPS values for different disk types

DISK SPEED (RPM)	EXPECTED AVERAGE IOPS
5400 RPM	50
7200 RPM	125
10,000 RPM	120
15,000 RPM	180
Solid State Disk (SSD)	2,000–4,000 (or higher)

The values you see in Table 7.1 might be somewhat different (but still probably pretty close) to values you've seen elsewhere. Vendors may alter these numbers slightly, but for the most part these are industry-accepted average values for the listed drive times. Remember when we mentioned the phrase "numbers without context are meaningless?" The average IOPS values listed in Table 7.1 are just that—without context; they are essentially meaningless to you. The table does not give any information about the type of workload that was run to generate those IOPS. More than likely the workload was a sequential read operation, meaning an I/O operation that is relatively easy for the disk to execute. If you were looking at random write operations, you would see very different values. That's not to say, however, that the values you see listed there are wrong. It just means that they may not be applicable to you, depending on your workload profile.

Putting aside the fact that these values may not apply to your workload, they provide the basis for calculating expected IOPS based on the type of disks you're using. To calculate IOPS, it should be as simple as multiplying the number of drives you have by the expected average IOPS, right? In other words, if you have six drives that are 10,000 RPM, then you should expect to get 720 IOPS (6 × 120), right? Unfortunately it is not that simple; there are several factors that can impact the total IOPS available. Some factors are environmental, such as whether the I/O operations are reads or writes, whether the data is being read or written sequentially or in a random fashion (resulting in reduced performance), and the block size of the data in question.

Additionally, the use of RAID introduces another wrinkle into IOPS planning. When RAID is used, multiple disks are grouped into a single logical unit for both availability (protection from drive failure) and performance reasons. When data has to be written to the group of disks, there can be an increase in the actual amount of I/O operations that have to happen at the storage layer (as opposed to those issued from the operating system or application) in order to actually write that data to disk. That increase in I/O operations is known as the RAID penalty (or the RAID write penalty). Generally speaking, when RAID configurations offer some level of redundancy, there is a penalty when the data is written because either it must be written in multiple places or parity must be calculated to ensure redundancy. Table 7.2 lists the RAID penalty for the types of RAID we'll cover in the following sections, and we'll go into more detail about how this penalty affects each type of RAID configuration when we describe them. You'll notice that read operations do not have a penalty with RAID and are typically much faster than they are without RAID.

TABLE 7.2:   RAID penalty for different RAID configurations

RAID Configuration	Write Penalty
RAID-0	1
RAID-1	2
RAID-10	2
RAID-5	4
RAID-6	6

RAID-0

RAID-0 is about as basic a RAID configuration as you're likely to find. It consists of two (or more) disks in a *stripe*, meaning data is broken down and written evenly across the disks. The disk space of the disks in this configuration is added together, meaning if you combine two 1 TB drives in a RAID-0 configuration, the resulting logical volume will be 2 TB. RAID-0 offers the best performance of all of the different RAID levels, but it does so at the cost of redundancy. In this configuration there is no redundancy whatsoever, so if a single drive fails, you are certain to lose data.

In almost all circumstances, RAID-0 should not be used for production workloads. In fact, the only reason it is mentioned here at all is to set a foundation for RAID-10, which has a RAID-0 component (more on this later).

RAID-1

In a RAID-1 configuration, data is *mirrored* across two (or more) disks. The data is identical on both drives (which is why it is referred to as a mirror), which provides redundancy should one of the drives in the RAID-1 mirror fail. It also provides an added benefit in that either of the drives is capable of servicing a read request, offering a performance improvement for read operations. Write operations, however, have to be written to both drives before the storage can report a successful write back to the operating system. Since the data has to be written twice, the penalty is a second write I/O operation that must occur at the storage layer. In other words, if a workload generates 50 IOPS of write activity, the storage array must process 100 IOPS to write that data to the disks (50 IOPS on each disk).

RAID-1 is often used on servers where ESXi is installed locally on the hard drives. Today, ESXi supports many different methods of installation, whether it be on internal USB or SD cards or stateless installations with no disk drives at all. Though it is less common to see ESXi installed on actual hard drives these days, if your design calls for it to be installed on local hard drives, then RAID-1 offers a good compromise of cost and disk protection.

RAID-10

Recalling the concepts discussed for both RAID-0 and RAID-1, RAID-10 (sometimes referred to as RAID 1+0) is a combination of both RAID types. It is a stripe of mirrors, or a mirrored set of data that is striped across multiple disks. RAID-10 offers excellent read performance because it can read from the mirrored pairs at the same time. It also offers good write performance because data is striped across multiple disks. RAID-10 offers this great performance at the cost of total number of disks required to support redundancy. RAID-10 requires at least four disks, two of which are allocated for redundancy, leaving only two for capacity. This disk requirement makes RAID-10 one of the most expensive RAID configurations.

Typically, organizations use RAID-10 when they have high demands for performance, availability, or both. In a RAID-10 configuration, multiple drives can fail (provided they are in different groups) without impacting availability or causing data loss. RAID-10 is frequently used in applications such as email servers or database servers due to the high I/O performance that it can deliver.

RAID-10 has the same RAID penalty as RAID-1, so the previous example holds true here as well. If your environment has applications that have very high I/O demands, RAID-10 should be something to consider.

RAID-5

In a RAID-5 configuration, data is striped across all drives along with parity. Parity is essentially a duplication of the data that is already striped across the drives and is used to allow for a drive failure without data loss. Because both data and parity are striped across all drives, RAID-5 is also known as a distributed parity configuration. There are other RAID configurations that store all parity information on a specific disk in the group, but RAID-5 distributes the parity across all of the disks.

RAID-5 has become extremely popular in servers and SANs due to the relatively low cost and the low level of complexity for providing redundancy. In a RAID-5 configuration, you lose one disk's worth of data to account for the parity copy. That means that if you use the minimum of three drives in your RAID-5 configuration, you'll have a total of two drives' worth of capacity. It is often very easy to allocate a disk out of your group for parity without losing too much capacity, especially with the increasing size of drives available today.

RAID-5 offers great read performance, but write performance is significantly impacted because of parity. RAID-5 has a RAID penalty of 4, meaning that every write operation generated by a virtual machine must be matched by a total of four I/O operations on the storage array. If your virtual machine generates 50 IOPS of write activity, the storage array needs a total of 200 IOPS of actual operations. This penalty can significantly impact write performance if virtual machines are very heavily skewed toward write operations.

To see the impact in a more realistic example, let's assume a virtual machine generates 500 IOPS of disk activity and that it's an even split of 50 percent reads and 50 percent writes. To determine how many IOPS will generate on the backend, we just need to do a little math. Because there is an even split between reads and writes, that means there are 250 read I/Os and 250 write I/Os. However, with a RAID penalty of 4, that means that it takes 1,000 IOPS (250 IOPS × 4) on the backend for those 250 write I/Os. Add in the 250 read I/Os and you can see that a single VM generating 500 IOPS of disk activity (reads and writes) actually generates 1,250 IOPS on the backend. This example should help illustrate just how severe the RAID penalty for RAID-5 can be.

Despite the heavy RAID penalty, RAID-5 is still a good option for providing redundancy as well as good performance for virtual machines. VMs that frequently perform read operations will benefit from the performance of RAID-5, while write-heavy applications will likely perform better under other RAID configurations (such as RAID-10).

RAID-6

The last RAID configuration we'll cover here is RAID-6. RAID-6 is very similar to RAID-5 in that it stripes data and parity across all drives, but with RAID-6 a second stripe of parity is distributed. This allows for up to two drive failures within the group without incurring any data loss, making RAID-6 a distributed *double parity* configuration.

RAID-6 has a RAID penalty of 6, meaning it incurs two additional write operations above RAID-5 for every write. That means that in our earlier example, if a virtual machine issues 50 write IOPS, the storage array will actually need 300 I/O operations to commit that data to disk.

RAID-6 is useful for organizations that have high uptime requirements and/or critical data that needs the extra redundancy. Extremely write-heavy workloads suffer under RAID-6, so make sure you properly understand your workloads before using this configuration.

DOES RAID CONFIGURATION MATTER ANYMORE?

Now that we've covered the most common RAID types and the RAID penalty associated with each, it makes sense to stop and ask how much of this really applies to vSphere performance. The reality is that today, determining the available performance from a storage array is much more complicated than simply multiplying IOPS per drive while factoring in the RAID penalty. Modern storage arrays use a multitude of technologies and features that can all but eliminate the RAID penalty.

First, most modern storage arrays use some level of cache to help improve performance. The cache layer is typically a layer of SSDs (or in some cases, RAM) that is used to quickly commit and acknowledge back to the source that the write was successful. At some point the data is written from the cache layer back to the slower disks without forcing the source (in this case, a virtual machine) to wait for that operation to be completed. Using SSDs, which are significantly faster than even the fastest spinning disk, can significantly improve performance. Taking it one step further, some storage arrays offer the ability to automatically tier your data from slower disks to faster disks depending on how frequently they access data. This operation is transparent to the end user and to the vSphere layer and can help make sure that "hot" (active) data is always on the fastest possible disks while "cold" (static) data sits on slower, larger disks.

Another feature of modern storage arrays is the ability of the array to coalesce writes before actually writing them to disk. The hardware in the storage array is capable of taking the data that is sitting in cache and reorganizing it into larger blocks of sequential data that can be more quickly written to the disks. Even if the data that comes into the cache is random, the data is coalesced into sequential data before it is written out to disk. Not only can this operation improve performance, it can also reduce the impact of the RAID penalty.

Finally, there are numerous vendors and startups with caching solutions that sit outside the storage array and offer similar capabilities. Some work by leveraging a virtual appliance inside your vSphere environment, while others actually work at the vSphere level. VMware itself also offers this kind of functionality with the vFlash Read Cache, which we'll cover in more detail later.

Simply put, it's no longer simple to figure out how many IOPS your disks can provide. The good news is that storage vendors are putting these technologies in place to help improve overall performance, so it's less for you to worry about. The best advice is to work with your particular storage vendor to understand how their technologies work and how best to take advantage of them in your vSphere environment.

Flash Infrastructure Layer

Flash storage is a significant disruptor in the storage industry. Flash storage typically comes in two flavors: in a solid-state disk format that uses the server's disk interface and on a PCIe card that uses the faster PCI bus. In either configuration, they are many times faster than even the fastest spinning disks and can deliver higher IOPS at lower levels of latency. They are making it possible for organizations to virtualize business-critical applications without having to devote as many disks to satisfy performance and capacity requirements.

VMware has also begun investing in flash technology and has had flash-related features in the product since vSphere 5. vSphere lets you allocate SSD storage to improve the performance of VMkernel swap by using the "swap to host cache" feature discussed in Chapter 5, "Memory." And as mentioned, new in vSphere 5.5, VMware has provided the vFlash Read Cache that lets you allocate SSD storage (either SATA or PCI based) to be used as a cache layer to improve read performance. Additionally, VSAN requires the use of at least one SSD to improve both read and write performance.

The key point to understand is that this is likely to be just the beginning of the SSD-related technologies that will be incorporated into future releases of vSphere. If you are in a position to purchase new server hardware, you should strongly consider purchasing servers with one or more SSDs to take advantage of today's features while making sure you can use whatever VMware comes up with next.

Networking for IP Storage

You've just finished reading the networking chapter (Chapter 6, "Network") and you're an expert, right? If so, great, but that doesn't mean you can skip this section! IP storage technologies all rely on Ethernet networking and have some special considerations that you should be aware of when designing your physical storage.

In Chapter 6 we discussed the need to have redundancy at each functional component of your network. That includes the networking required to connect your ESXi hosts to your iSCSI or NFS storage. Redundancy is crucial to maintaining uptime in your vSphere environment because a loss of connectivity to storage can result in a very large outage, especially if you have high consolidation ratios.

It doesn't end with physical redundancy, however. You should strive to isolate, to the extent possible, all facets of the networking from your ESXi hosts to the backend storage. Keep the physical network cards used for IP storage separated from other functions on your ESXi hosts, using them only for storage networking. In scenarios where NICs on ESXi hosts aren't plentiful, you may think it makes sense to combine IP storage traffic with other traffic, such as management, vMotion, or virtual machine traffic. Though this will provide redundancy for multiple functions, you are likely to suffer performance problems if there is contention for network resources. And certain operations like vMotion or Multi-NIC vMotion can consume nearly all of the available bandwidth on your NICs, which can cause serious performance degradation if those NICs are also being used to connect to IP storage. Instead, utilize technologies like Network I/O Control (NIOC) or traffic shaping in vSphere (both covered in Chapter 6) to help control resource usage on physical network cards when you are using servers where network cards are not plentiful.

Isolating network traffic for IP storage does not end with using dedicated physical NICs, however. You should also further isolate the traffic at the logical level by using dedicated VLANs for IP storage. Create dedicated VLANs for your iSCSI or NFS storage so that only storage traffic can traverse those networks. That can reduce the incidence of a network broadcast storm interfering with storage traffic. Additionally, having any kind of network routing of your storage traffic can introduce latency and reduce performance. Using dedicated VLANs for storage traffic eliminates the requirement to route storage traffic and can improve overall storage performance for your ESXi hosts.

Where possible, dedicating physical network switches for IP storage can also help to further isolate traffic and reduce latency. This is not always possible and can become costly with certain scenarios, but if it's possible, it can help improve storage performance.

VLANs Alone Are Not Enough

Remember that simply creating a VLAN and assigning it to physical network cards that are being used for other purposes, such as vMotion, is not enough. VLANs offer logical separation of network traffic but cannot solve the problem of physical network cards that are saturated and experiencing performance degradation. When using IP-based storage, you should have dedicated physical NICs as well as VLANs to provide separation at both the physical and logical layers whenever possible.

MULTIPATHING

Using multiple interfaces, either fibre channel or Ethernet, between your ESXi hosts and the storage network is key to ensuring both availability and performance. Simply having multiple interfaces, however, is only part of the story. You'll also need to use multipathing in ESXi to make sure the hosts know how to properly use each interface. Multipathing is a technology that controls how the ESXi hosts use the interfaces to communicate to the backend storage. A path represents a single physical connection between the ESXi host and the storage array, such as a fibre channel port or Ethernet port.

ESXi supports several Native Multipathing (NMP) policies, referred to as Path Selection Policies (PSPs). Each PSP controls how the physical uplinks are utilized to communicate to the backend storage, and the type you use often depends on the type of storage array you're using. Table 7.3 lists the NMP PSPs supported by vSphere 5.5.

TABLE 7.3: Path Selection Policies in vSphere 5.5

NAME	DESCRIPTION
Most Recently Used (MRU)	Uses the first functional path that the ESXi host discovers during boot. Continues using this path until the path goes down. When the path becomes available again, ESXi continues using the new path until another failure occurs.
Fixed	Uses the first functional path that the ESXi host discovers during boot. Continues using this path until the path goes down. When the path becomes available again, the ESXi host resumes using the original selected path.
Round Robin	Uses all paths in an automatic, round-robin method that distributes load down all paths evenly. This is the only PSP that effectively utilizes all paths.

Though the Round Robin PSP seems like the obvious choice, it is not always ideal in all scenarios. In versions of vSphere prior to vSphere 5.5, the Round Robin PSP was not supported when used to support logical unit numbers (LUNs) that were part of a Microsoft Windows failover cluster. Additionally, not all storage vendors support the use of Round Robin and instead require either the Fixed or MRU PSP. Check with your particular storage vendor to determine what the most appropriate PSP is for your configuration.

vSphere also supports PSPs that are not part of the NMP included with ESXi. EMC and Dell are among the vendors that offer a custom PSP that is installed on ESXi hosts and manages the multipathing instead of using VMware's NMP. Typically, vendor-provided PSPs are tuned to work best with the vendor's storage and can provide better performance than the NMPs in ESXi, so if your storage vendor provides a third-party PSP and you have the appropriate license level (both vSphere licensing and vendor licensing), then you should strongly consider using it.

To adjust the PSP on an individual datastore on an ESXi host, use the following procedure:

1. Launch the vSphere Web Client and connect to vCenter Server.

2. From the Home view, select Hosts And Clusters and find the ESXi host connected to the appropriate storage.

3. Select Manage, and click the tab labeled Storage. Select Storage Devices, and select the storage device that you wish to modify from the list.

4. Under Device Details, scroll down and select the button labeled Edit Multipathing.

5. From the Path Selection Policy drop-down list, change the option to the appropriate policy, as shown in Figure 7.1, and click OK.

FIGURE 7.1
Changing the Path
Selection Policy on a
VMFS datastore

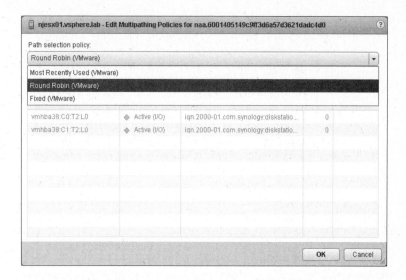

Designing vSphere Storage

After you've designed your physical storage to meet the performance demands of your
virtual machines, you're well on your way. Physical storage is one half of the story, and the
other equally important half is designing vSphere and its various storage features. Storage has
become arguably the most important resource, from a performance perspective, in vSphere
environments today. And thankfully, never before have there been so many storage innovations
within vSphere to help address this need.

In the following sections, we'll cover the newer storage-related features in vSphere and
how to use them to get the best possible performance out of your virtual machines. Some of
these features have been in the vSphere platform for some time and others are available only in
vSphere 5.5 or later.

Why Is Storage So Important?

Before we dive into vSphere's numerous storage-related features, it makes sense to take a
step back and talk about the problem we're trying to solve. Why has storage become such an

important piece of the performance puzzle for vSphere environments? Do virtual machines inherently generate more I/O than their physical counterparts?

Consider the way storage has typically worked for physical servers in the past. Let's say you have a physical database server connected to LUNs (logical unit numbers) on a SAN. The storage for that server is typically allocated just for that server, with dedicated disks and RAID configurations to meet the demands of that particular server. Those disks have to process I/O only for that one server generating one type of workload profile (sequential or random reads and writes). Architecting storage in this way allowed for better control over I/O but isn't terribly efficient in terms of overall utilization. Modern storage arrays allow you to virtualize the storage and create multiple LUNs on a single RAID group, but even with these technologies, physical servers are still often allocated with their own dedicated LUNs and disks on the SAN.

Now consider the way storage is allocated to ESXi hosts. LUNs are provisioned and presented to ESXi hosts, with multiple virtual machines running on the same LUN. Not only is this generating more I/O than a single server, it's also harder to size the storage due to the different workload profiles of each server. Some virtual machines could be generating random reads while others are generating sequential writes. Even if all of the virtual machines on the same volume are generating sequential I/O, because this I/O is coming from multiple virtual machines, it is essentially randomized when it hits the storage array. This combining of different I/O profiles on the same LUNs/disks on the SAN is known as the I/O blender effect.

Figure 7.2 illustrates, at a basic level, the I/O blender effect. In this example, three virtual machines are running on an ESXi host. Each virtual machine is generating sequential write I/O depicted by the letters *A*, *B*, and *C*. From the virtual machine's perspective, the I/O being generated is sequential in nature and as such should be easier for the storage array to handle than random I/O. Unfortunately, even though all virtual machines are generating sequential write I/O, the likelihood that all of the actual data from these virtual machines exist in the same place on the disks is very low. As such, once the write I/O operations reach the SAN, they have effectively "gone through the I/O blender" and come out as random write I/O instead. The I/O blender effect reduces performance because random I/O is generally slower than sequential I/O. Cache layers and write coalescing can help solve the I/O blender effect, again highlighting the importance of these features in your storage. Proper storage tiering, or placing known workload types on specific storage tiers, can also help separate out different I/O types and reduce the impact of the I/O blender.

In addition to the features found in enterprise storage arrays, vSphere offers features that can help reduce the impact of the I/O blender effect. The I/O blender will likely remain a problem for the future, though newer technologies (such as all flash SAN arrays and hyperconverged solutions like VSAN, for example) can help reduce the impact on virtual machine performance.

VAAI

To help reduce the impact of the I/O blender, VMware introduced a set of application programming interfaces (APIs) called vStorage APIs for Array Integration, or VAAI. VAAI is a technology that allows the ESXi host to offload certain storage-related functions directly to the storage array rather than processing these tasks at the host level and transmitting storage commands over the fabric (fibre or Ethernet). Offloading tasks directly to the storage helps reduce the amount of storage bandwidth, memory, and CPU utilized on the ESXi host. VAAI accelerated operations complete faster and help to improve overall performance.

VAAI supports several *primitives,* or operations, that can improve overall storage performance. Table 7.4 lists the VAAI primitives that can accelerate storage-related tasks.

FIGURE 7.2
Illustrating the I/O
blender effect

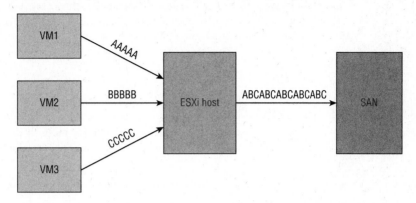

TABLE 7.4:   VAAI primitives in ESXi 5.5

NAME	DESCRIPTION
Atomic Test & Set (ATS)	ATS is a locking mechanism that allows an ESXi host to perform metadata updates of a VMFS volume without significantly impacting other hosts sharing the same volume. Before ATS, ESXi used SCSI reservations that could impact the performance of other ESXi hosts and running virtual machines because they were essentially locked out of accessing data on the LUN until the SCSI lock had been lifted.
Clone Blocks/Full Copy/XCOPY	The XCOPY primitive is used when virtual machines are either cloned or migrated (using Storage vMotion). Without this primitive, the ESXi host is responsible for sending all required blocks over the storage interface (FC or Ethernet). When this primitive is used, the copy operation is offloaded directly to the storage array, reducing CPU and storage network utilization on the ESXi host. Clones or migrations that are offloaded using this primitive often complete much faster.
Zero Blocks/Write Same	The Write Same primitive is used when creating virtual machine disks in the eager-zeroedthick format. In this format, all blocks on the disk are zeroed out at creation instead of when data needs to be written to the block. Just as with cloning, when the eagerzeroedthick disk is created, the ESXi host must send all zeroed-out blocks over the storage network to the storage array. The Write Same primitive allows this operation to be offloaded to the array, significantly reducing the time it takes to create eagerzeroedthick disks.

NOTE The primitives listed in Table 7.4 are only those that have a direct impact on performance. There are several other primitives that are used to help in storage management, including alerting if a thin provisioned volume is close to consuming all available space or reclaiming deleted blocks on a thin provisioned volume. VMware has an excellent white paper on all VAAI primitives that can be downloaded at the following location:

```
www.vmware.com/files/pdf/techpaper/VMware-vSphere-Storage-API-Array-
Integration.pdf
```

VAAI is enabled by default in vSphere 5.5, and there is very little reason not to use it to accelerate storage operations. The storage array in use needs to support VAAI in order to take advantage of these features, and thankfully, today many modern storage arrays support this functionality. To verify that VAAI is enabled on your ESXi hosts, use the following simple procedure:

1. Launch the vSphere Web Client and connect to vCenter Server.

2. From the Home view, select Hosts And Clusters and find the ESXi host connected to the appropriate storage.

3. Select Manage, and click the tab labeled Settings. Select Advanced System Settings under the Systems heading in the menu on the left.

4. Verify that the following advanced system settings all have a value of 1 (the first two are shown in Figure 7.3).

   DataMover.HardwareAcceleratedMove

   DataMover.HardwareAcceleratedInit

   VMFS3.HardwareAcceleratedLocking

5. Alternatively, you can connect directly to your ESXi host and issue the following three commands to verify that these values are set to 1:

```
esxcli system settings advanced list -o /DataMover/HardwareAcceleratedMove
esxcli system settings advanced list -o /DataMover/HardwareAcceleratedInit
esxcli system settings advanced list -o /VMFS3/HardwareAcceleratedLocking
```

There have been instances in the past where bugs in storage arrays have caused performance issues when VAAI is enabled. If your storage array has a bug and VAAI needs to be disabled, follow the preceding procedure but change the values of each of the configurations from 1 to 0 to disable VAAI.

If the storage array you are using supports VAAI and you have the feature enabled on your ESXi hosts, you're more likely to have better overall storage performance. Features like Storage vMotion and clones will complete faster, and you'll be able to create eagerzeroedthick disks much faster. As stated, there is almost no reason not to use VAAI if your array supports it.

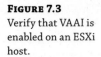

FIGURE 7.3
Verify that VAAI is
enabled on an ESXi
host.

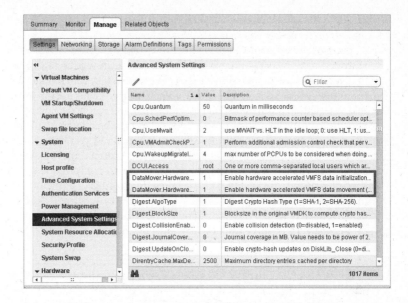

Storage I/O Control

Back in Chapter 6, we talked about a technology in vSphere called Network I/O Control (NIOC) that can be used to solve the "noisy neighbor" problem. If a single virtual machine (or several virtual machines) starts consuming too much network bandwidth, NIOC can enforce fairness and prevent one virtual machine from monopolizing network resources.

The same noisy neighbor problem also exists in the world of storage. To combat that problem, VMware introduced Storage I/O Control (SIOC) in vSphere 4.1. SIOC works similarly in theory to NIOC in that it enforces fairness among virtual machines accessing and sharing the same VMFS datastores. It allows you to take the entire set of a datastore's resources (the I/O it can provide at a given latency) and divide it up evenly among the virtual machines running on it. Enabling SIOC on a datastore ensures that all virtual machines on all ESXi hosts have access to the same amount of the datastore's resources and prevents a single VM from consuming too many disk resources.

Storage I/O Control enforces fairness by using the same method as other resource controls within vSphere. That is, shares are assigned on each virtual machine and those shares are used to determine which virtual machines get priority access to storage resources. Fairness in access to storage resources is invoked only when the latency for a datastore approaches an upper limit that you define or a specific latency value that you can define. SIOC is capable of looking at the performance of the datastore and figuring out the best latency threshold to use, making the process of figuring out the threshold much simpler. If you have a specific application or requirement for a certain latency level, that level can be set manually as well. The default values for SIOC have been tested and tuned and generally do not have to be changed unless you have a specific reason to do so. High latency on a datastore is usually a very bad thing and often results in a drop in performance that can be very visible to applications and end users. Throttling the performance of a high I/O virtual machine to bring the latency back down to acceptable levels can have a very positive impact on overall performance.

STORAGE I/O CONTROL CAN MANAGE ONLY VMFS VOLUMES

When Storage I/O Control detects I/O activity on a storage device that is not being generated by virtual machine I/O (or is generated from a legacy host that does not support SIOC), it considers this a "Non-VI Workload" and may trigger an alarm within vCenter. Storage I/O Control is capable of throttling access to storage resources only for virtual machines under its control (within management of vCenter). External workloads, such as LUNs that are created on the same disk spindles as the VMFS volumes, can introduce I/O load that Storage I/O Control cannot manage.

When using Storage I/O Control on a particular VMFS datastore, make sure the LUN does not share disk spindles with other systems outside of the virtual infrastructure. This will reduce complexity and make it easier for Storage I/O Control to manage access to disk resources. Normally, Storage I/O Control can still work under this configuration, but it is best to avoid it whenever possible.

You can find more information on this particular setup at http://kb.vmware.com/kb/1020651.

Storage I/O Control is configured on each datastore and is disabled by default. To enable SIOC and configure a threshold value, follow this simple procedure:

1. Launch the vSphere Web Client and connect to vCenter Server.

2. From the Home view, select Storage and find and select the datastore on which you want to enable Storage I/O Control.

3. Select Manage, and select the Settings tab. Then click the button labeled Edit next to Datastore Capabilities.

4. Select the check box labeled Enable Storage I/O Control, as shown in Figure 7.4. You also have the option to modify the congestion threshold to either a certain percentage of peak throughput or a specific latency value.

FIGURE 7.4
Enable Storage I/O
Control and modify
the Congestion
Threshold values.

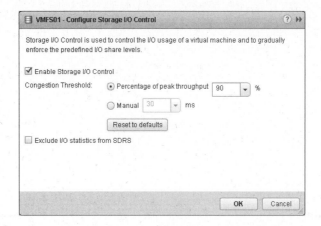

Once Storage I/O Control has been enabled, you next need to define share values on your virtual machines that require higher-priority access to storage resources. These share values are assigned on a per-VM basis, and it can be a lengthy process to assign to multiple VMs at once, but once the value is assigned, it shouldn't need to be changed. You should only have to configure custom share values if you need to assign priority to specific virtual machines. Otherwise, the default values should enforce fairness among your virtual machines. The default values for shares are 500 for Low, 1,000 for Normal, and 2,000 for High. There is also a Custom value for shares that allows you to assign whatever value you want.

Limits like those found for CPU and memory can also be assigned on a per-VM basis. Virtual machines can have IOPS limits assigned and enforced to control how many total I/O operations they can generate. This value must be configured on all virtual hard disks if the VM has more than one. As with CPU and memory limits, IOPS limits can be a dangerous thing, so they should be configured only if absolutely required. In general, using SIOC to enforce fairness in access to storage resources is likely to be a better solution than setting individual VM IOPS limits.

To assign share values to individual virtual machines, repeat the following procedure for each virtual machine that requires custom share values:

1. Launch the vSphere Web Client and connect to vCenter Server.

2. From the Home view, select either Hosts And Clusters or Virtual Machines And Templates, and find and select the virtual machine on which you want to configure share values.

3. Right-click on the virtual machine and select Edit Settings to bring up the virtual machine's configuration.

4. Expand the virtual machine's hard disk(s), and select the drop-down box labeled Shares to set a share value of either Low, Normal, High, or Custom, as shown in Figure 7.5.

You might be wondering how Storage I/O Control works when used in combination with a storage array that supports automatic tiering. Arrays that support automatic tiering can automatically move "hot data," or data that is active and consuming a lot of I/O, to faster tiers of storage such as SSDs while moving "cold data," or data that is infrequently accessed, down to slower spinning disks. Can Storage I/O Control work in conjunction with arrays that support this feature? The answer is yes—SIOC looks only at storage congestion and latency values. Those values can become elevated on any tier of storage if enough virtual machines are generating high I/O activity. Even on arrays that support auto-tiering, SIOC can help smooth out performance and not allow a single virtual machine consuming a lot of I/O to degrade the performance of others. If you plan on using an array that supports this feature, check out the *VMware Storage/SAN Compatibility Guide* to see if your array has been specifically certified to be compatible with SIOC. There are different guides for each version of vSphere and they can be found at the following location:

www.vmware.com/resources/compatibility/search.php?deviceCategory=san

Some arrays offer what is known as sub-LUN tiering, or tiering that can move individual blocks of data between storage tiers. Storage I/O Control determines the characteristics of each datastore by using an injector that introduces random read I/O to each datastore (during idle periods) and measures the resulting latency. This data is then used in conjunction with Storage Distributed Resource Scheduler (covered in the next section) to make intelligent placement and migration recommendations. When sub-LUN tiering is used on the storage array, the injector can get unpredictable results during read I/O testing. It is for this reason that it is typically best to work with your storage vendor to determine how to best configure SIOC when using arrays that support sub-LUN tiering technology.

Even if you don't go through the effort of configuring share values to individual virtual machines, SIOC can still help enforce fairness and make sure that virtual machines get access to the storage resources. Unless there is a specific reason not to enable SIOC, it makes sense to enable it for all datastores to help make sure virtual machines have access to the storage resources they need.

DO YOU REALLY NEED STORAGE I/O CONTROL?

We often come across this common objection to using Storage I/O Control: "All of my virtual machines need equal access to storage resources, so why should I use Storage I/O Control at all?" The logic here is that if all virtual machines need equal access to the VMFS datastore, then Storage I/O Control won't be used and as such is not needed.

Thinking about this for a second, you can probably see why this logic is flawed. The only way to ensure equal access to storage resources for all virtual machines is to actually enable Storage I/O Control. Without it, one virtual machine could end up consuming far too many disk resources and cause performance problems on other virtual machines, even those running on different ESXi hosts. Simply enabling Storage I/O Control, even without modifying share values, will enforce fairness in access to storage resources and meet the requirement of making sure all VMs get equal access to the storage.

Storage Distributed Resource Scheduler

Storage Distributed Resource Scheduler, or Storage DRS, was introduced in vSphere 5.0 as a way to automatically manage and balance storage resources in much the same way that DRS manages compute (CPU and memory) resources. Before we get to Storage DRS, however, we need to talk about the concept of a datastore cluster. A datastore cluster is a cluster of multiple datastores managed as a single object, just as hosts are managed in a cluster. Datastore clusters contain multiple datastores of the same type, either VMFS or NFS, with configuration managed from a single entity within vCenter.

To use Storage DRS, there must be at least one datastore cluster in your environment. Once datastores have been added to a datastore cluster, Storage DRS can begin to manage the virtual machines on those datastores and perform the following tasks to help simplify storage management and performance:

◆ I/O load balancing of virtual machines across multiple datastores within a datastore cluster. When an I/O threshold has been exceeded, Storage DRS can invoke Storage vMotion to migrate the virtual machine disk files from one datastore to another within a datastore cluster. Storage DRS performs this monitoring of I/O load on an ongoing basis (every eight hours, a configurable value) and can help keep your virtual machines running optimally on the right datastore.

◆ Initial placement of new virtual disks that have been created based on both the current capacity of the datastore and the I/O workload. Storage DRS reduces the burden of managing individual datastores to see which is the most appropriate to use when creating new virtual disks. Administrators can simply create a new virtual disk (or virtual machine) and select the datastore cluster object and Storage DRS will decide where to place the virtual machine disk files.

◆ Storage DRS can also manage the capacity of datastores within the datastore cluster, performing Storage vMotion migrations when datastores exceed a specific capacity threshold. This again eases the burden of managing space on individual datastores, which can be a burden in large environments with many datastores.

Storage DRS also has the capability to control the placement of virtual machine disk files by enforcing affinity or anti-affinity rules. These rules operate just like DRS rules do for virtual machines in that they control whether virtual machine disk files should always remain on the same datastore (affinity) or should never remain on the same datastore (anti-affinity). These rules can be useful to help with both performance and availability of applications. For example, consider a virtualized deployment of Microsoft SQL Server 2012 where the organization is utilizing AlwaysOn Availability Groups (AAGs) to keep multiple copies of each database. In that scenario, you can use VMDK anti-affinity rules to make sure the VMDKs housing the primary replica of the databases do not end up running on the same datastore as the VMDKs that house the secondary replica(s). Separating out the VMDKs not only helps with virtual machine performance but also reduces the impact of a datastore outage.

The first step to utilizing Storage DRS is to create a datastore cluster. Luckily, the process of creating a datastore cluster is about as easy as creating a host cluster; you only need to answer a few simple questions to get the cluster configured. To create a datastore cluster, use the following procedure:

1. Launch the vSphere Web Client and connect to vCenter Server.

2. From the Home view, select Storage.

3. Right-click on the datacenter object and select New Datastore Cluster.

4. Give the datastore cluster an appropriate name, and make sure the check box labeled Turn ON Storage DRS is selected. Click Next to continue.

5. Select the Automation level for Storage DRS. In No Automation (Manual Mode), Storage DRS will make recommendations for virtual machine migrations but will not automatically perform them. In Fully Automated mode, virtual machine files can be migrated automatically using Storage vMotion. Click Next to continue.

6. Under the I/O Metric Inclusion section, select the check mark next to Enable I/O Metric For SDRS Recommendations. If you are using a storage array that performs automatic rebalancing of data between tiers, it may make sense to disable this feature and allow the array to handle the movement of data at the block level. Storage DRS can still be used to automatically manage initial placement and datastore capacity. It is always best to work with your storage vendor to understand the capabilities of your array and their recommendations for Storage DRS configuration.

7. Under Storage DRS Thresholds, you can adjust the threshold values for the Utilized Space and I/O Latency options, as shown in Figure 7.6. The default values of 80 percent

for utilized space and 15 ms for latency are usually acceptable values if you are unsure of what to choose. These settings can be changed after the datastore cluster has been created.

8. Expanding the Advanced Options section allows you to configure additional settings, such as the frequency with which Storage DRS checks for imbalances, as shown in Figure 7.7. The frequency with which Storage DRS checks for imbalances can be as little as every 60 minutes, but keep in mind that performing frequent Storage vMotion migrations can introduce I/O and latency and impact performance. Only adjust this value from the default if you are comfortable with the impact of making the change. When you are done making changes, click Next to continue.

FIGURE 7.6
Configuring Storage
DRS thresholds

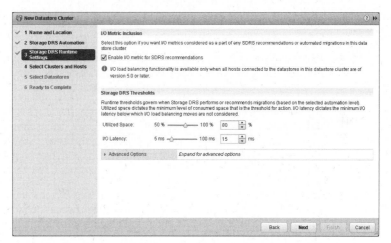

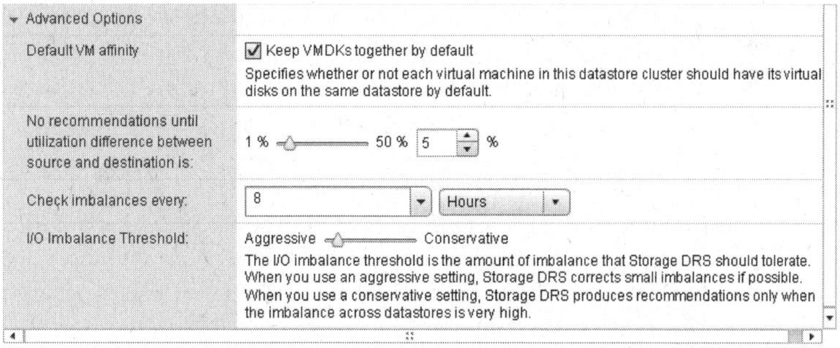

FIGURE 7.7
Configuring Storage
DRS advanced options

9. Select the host cluster that is connected to the datastores in the datastore cluster. Click Next to continue.

10. Select the datastores that will be included in the cluster. Click Next to continue.

11. Review the settings and then click Finish to create the datastore cluster.

NOTE Once you enable Storage DRS, Storage I/O Control is automatically enabled on the datastores in the datastore cluster. SIOC is used to monitor the I/O on the datastore and make placement and migration recommendations. It's worth noting, however, that these two technologies are more complementary than cooperative. SIOC is designed to provide an immediate fix for storage contention, whereas Storage DRS provides more long-term solutions and is invoked much less frequently.

That's all there is to it. You now have a datastore cluster created and Storage DRS enabled to automatically balance out virtual machine disk files to satisfy capacity and performance requirements. It may be simple to set up, but there are still some good practices you should follow when creating datastore clusters:

♦ You cannot combine different datastore types within the same datastore cluster. For example, you cannot combine block-based datastores (FC or iSCSI) with NFS datastores.

♦ Using datastores of varying sizes within a datastore cluster will work, but it will reduce the effectiveness of Storage DRS to balance out storage capacity. When possible, try to use like-sized datastores as part of your datastore cluster.

♦ It is possible to combine datastores of different types (such as SATA and SSD backed datastores) or different storage tiers, but this complicates Storage DRS's ability to satisfy performance requirements and could cause unnecessary migrations to satisfy capacity constraints. If you have multiple tiers of storage, it makes sense to create separate datastore clusters for each.

♦ Using datastores from different storage arrays within the same datastore cluster is also possible, but it's not recommended unless the arrays are configured identically.

♦ Perhaps most important, it is not wise to utilize datastores backed by the same physical disks within the datastore cluster if you are planning to use Storage DRS to balance out I/O demand. Using datastores backed by the same physical disks will make it impossible for Storage DRS to balance out I/O load because I/O saturation at the disk level cannot be solved by simply moving virtual machines between datastores. It is appropriate to do this only when you are concerned with just balancing out capacity and not I/O performance.

Profile-Driven Storage

Profile-Driven Storage is a feature in vSphere that provides a policy-based approach for defining and maintaining storage compliance for virtual machines. Once defined, these capabilities become visible when you're creating new virtual machines or adding new datastores to a datastore cluster, making it easy to make sure the proper datastores are used based on the requirements of the virtual machine. Ongoing compliance checks also notify administrators when virtual machines are not running on the appropriate storage based on their requirements. Additionally, these storage profiles can be accessed from other VMware applications, like VMware vCloud Director.

It all sounds good, but how does vSphere actually know what the capabilities of the storage array are? Let's find out.

VASA

vSphere supports a set of APIs known as the vSphere APIs for Storage Awareness, or VASA. Using VASA, a storage array can advertise particular features about its configuration (such as RAID configuration and thin provisioned LUNs) and have those capabilities automatically associated with the appropriate datastores. Once these capabilities are discovered, they are visible within the vSphere Web Client and can help an administrator make informed choices about where to store virtual machine disk files to meet SLAs.

VASA was introduced with vSphere 5 and is still gaining traction among mainstream storage vendors. VAAI, by comparison, is supported by numerous storage vendors and many different storage arrays. As more storage vendors start to see the benefits of VASA, they will hopefully begin to include VASA support.

VASA requires the use of Storage Providers, which are third-party software plug-ins typically written by the storage vendor. Storage Providers act as a "middle-man," communicating between the backend storage array and vCenter. They communicate the capabilities and status of the array back to vCenter, which can use that information to help make intelligent placement decisions for virtual machines.

User-Defined Storage Capabilities

If a storage array does not support VASA (or if an administrator prefers manual configuration), vSphere administrators can also assign storage capabilities manually. User-defined storage capabilities can actually go beyond what VASA can provide, allowing administrators to define any capability they choose. Considering the current level of VASA support, it is likely that you will have to define at least some storage capabilities manually.

Administrators assign properties to a particular object by assigning tags, or custom properties, to their datastores or datastore clusters. Tags are simply a way to assign properties to a datastore and can be defined as literally anything you want. You could, for example, create a tag called Jerry's Storage Only and assign that tag to a datastore, making it clear that only Jerry should be using that storage. To get any value out of this feature, however, it makes sense to create logical, easy-to-understand tags that make sense from an operational perspective. Good examples of tags include those describing service levels, storage device capabilities, or features of the storage such as Replicated or Deduplicated.

To assign a tag to a datastore or datastore cluster, use the following procedure:

1. Launch the vSphere Web Client and connect to vCenter Server.

2. From the Home view, select Storage.

3. Right-click either the datastore or datastore cluster on which you want to assign the tag and select Assign Tag.

4. Select the icon that looks like a tag with a green plus sign next to it (New Tag). Assign an appropriate name and description for the tag, keeping in mind that you will use this tag later when creating storage policies. Then choose the appropriate category or create a new category. In this example, we'll create a tag called SATA Disk and a category called Tier 3 Storage, as shown in Figure 7.8.

5. Click OK to complete the process of creating the tag and assigning it to the datastore or datastore cluster.

FIGURE 7.8
Creating a tag on a datastore cluster

VM STORAGE POLICIES

Once your datastore capabilities have either been discovered through VASA or assigned manually through the creation of user-defined tags, you can create VM storage policies to make managing virtual machine storage easier. Storage policies are user-defined policies that allow you to group particular virtual machines based on characteristics that you define. For example, you can create a storage policy for Tier 3 virtual machines that are low priority, and associate that policy with datastores that are backed with SATA disks. We'll run through that exact example next.

By default, VM storage policies are disabled and must be enabled for the appropriate clusters or hosts. After policies have been enabled, it's time to create a VM storage policy and show how that can make managing virtual machine placement on specific datastores much easier.

To create a VM storage policy, use the following procedure:

1. Launch the vSphere Web Client and connect to vCenter Server.

2. From the Home view, select VM Storage Policies.

3. Select the icon that looks like a piece of paper with a green plus sign to create a new VM storage policy.

4. Enter an appropriate name and description for the VM storage policy. Remember that this name and description should be meaningful to the people who will ultimately use it. After entering a name and description, click Next.

5. The next screen is an informational screen describing how rule sets work. After reading the information, click Next.

6. Select the button labeled Add Tag-Based Rule to bring up the Add Tag-Based Rule screen. From the Categories drop-down, select the category you created in the previous section. Then select the appropriate tag or tags that were created in the previous section, as shown in Figure 7.9. Click OK to continue, and then click Next to proceed.

FIGURE 7.9
Adding a tag-based rule in a VM storage policy

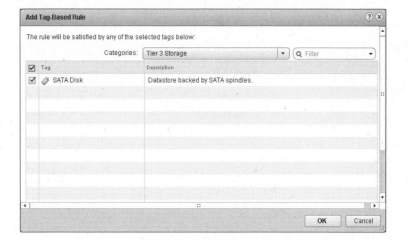

7. Select the matching resources to add to the policy. In this example, we're selecting a datastore cluster, as shown in Figure 7.10. Once the resources have been selected, click Next.

8. After reviewing the configuration of your storage policy, click Finish.

Now that we've created a storage policy, let's see it in action. When creating a new virtual machine, we are given the opportunity to pick a VM storage policy when choosing where to place the virtual machine disk files. As shown in Figure 7.11, when we select our newly created policy called Tier 3 Virtual Machines, only the datastores with matching characteristics are displayed. All other datastores are not visible.

FIGURE 7.10

Selecting matching
storage resources for a
VM storage policy

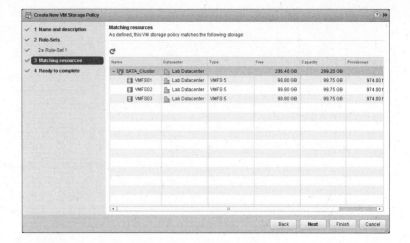

FIGURE 7.11

Selecting the appropri-
ate VM storage policy
for a new virtual
machine

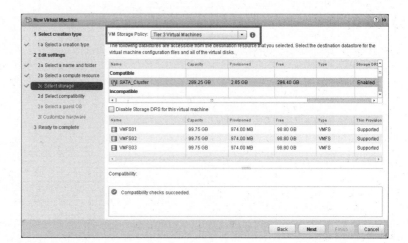

WHY USE PROFILE-DRIVEN STORAGE?

Profile-Driven Storage is primarily a management tool to make placement of virtual machine
disks easier and to help enforce your organization's service levels. Because it's primarily a management tool, why are we talking about it in a book about performance? After all, assigning a
tag labeled SSD on a datastore backed by SATA disks does not suddenly make the datastore perform better (but that sure would be nice).

Profile-Driven Storage will not make your vSphere environment perform better on its own,
but it will help vSphere administrators make better decisions when creating or migrating
virtual machines. VMs that are placed on incorrect datastores based on their profile can lead

to underperforming VMs that might be harder to troubleshoot. For example, Profile-Driven Storage can help make it obvious what storage should be used when an administrator is deploying a new virtual machine for a Tier 1 workload. Without Profile-Driven Storage, the administrator is more likely to make a mistake and choose the wrong datastore or datastore cluster for that virtual machine.

Another benefit of using Profile-Driven Storage is that it can alert you when virtual machines are out of compliance with their assigned VM storage policy. For example, if an administrator performs a Storage vMotion on a virtual machine and moves it to a datastore that does not have the same capabilities as the original datastore, the VM becomes out of compliance and the administrator is alerted to this condition.

Remember, VM storage policies and user-defined tags can be created for any capability that you want. By defining capabilities that make sense to your organization and using clear language in the names and descriptions, you can make it easy for administrators to make the right decisions when creating or moving virtual machines and help to maintain good performance in your environment.

Datastore Size

Perhaps one of the oldest design discussions in VMware virtualization, back in the earliest days of ESX, is this: how large should I make my datastores and how many virtual machines should I run per datastore? There are administrators and architects on all sides of this discussion, often swearing by their positions. For example, for years a common recommendation for VMFS datastore sizing was "500 GB VMFS volumes and no more than 15 VMs per datastore." When faced with recommendations like these, hopefully you'll think back to our favorite phrase, "Numbers without context are meaningless."

The truth is, without knowledge of the workload profile of the virtual machines, there is no way of knowing how many should run per datastore. Combine that with the fact that technologies in vSphere like Storage DRS can automatically move VMDKs among datastores, and you'll see that hard limited recommendations like that are not recommended.

There are a number of reasons that having a standardized datastore size and number of virtual machines per datastore is something of an antiquated recommendation:

- ♦ Storage DRS is capable of automatically moving VMDKs to solve both capacity and performance issues. Automating the movement of VMDKs on your datastores makes it almost impossible to know how many VMs are running on a single datastore at any time. More important, you don't really need to know the actual number, provided performance is being managed via Storage DRS and Storage I/O Control.

- ♦ Without knowing the type of I/O generated by the virtual machines, you can't make an intelligent decision about datastore placement. Instead, it is better to let Storage DRS and Storage I/O Control handle the placement and movement based on actual utilization.

- ♦ vSphere now supports datastores up to 64 TB in size. With datastores that large, limiting the number of virtual machines would be wasteful. Additionally, VMDKs can now be up to 62 TB in size, which necessitates very large datastores.

- ♦ Limiting the number of virtual machines on a datastore used to be more important prior to the introduction of VAAI. With large numbers of VMs on a single datastore, VMFS metadata updates caused SCSI reservations that reduced the performance of all other VMs on the datastore. VAAI has virtually eliminated that problem, so having more VMs on a datastore is less of an issue.

◆ There are uses cases like VDI that necessitate large numbers of VMs, so putting an artificial limit on the number of VMs per datastore would make these use cases difficult to manage.

As you can see, there are many reasons using a datastore sizing methodology that limits the number of VMs per datastore is not always ideal. Instead, a better strategy is to choose a datastore size that accommodates the requirements of your virtual machines while leaving room for things like growth and virtual machine snapshots. Then use both Storage DRS and Storage I/O Control to manage the performance and capacity of your datastores. Your storage vendor may also offer guidance on datastore sizing based on the particular features offered by its products.

Remember that the size of a virtual machine is more than just the size of the VMDKs. You need to factor in the size of the VMkernel swap file, which is equal in size to the configured memory of the virtual machine (minus any defined memory reservation). There are also virtual machine configuration files and log files that consume space on the disk. And if you plan on using virtual machine snapshots, you should account for extra overhead as well. Though there is no "rule" defining how much overhead you should reserve for snapshots, 20 percent is a reasonable amount to reserve in most cases. If you use snapshots more frequently, a higher number may be more appropriate.

vFlash Read Cache

Flash storage has become a large disruptor in the storage industry, providing levels of performance many times faster than the fastest available spinning disk. Vendors are including flash as a storage tier in an array that also uses spinning disks, and others are offering entire arrays with nothing but flash. Flash is also being used as a cache layer to improve performance of disk I/O before it hits spinning disks. And beyond that, other vendors are offering flash on a PCIe card for extreme performance use cases.

Not wanting to be left out of the flash party, VMware has introduced features that leverage flash starting with vSphere 5. In vSphere 5.5, VMware has introduced the vFlash Read Cache, or vFRC, as a way to leverage flash storage to improve virtual machine performance. vFRC consists of flash stored locally in an ESXi host, either as a SAS-/SATA-based SSD or PCIe-based flash, that is presented to individual virtual machines to use as a read cache. Using flash in this capacity can greatly improve the performance of virtual machines that consume a lot of read I/O. In some cases, as you'll see, it can even improve performance for virtual machines that are heavily write I/O bound.

vFRC is configured on a per-virtual-hard-disk level (on each virtual machine) rather than via a global setting that applies to all virtual machines. Though this introduces some administrative overhead in configuring vFRC, because it must be enabled on each virtual disk on every VM that requires it, the benefit is that you can tune the configuration to each specific workload. This is especially useful for virtual machines that have multiple hard disks and only some, but not all, of the disks can benefit from vFRC. By assigning the cache at the virtual hard disk level, you are not forced to share the cache with read I/Os that do not need to be accelerated. A good example of this scenario would be a database server, where optimizing the read I/Os for the database VMDK is beneficial while reads on the operating system or log VMDKs would not be beneficial and would waste flash storage space.

For each virtual disk file, vFRC requires you to configure cache size and cache block size:

◆ Cache size is the actual size, configured in megabytes or gigabytes, of the flash cache devoted to each virtual machine. The cache size needs to be large enough to accommodate the amount of read requests performed by the virtual machine but not so large that it consumes precious flash storage unnecessarily.

◆ Cache block size is the size of the blocks of data that will be entered into, and subsequently read from, the vFRC. It is important to size the vFRC cache block size correctly based on the actual workload profile of the virtual machine. An incorrectly sized cache block size will reduce the effectiveness of vFRC and reduce any potential performance gains.

Each host must have flash storage configured in order for vFRC to be effective. When each host in the cluster has flash storage available for use as vFRC, virtual machines can vMotion between hosts while retaining the data in their cache. During a vMotion operation on a VM configured with vFRC, you are presented with the option of either migrating the cache with the virtual machine or dropping the cache altogether, as shown in Figure 7.12. Migrating the cache will help the virtual machine maintain good performance but at the cost of a longer vMotion migration. Dropping the cache will allow the vMotion to complete more quickly but could impact the performance of the virtual machine because the cache has to rebuild on the new host. For it to be possible to migrate the vFRC for a virtual machine, the destination host must have enough flash storage available to accommodate the migrated cache.

vMotion also supports the ability to only migrate the contents of the vFRC for individual virtual hard disks on a virtual machine. When migrating a virtual machine, there may be scenarios where it makes sense to drop the contents of the cache for certain virtual hard disks while retaining it for others. This is another reason that really knowing and understanding your workload profile can help you make informed decisions and maintain good performance.

Determine vFlash Read Cache Size

The first step to using vFlash Read Cache is to determine the vFRC cache size for your virtual machines. This is not an arbitrary number, so having some knowledge of your workload is important here. It might be tempting to assign a large amount of flash to the vFRC for a particular VM if you are unsure of what to assign, but that can end up reducing overall performance for a few reasons:

◆ Assigning too much flash storage for vFRC takes away cache that could have otherwise been used for other workloads. If you assign a lot more cache to a virtual machine than it can use, you are potentially taking flash away from another VM that might benefit.

◆ A large vFRC can take a significantly long time to vMotion, increasing the time it takes to evacuate a host when using maintenance mode or for load-balancing purposes. The vFRC file that is created on flash storage is similar to a thick provisioned disk, meaning all blocks are allocated even if they are not in use. For example, if a virtual machine has a 10 GB vFRC but is only utilizing 1 GB of it, a vMotion operation would still need to migrate all 10 GB over the vMotion network (in addition to the contents of the VM's RAM).

◆ In the event of a host failure, vSphere HA is able to restart a virtual machine configured with vFRC only if enough flash resources are available on the other host. If none of the hosts have enough flash resources, the virtual machine(s) is not powered up.

FIGURE 7.12
vFlash Read Cache can
be migrated with a vir-
tual machine during
vMotion or dropped
and started fresh on
the new host.

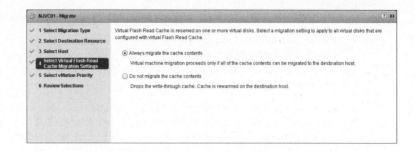

As you can see, choosing the correct read cache size is not trivial. It is important to really know the type of workload that you're running before configuring vFRC so you can set the cache size correctly. VMware recommends, in the absence of other detailed application data, starting with an approximate value of around 20 percent of the VMDK size (or the application's dataset, such as the size of the database) as a starting point. Having some knowledge of the application is helpful here. For example, if you know that you're working with a database that is 20 GB in size and you wish to try to cache the entire database, you would make the cache size 20 GB.

It is not always possible to size the cache correctly when it is created. We'll discuss how you can monitor the vFRC to determine if the size needs to be adjusted in just a few pages.

DETERMINE vFLASH READ CACHE BLOCK SIZE

The other piece of the vFlash Read Cache puzzle is determining the proper block size. Once again, knowing the application can help, so working with application owners may be required. If you don't have any other method of determining the correct block size, however, there is one available in ESXi to figure this out.

For years, the ESX/ESXi platforms have included a tool called vscsiStats that can be used to gather a great deal of storage data on each individual virtual disk of a virtual machine. While tools like esxtop/resxtop and vCenter are good at providing real-time data on storage latency and throughput, they do not go down to the individual I/O level as vscsiStats does. You'll recall we covered vscsiStats back in Chapter 2. One of the pieces of information that vscsiStats can provide is the most common block size for the I/Os generated during the time the disks were monitored. You can use this data to determine the most appropriate block size for vFRC on each virtual disk.

To use vscsiStats, use the following procedure. Note that vscsiStats is a somewhat resource-intensive monitoring tool, so it shouldn't be run for extended periods of time if resources are constrained on your ESXi host.

1. Connect to the console of your ESXi host and log in as a user with elevated privileges.

2. Run the following command to determine the world_group_id of the virtual machine you wish to monitor:

   ```
   /usr/lib/vmware/bin/vscsiStats -l
   ```

3. Start the data collection by running the following command:

   ```
   /usr/lib/vmware/bin/vscsiStats -s -w <world_group_id>
   ```

For example, if the world_group_id of the virtual machine is 3137850, the command would look like this:

```
/usr/lib/vmware/bin/vscsiStats -s -w 3137850
```

4. The data collection will run for about 30 minutes and automatically stop. If you wish to collect data over a longer period of time, you can issue the same command as in step 3 to continue data collection for another 30 minutes and the data will append to the previous 30 minutes. Keep in mind the performance impact of vscsiStats, so don't run the tests for an extended period of time if the ESXi host utilization is high.

5. Once the data collection has completed, you can export the gathered data into a comma-separated values (CSV) file for analysis in tools like Microsoft Excel. To export the data to CSV format, issue the following command:

```
/usr/lib/vmware/bin/vscsiStats -w <world_group_id> -p <histo_type> -c
>outputfilename.csv
```

There are several histo_type values supported by vscsiStats. They include all, ioLength, seekDistance, outstandingIOs, latency, and interarrival. For determining the most common block size, use the histo_type called ioLength:

```
/usr/lib/vmware/bin/vscsiStats -w 3137850 -p ioLength -c > ioLength.csv
```

Once the data capture is complete, copy the CSV output file (in this example, ioLength .csv) to your computer for analysis in an application like Microsoft Excel. The relevant output of vscsiStats for vFRC is called "Histogram: IO lengths of Read commands" and shows how many read commands were issued at each block size. Figure 7.13 shows an example out of vscsiStats, clearly indicating that the block size 8,192 (8 KB) is the most frequently read block size for this particular workload. From this data, we can see that 8 KB is the most appropriate cache block size for vFRC.

FIGURE 7.13
Histogram from vscsiStats showing size of read I/Os on a virtual machine

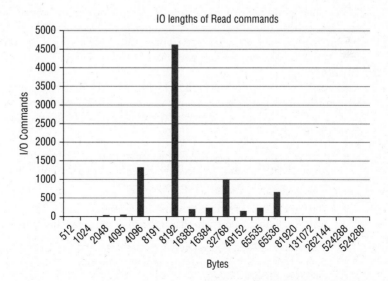

The impact of choosing the wrong cache block size can be seen in the overall performance of vFRC. Choosing a cache size that's too small or too big can result in reduced effectiveness for the cache and a lower overall performance benefit. For example, let's say you've chosen 4 KB as the block size but the most common read block size is actually 512 KB. To write 512 KB blocks to the vFRC, they must first be broken into smaller 4 KB blocks. Those blocks may not end up on contiguous segments of the disk, causing a delay when they need to be read out of the cache. This delay can significantly reduce the effectiveness of the vFRC.

Similarly, sizing the cache block size too large can have a negative effect on performance. Let's use the same scenario, except reversed: Let's say we have configured a vFRC with a 512 KB block size but the most common read block size is actually 4 KB. Once the cache fills up with data, any new data will require that previously cached data is evicted, or removed from the cache. In this scenario, the vFRC would have to evict 512 KB of data in order to store the new 4 KB block of data that was just read. Not only is this an inefficient use of cache storage, it is also more likely to reduce performance because valid data may end up being evicted from the cache.

As you can see, choosing the wrong cache block size can reduce the effectiveness of vFRC and should be avoided whenever possible. If the block size of the application is not well known, use vscsiStats to determine the most common read block size so that you can configure the vFRC properly.

CHOOSE YOUR FLASH DEVICE

vFRC supports both flash devices that are attached via SATA/SAS connections and PCIe cards. Typically, PCIe cards perform significantly faster than SATA- or SAS-attached flash storage due to the speed of the PCIe bus, offering much greater performance but also for a higher cost. Since vFRC supports both types of flash devices, choose the one that meets your performance requirements the best.

MONITOR vFLASH READ CACHE EFFECTIVENESS

You've done your homework and determined the proper cache size and cache block size and you've just configured vFRC on a virtual machine. Now what? How do you know whether it's helping to improve performance? Maybe you'll know because the end users and application owners will bring you cake and your boss will give you the rest of the day off. Maybe, but probably not.

Instead, VMware provides two different methods for determining how well the vFRC is performing on your virtual machines. First, there are vFRC performance counters that are exposed in vCenter. These counters are part of the virtual disk object and present the following three statistics:

◆ Virtual Flash Read Cache I/Os per second for the virtual disk: the number of read I/Os per second that are being serviced by the vFRC. A high number here is a good indication of how frequently the cache is being accessed.

◆ Virtual Flash Read Cache throughput for the virtual disk: the amount of data being read from the vFRC. Again, a high number indicates that the cache is being used frequently.

◆ Virtual Flash Read Cache latency for the virtual disk: the amount of read latency when the disk is being read. Note that this latency is presented in microseconds, not milliseconds as it is typically presented.

To view these stats in vCenter, follow these simple steps:

1. Launch the vSphere Web Client and connect to vCenter Server.

2. From the Home view, select the Hosts And Clusters view or the VMs And Templates view. Find and select the virtual machine you wish to monitor.

3. Select the Monitor tab, and then select Performance. Change the view from Overview to Advanced.

4. Change the chart type to virtual disk, and click Chart Options to add the three vFlash Read Cache counters listed previously. Note that you will need to remove the default latency counters first before you can display the vFRC counters. Once you've selected the counters, click OK to display the vFRC usage, shown in Figure 7.14.

The second method of gathering vFRC usage statistics is via the ESXi console and the `esxcli` command. This command gives much more detail and statistics about how the vFRC is being used and can be helpful in determining if the cache is actually helping improve the VM's performance.

To access the `esxcli` command, use the following procedure:

1. Connect to the console of the ESXi host on which the VM you wish to monitor is running and log in as a user with elevated privileges. Alternatively, you can use the vSphere CLI from a Windows or Linux workstation.

2. Run the following command to determine the name of the cache file for your virtual machine:

   ```
   Esxcli storage vflash cache list
   ```

3. Using the cache file name you determined in step 2, issue the following command to view statistics about cache usage:

   ```
   Esxcli storage vflash cache stats get -c <name_of_cache_file>
   ```

   For example, if the cache file is named `vfc-3069824598-NJVC01`, you would issue the following `esxcli` command:

   ```
   Esxcli storage vflash cache stats get -c vfc-3069824598-NJVC01
   ```

Figure 7.15 shows the output of the `esxcli` command. Useful data such as `Read: Cache hit rate (as a percentage):` can show how frequently the cache is being used, with a higher percentage being a more frequently accessed cache. You can also view total IOPS, latency, and statistics about cache block evictions.

You can use the output of this command to view how effectively the cache is performing and also to determine if the total cache size is too big or too small. Let's say you've started conservatively and created a vFRC size of 6 GB with a block size of 8 KB for a particular VMDK. By dividing 6 GB (in bytes) by 8 KB (in bytes), you determine the total number of blocks in the cache:

$$6,442,450,944 / 8192 = 7,86,432 \text{ total blocks in our vFRC}$$

FIGURE 7.14
Virtual Flash Read
Cache counters in
vCenter

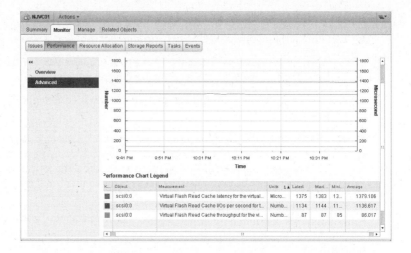

FIGURE 7.15
Output of `esxcli`
command to view
Virtual Flash Read
Cache counters
statistics

Looking at Figure 7.15, you can see the total number of blocks in use in the cache is 476,845 (represented by `Mean number of cache blocks in use:`). If the number of blocks in the cache is significantly lower than the number of blocks in use, as it is in our example here, you can surmise that your vFRC size is probably too large and it can be reduced. If the number of blocks in use and the total block size are equal, either you have a perfectly sized vFRC or, much more likely, you need to increase the size of the cache. Before you increase the size of the cache, it makes sense to know how effective the cache actually is for the particular workload. If the workload is primarily performing random read I/O, then the cache could be filling up with blocks but not frequently accessing them again. To determine if that is the case, look at the field `Read: Cache hit rate (as a percentage):` to see your cache hit rate. If it is low, such as the 25 percent rate you see in Figure 7.15, it could be an indication that the vFRC is sized too large or the workload simply isn't a good use case for vFRC in the first place.

Next, we need to look at the number of blocks that are being evicted from the vFRC. Blocks are evicted to make room for new blocks, so a large number of cache evictions could be an indication that the vFRC is sized too small. Look at the field labeled `Evict: Mean blocks per I/O operation` to see how many cache block evictions are taking place. A high value could indicate that the cache is too small, but you should verify how effective the cache is by looking at the cache hit rate before making any changes. It could also indicate an incorrectly sized cache block size as discussed earlier.

You may need to continue to monitor these vFRC stats over time as you increase or decrease the size of the cache until you find a balance that works for the workload. For example, if you decrease the size of the cache and notice that there are more cache evictions taking place, it's likely that the cache is now too small. Similarly, if you increase the size and notice that evictions go down but the overall cache hit rate is not increasing, it may not be necessary to increase the size of the cache.

Monitoring how frequently the vFRC is being used for a virtual machine is important as an ongoing task in order to most efficiently use your flash storage. If a virtual machine is not making effective use of the cache or is only using it infrequently, it may make sense to remove the cache and assign it to other virtual machines that will use it more frequently and benefit from the performance gains.

Choose Appropriate Workloads for vFRC

Choosing workloads that are good candidates for vFRC is the best way to make the most effective and efficient use of this feature. For a virtual machine to be a good candidate for vFRC, it should meet the following criteria:

- The workload should have a large percentage of its I/O as read I/O. vFRC, as the name implies, accelerates only reads, so write-heavy workloads will not benefit.

- The virtual machine should access the same data frequently, allowing subsequent reads to come out of the cache instead of from the disk. Workloads that read random bits of data, infrequently reading the same data over and over, will not see as much benefit from vFRC as those that read the same data frequently.

- The working set data, or the data that is accessed frequently, should be small enough so that it can fit within the configurable size of the vFRC. In other words, if the active working set of data on the virtual machine is 150 GB and you only have 120 GB of available flash storage, data will frequently need to be evicted from the cache to make room for newly cached data. In that scenario, you are unlikely to see a large performance gain.

Despite the fact that the vFRC is only a read cache, it can actually indirectly improve write performance. Consider the scenario of four virtual machines on the same backend storage where two are read I/O heavy and two are write I/O heavy. Under normal circumstances, the storage array must handle both the read I/O and the write I/O. If vFRC is configured on the two read-heavy virtual machines, the read I/O can be offloaded to the cache while the storage array only has to handle the write I/O. This reduction in total I/O can help reduce the burden on the storage array and improve write performance.

Caveats for Using vFlash Read Cache

Up until this point you thought vFRC was nothing but rainbows and unicorns, right? The truth is that vFRC is a great feature for improving performance, but it is also the first iteration of the feature as of vSphere 5.5. There are some caveats that you should be aware of before implementing vFRC in your environment:

◆ vFRC is not compatible with VMDKs that are larger than 16 TB in size.

◆ For a virtual machine to take advantage of vFRC, it must be running VM version 10 compatibility mode (ESXi 5.5 or later). While this in and of itself is not a bad thing, VM version 10 virtual machines can be edited only in the vSphere Web Client, which some folks may find undesirable, especially in situations when vCenter is unavailable. If vCenter is unavailable and you need to modify the VM's settings, you need to manually edit the VM's configuration file (VMX file).

◆ As stated earlier, vSphere HA will not automatically restart a failed vFRC virtual machine if other hosts in the cluster do not have enough free flash storage available to accommodate the vFRC cache file. Unlike with CPU or memory, vSphere DRS cannot defragment the cluster, or perform vMotion migrations to free up enough flash resources to accommodate the virtual machine.

◆ vSphere DRS will not automatically load balance virtual machines that have vFRC configured except under certain specific conditions, such as when a host goes into maintenance mode or to fix a DRS rule violation (affinity or anti-affinity).

NOTE The Release Notes for vSphere 5.5 lists these and other known issues with the first generation of vFlash Read Cache. If you plan on using vFRC in your environment, you should review the Release Notes to make yourself aware of these issues. You can find the vSphere 5.5 Release Notes at the following location:

`www.vmware.com/support/vsphere5/doc/vsphere-esx-vcenter-server-55-release-notes.html`

vFlash Read Cache is a great new feature of vSphere 5.5 and offers the promise of significantly improving virtual machine performance. If you have flash capacity in your ESXi hosts, you should test and determine whether your virtual machines can benefit from using vFRC. Though there is some upfront work in determining the proper cache size and cache block size, the improved performance for a good candidate workload will more than make up for it.

Read More about vFlash Read Cache

VMware has released a paper entitled "Performance of vSphere Flash Read Cache in vSphere 5.5" that covers some technical information about vFRC and reviews the results of several performance studies on the effectiveness of vFRC. You can download the paper at the following location:

`http://blogs.vmware.com/performance/2013/10/vfrc_vsphere55.html`

In addition, VMware has also released a great "Frequently Asked Questions (FAQ)" document answering common questions about vFlash Read Cache. You can read the FAQ here:

`www.vmware.com/files/pdf/techpaper/VMware-vSphere-Flash-Read-Cache-FAQ.pdf`

Virtual SAN

We touched on Virtual SAN, or VSAN, a little earlier when we talked about the different storage options available. VSAN deserves its own section because it is different from the others in that it is neither VMFS nor NFS—it is a completely different architecture that requires at least vSphere 5.5. And yes, that's an uppercase V in VSAN. Despite the fact that the names of numerous vSphere technologies include a lowercase v (such as vMotion, vFlash, and vCPU), VMware decided to use an uppercase V in VSAN.

VSAN works by taking the local disks in ESXi hosts and combining them to create a common datastore that is accessible by all hosts in the cluster. The data is replicated between hosts so that an individual host is not a single point of failure. VSAN requires a dedicated VMkernel port on each ESXi host, and it uses that network to replicate the data blocks that make up the virtual machines hosted on the VSAN datastore. It is possible to use either 1 Gb or 10 Gb NICs for VSAN, but using 10 Gb is ideal, especially as the number of virtual machines grows.

At a minimum, VSAN requires one hard disk (non-SSD) and one SSD in order to create a VSAN datastore. The server also needs a hard drive controller capable of pass-through, allowing it to present the characteristics of each individual disk drive to the operating system (or in this case, vSphere). VSAN uses the drives in a way that's similar to the way a hybrid SAN uses both kinds of storage. That is, the faster SSD is used as a caching layer for reads and a buffer for writes while the larger spinning disks are used to satisfy disk capacity requirements. Additional hard drives can be used to improve performance in certain scenarios, but SSDs can only be used for caching, and they do not contribute to the overall storage capacity.

NOTE The following sections are not intended to be a deep dive on the architecture of VSAN. Instead, we'll focus on how the configuration of VSAN can impact the performance of virtual machines. A deeper look into the architecture and management of VSAN can be found at www .vmware.com/resources/techresources/10391.

DISTRIBUTED RAID

Earlier in this chapter we covered the common RAID configurations and the impact they can have on virtual machine performance. If you're going to use VSAN, however, you can forget all of that—VSAN doesn't use traditional RAID configurations.

Each ESXi host that participates in the VSAN cluster requires a disk controller. It is possible to use a RAID controller, but the controller must be in pass-through mode or HBA mode. These modes allow the RAID controller to pass through the hard drives as individual disks rather than grouping them together as one logical disk as is normally done with RAID configurations. This is important because with VSAN, vSphere is managing the disk configuration and needs to be able to recognize things like a single disk failure.

This configuration can be thought of as distributed RAID, where the cluster can now tolerate the loss of an entire ESXi host rather than just the loss of a disk or disks in a traditional RAID configuration. VSAN can accomplish this because data is replicated between the hosts in the VSAN cluster based on policies (which we'll cover next), eliminating a host, hard drive, or network as a single point of failure. The replication that VSAN leverages is known as synchronous replication, meaning that writes to the storage have to be acknowledged on the hard drives on which the virtual machine is running but also on all ESXi hosts that are hosting a replica before the write can be acknowledged back to the virtual machine. Using synchronous replication guarantees that all hosts in the VSAN cluster have the same copy of the data so the loss of a single host (or disk) does not cause a failure of the virtual machine.

THE IMPORTANCE OF NETWORKING IN VSAN

VSAN relies on synchronous replication to replicate data between ESXi hosts, placing a burden on the network. Synchronous replication technologies like VSAN are very intolerant of latency, and increased latency at the network level can result in severely degraded performance that is visible to end users.

If you plan on using VSAN, strongly consider using 10 GbE NICs on your ESXi hosts for replication. In addition, the concepts discussed in Chapter 6 for maintaining good networking performance on your ESXi hosts are very applicable here.

SOLID STATE DISKS

Unlike vFlash Read Cache, which we discussed earlier, the role of the SSD in VSAN is twofold: it serves as a read cache as well as a write buffer. In both, the goal is to improve performance by allowing the cluster to scale out using cheaper spinning disks for capacity while using SSDs to increase read and write performance.

The read caching done by VSAN is not that different from the way vFRC utilizes SSDs. The major difference between the two, however, is that VSAN is a distributed technology whereas vFRC stores cache data only on a single host. What that means in real terms is that the data being read on the virtual machine on one host might exist in the read cache sitting on another host. VSAN uses a directory of the blocks that have been cached, distributed across all hosts in the cluster, to know which host has the particular set of cached blocks. Just as with the vFRC, if the data does not exist in VSAN's read cache, then it is retrieved from the hard drives and stored in the cache for subsequent read activity.

When it comes to writing data, VSAN leverages SSDs as a buffer to increase performance before writes are destaged, or written back to the slower spinning disks. In simple terms, that means that all writes are committed and acknowledged on the SSD and then destaged to the spinning disks afterward. However, to guarantee availability, the cache must be written to both the local cache and the SSD in the other hosts in the cluster. Because SSDs are much faster than even the fastest spinning disk, using SSDs as a write buffer can reduce latency and improve performance.

STORAGE POLICIES

VSAN is designed to be a true implementation of software-defined storage, or storage that can be managed as a resource through policies defined in vSphere. To that end, VSAN makes heavy use of VM Storage Policies (similar to the storage policies described earlier) to define specific properties about the storage that an administrator uses when deploying and managing virtual machines. With VSAN, an administrator can define a specific set of requirements for availability, performance, and sizing and allow vSphere to manage the placement of VMDKs and choose the correct datastore when deploying a new virtual machine. To help determine the capabilities of the underlying storage hardware, VSAN leverages VASA to expose details about the hardware to allow those capabilities to be included in storage policies.

Storage policies are configured using the same method we described earlier in this chapter. VSAN has several capabilities that are defined to control availability, performance, and sizing requirements. These requirements are then assigned to VMs on a per-VM basis, meaning that different VMs can have different requirements and as such will automatically get assigned to different VSAN datastores.

Number of Failures to Tolerate

The capability Number of Failures to Tolerate controls how many VSAN resources (host, disk, or network) can fail and not decrease availability of the virtual machine. By default, each virtual machine has at least one replica copy on another set of disks within the VSAN cluster. The Number of Failures to Tolerate capability allows you to specify an additional number of failures that can be tolerated before the availability of the virtual machine is compromised.

If you have a somewhat large VSAN cluster, it might be tempting to set this to a relatively high number to help ensure availability of your virtual machines. In reality, it makes sense to increase this value only if the VM's specific availability requirements dictate it. Remember, VSAN uses synchronous replication and all writes must be acknowledged to all hosts that maintain a replica copy of the virtual machine. Increasing this number for a large number of virtual machines will increase network traffic on your VSAN network and potentially introduce latency, especially with write I/O–heavy workloads. Increase this value only for the virtual machines that really need it.

Number of Disk Stripes per Object

The capability Number of Disk Stripes per Object controls the total number of physical disks on which each virtual machine replica is distributed. If you think about how striping data across multiple disks in a typical RAID configuration works, you might think that increasing this number will improve performance. It's possible that increasing this number will improve performance, but not in the same way that striping works on traditional RAID configurations.

The key thing to remember about disk stripes when thinking about virtual machine performance is that VSAN uses fast SSDs for both read caching and write buffering. Since SSDs are always faster than spinning disks, increasing the number of disk stripes may not automatically make the VM perform better. If the virtual machine is extremely write heavy where it is saturating the SSD and writes cannot be destaged to disk fast enough, increasing the disk stripe value might improve performance.

Similarly, if the virtual machine is read heavy and reads cannot be serviced from the read cache, having a larger number of disk stripes may help improve performance. In this way, disk stripes do act more like traditional RAID configurations in that data can be read from more than one disk at a time and performance can be improved.

Of course, increasing the disk stripes comes at a cost of higher storage consumption per virtual machine. In general, the default value of one is applicable for most workloads. Before increasing stripe count, make sure to properly monitor your virtual machines to make sure they can really benefit from additional disk stripes. For example, if the workloads are primarily read heavy and most reads are being serviced by the read cache, increasing the disk stripes is unlikely to improve performance.

Flash Read Cache Reservation

Flash Read Cache Reservation allows you to configure a specific amount of flash storage to reserve for virtual machines as a read cache. A reservation works just like a reservation for other resources in that the resource is reserved for the sole use of a virtual machine, taking the potential resource away from other virtual machines.

A reservation can be useful in scenarios when workloads are read heavy and you know they will benefit from having more read cache available to them than other virtual machines. Increasing the read cache of read-heavy workloads can also have the effect of increasing write performance since fewer I/Os need to be devoted to reads on the backend hard drives. Of course, configuring a reservation is not actually required in order for VSAN to cache reads for virtual machines. In most circumstances, allowing VSAN to manage access to read cache resources is the ideal configuration because it is simpler and allows more fair access to the read cache for all virtual machines.

Object Space Reservation

Object Space Reservation allows administrators to define whether virtual machine data is stored as thin or thick on the backend (non-SSD) hard drives. By default, all data on the VSAN is stored as thin, but administrators can define a percentage to determine how much of the virtual disk's space will be reserved on the VSAN datastore. This is a useful configuration because some applications do not support thin provisioning technologies.

DESIGNING VSAN FOR PERFORMANCE

VSAN offers the promise of software-defined storage and may allow administrators to better control availability and performance for virtual machines. However, you'll be successful with VSAN only if it can deliver the performance required by your organization's virtual machines. With that in mind, the following list highlights some key things to remember when designing VSAN for performance:

- Whenever possible, use 10 GbE networking for VSAN. The synchronous replication requirement means that there could be a significant amount of data transmitted over the network. Using 10 GbE networks can help eliminate any network bandwidth bottlenecks.

- Utilize dedicated NICs for VSAN traffic. Don't allow other types of network traffic, such as vMotion or virtual machine traffic, to traverse the same physical NICs as those used for VSAN. Again, the synchronous replication requirement of VSAN demands low-latency transmissions, so sending traffic other than VSAN traffic down those NICs can introduce latency and reduce performance.

- Choose the right SSD for your environment. Remember that the SSD is shared between read cache and write buffering, so choosing large enough SSDs is key to making sure there is enough flash storage for each function. If there is not enough flash storage available, reads and writes may have to be serviced directly from the spinning hard disks, which will reduce performance.

- Just as with traditional storage and storage arrays, you can create multiple disk groups in VSAN based on the underlying capabilities of the disks. Keep this in mind when designing the storage in your ESXi hosts. It may make sense to once again use the concept of tiering

by configuring ESXi hosts with disks of varying speeds depending on overall requirements. Even though the SSDs should take care of read caching and write buffering,
there are times when data has to be written to or read directly from the underlying spinning disk.

Jumbo Frames for IP Storage

If your organization is using IP storage like iSCSI or NFS, configuring jumbo frames can help
improve storage performance. You'll recall from Chapter 6 that jumbo frames are Ethernet
frames larger than the standard 1,500 bytes and are typically 9,000 bytes in size. By increasing the amount of data that can be included in each Ethernet frame, you can reduce the total
number of frames that need to be transmitted and processed and improve performance. Using
jumbo frames does not always improve performance because it can be dependent on the workload, but configuring it for IP storage is usually recommended by storage vendors and network
administrators alike.

For jumbo frames to be effective, they must be configured at every level within the network
path. For example, for jumbo frames to improve performance for iSCSI storage, they must be
configured at the VMkernel adapter, the vSwitch (or dvSwitch), and the physical switches in
the network path to the backend storage and on the backend iSCSI storage itself. If any of the
devices within the path are not configured for jumbo frames, the frames are broken back into
standard frames and any performance benefit is lost. Even worse, performance can actually
degrade in that scenario. If you're going to use jumbo frames, and we think you should, make
sure you can work with the appropriate teams (vSphere, networking, and storage) to make sure
they are configured properly along the entire path.

Thankfully, configuring jumbo frames in vSphere is easy. To configure jumbo frames on a
distributed vSwitch and on the appropriate VMkernel adapters, use the following procedure:

1. Launch the vSphere Web Client and connect to vCenter Server.

2. From the Home view, select Networking.

3. Right-click on the dvSwitch and select Edit Settings.

4. Select Advanced to bring up the advanced options for the dvSwitch. Change the value of
    the MTU (Bytes) option from the default of 1500 to the appropriate jumbo frames value
    for your environment. You may need to work with your networking team to determine
    the correct value to enter here. Typically, entering 9000, as shown in Figure 7.16, is appro-
    priate. Click OK to complete the configuration of jumbo frames on your dvSwitch.

5. Select the Home view, and then select the Hosts And Clusters view.

6. Select an ESXi host, select the Manage tab, and then select Networking.

7. Select VMkernel Adapters on the left, and click the appropriate adapter (labeled vmk$n$,
    where n is the number of the adapter). Select the icon that looks like a pencil to edit the
    settings of the VMkernel adapter.

8. Select NIC Settings from the menu on the left, and change the MTU value to match the
    MTU value set in step 4. Click OK to save the settings, and repeat steps 6 through 8 for all
    appropriate VMkernel adapters.

FIGURE 7.16

Configuring jumbo frames on a dvSwitch

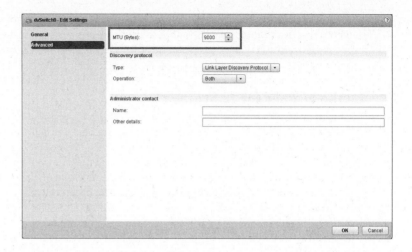

One more place where jumbo frames can be configured is inside the virtual machine. Certain scenarios may require the use of in-guest iSCSI, or connecting directly to iSCSI storage from within a virtual machine. If you are using in-guest iSCSI, it may make sense to configure jumbo frames inside the virtual machine.

Jumbo frames are supported on the default E1000 or E1000e virtual NIC as well as the higher-performance paravirtualized VMXNET3 virtual NIC. Jumbo frames can be configured on a virtual network card by editing the advanced properties of the NIC and modifying the Jumbo Packet value, as shown in Figure 7.17.

FIGURE 7.17

Configuring jumbo frames on a virtual NIC

As we discussed in Chapter 6, using in-guest iSCSI is generally not recommended. It completely bypasses the ESXi storage stack and relies on the guest to process all storage-related traffic. It also complicates the proper configuration of multipathing software. In general, using in-guest iSCSI is discouraged unless you have a specific requirement to do so. If you are going to configure jumbo frames inside a virtual machine, remember that it still must be configured end to end for it to be effective.

Finally, configuring jumbo frames when using VSAN can also improve performance. Though VSAN might not be the first type of storage you think of when you hear "IP storage," in reality it relies on the Ethernet network for synchronous replication of virtual machine data. Configuring jumbo frames can help improve the replication performance of VSAN.

Optimizing Virtual Machine Performance

Thus far we've talked about how to configure the various storage features of vSphere to get optimal performance. These settings are defined on the ESXi host and are designed to apply to multiple virtual machines at once. Beyond the ESXi host, there are decisions to be made on a per-VM level that can impact performance. In the following sections, we'll review some of these decisions and how they can impact the performance of your virtual machines.

Raw Device Mapping vs. VMDK Files

A common question that comes up when talking about virtual machine performance is whether to use raw device mappings (RDMs) or VMDK files for virtual machine storage. In fact, this question has persisted for many years across many versions of the ESXi platform. It's time to put the question to bed for good.

RDMs provide a way to present LUNs from a SAN directly to a virtual machine, exposing the raw SCSI disks rather than abstracting them into a VMFS datastore. RDMs are useful for applications that require direct SAN access, such as those that leverage SAN-based snapshots or replication. RDMs are also required for some Microsoft clustering configurations, though Microsoft appears to be moving away from shared disk clusters on its enterprise applications, so the need to use RDMs to support clustering may be reduced.

There seems to be a "best practice" that has circulated around for years stating that RDMs provide better storage performance than VMDKs. VMware has done several performance studies that prove that there is barely a measurable difference in performance between RDMs and VMDKs. In general, you should not make a decision on whether to use RDMs as opposed to VMDKs strictly on the basis of performance. RDMs are required for specific scenarios, but a high I/O workload is not one of those scenarios.

VMware has introduced many new features into the ESXi storage stack over the last few versions of vSphere, and nearly all of them require VMDKs rather than RDMs. In a way, using VMDKs future-proofs your environment against any new features that VMware may release in newer versions of vSphere. VMDKs are usually more flexible, offer better access to vSphere storage features, and are appropriate for nearly all workloads. Only those that require either Microsoft clustering or direct access to SAN technologies should leverage RDMs.

PERFORMANCE STUDIES OF RDM VS. VMDK

VMware has conducted performance studies of RDM vs. VMDK performance all the way back to ESX 3.x back in 2007. Even that study found very little measurable difference between RDMs and VMDKs. That study was repeated again for ESX 3.5, and a similar performance comparison was run on ESXi 5.1. All of the data shows that RDMs and VMDKs perform nearly identically.

You can read the complete details of these performance studies here:

`http://blogs.vmware.com/vsphere/2013/01/vsphere-5-1-vmdk-versus-rdm.html`

Virtual Disk Type

When provisioning storage for virtual machines, administrators have the option of selecting the virtual disk type for each VMDK. The virtual disk type represents how the virtual disk is provisioned on the VMFS datastore. There are three virtual disk types:

- Thin provisioned virtual disks have their storage space allocated and zeroed out the first time data needs to be written to the blocks on the disk. A thin provisioned virtual disk consumes only as much space on the datastore as there is data written to the disk. This makes thin provisioning a useful tool for managing storage, keeping in mind that once space is consumed, it may not automatically be removed if files inside the virtual machine are deleted. Also, the growing of the virtual disk file and zeroing out of blocks does incur a slight performance penalty.

- Thick provision lazy zeroed virtual disks have all of their space allocated at the time the virtual disk is created. Each block still needs to be zeroed out the first time data is written. Thick provisioned lazy zeroed disks can be provisioned quickly, but like thin provisioned, they incur a small performance penalty when zeroing out blocks on first write.

- Thick provisioned eager zeroed virtual disks have all of their space allocated and all blocks zeroed out at the time the disk is created. Since the blocks do not have to be zeroed out prior to data being written, eager zeroed thick disks offer the best performance of the three virtual disk types but at the cost of longer provisioning time when the virtual disks are created.

For the best possible performance, choose Thick Provision Eager Zeroed when creating new virtual disks, as shown in Figure 7.18. If you have already provisioned your virtual disk using either the thin provisioned or lazy zeroed format, you can still "upgrade" to eager zeroed format using two options.

- For thin provisioned disks, you can access the VMDK using the Browse Files option in the vSphere Web Client. When right-clicking on a thin provisioned VMDK, you will have the option to inflate the VMDK, meaning zero out all blocks and convert to eager zeroed thick format.

- Enable vSphere Fault Tolerance on a virtual machine that has either thin provisioned or lazy zeroed virtual disks. Fault Tolerance requires eager zeroed thick disks, so enabling this feature will cause ESXi to zero out all blocks on the virtual disks and convert them to eager zeroed thick format.

FIGURE 7.18
Configuring thick provision eager zeroed disks on a virtual machine

Improvements in vSphere can negate the performance differences of the virtual disk types. Remember VAAI from earlier in this chapter? One of the ways VAAI improves performance is by offloading the zeroing of virtual disk blocks to the storage array rather than having the ESXi host manage it. That can improve the zeroing performance, not only for creating disks using the thick provisioned eager zero format but also for zeroing out blocks on the first write for thin or lazy zeroed disks. For thin provisioned disks, VAAI also improves performance by managing locks during VMFS metadata updates, as is required when growing a thin provisioned disk.

NOTE   Back in the days of vSphere 4.x, VMware created a study to show the performance difference between thin and thick provisioned virtual disks. Though it is somewhat old, it is still helpful to show the slight difference in performance between the various virtual disk types. You can read the study at www.vmware.com/pdf/vsp_4_thinprov_perf.pdf.

Virtual SCSI Adapter

Virtual machines have virtual disks attached to them in much the same way as physical machines. That is, they are presented with a virtual hard disk controller that is used to manage access to virtual disks. Virtual hard disk controllers have the same limits as their physical counterparts in terms of the number of devices they support and performance characteristics. In vSphere 5.5, virtual hard disks can be presented to VMs in three different formats, as shown in Figure 7.19.

FIGURE 7.19
The three different types of virtual disks on a virtual machine

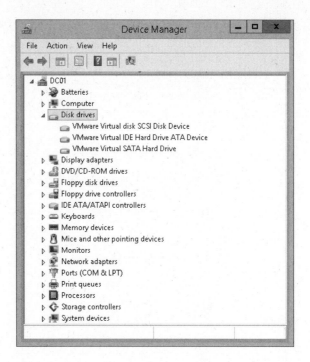

- ◆ Virtual SCSI (vSCSI) hard drives can be presented to virtual machines and controlled via virtual SCSI controllers. Just as with physical SCSI controllers, each controller can control a maximum of 15 SCSI devices, and vSphere 5.5 supports a maximum of four vSCSI controllers per virtual machine. That provides a maximum of 60 virtual hard disks per virtual machine.

- ◆ vSphere 5.5 introduced support for an Advanced Host Controller Interface (AHCI) that allows administrators to configure vSATA hard drive controllers on virtual machines. Each vSATA controller supports up to 30 virtual hard disks, and vSphere 5.5 supports a maximum of four vSATA controllers per virtual machine. That provides a maximum of 120 virtual hard disks per virtual machine.

- ◆ Virtual IDE controllers are still supported in vSphere 5.5, though they are primarily used for connecting virtual DVD-ROM drives to VMs. vSphere 5.5 supports one vIDE controller per virtual machine, supporting up to a maximum of four devices (either DVD-ROM drives or hard disks).

For the purpose of discussing performance, we will focus only on virtual SCSI hard drives and vSCSI controllers. There are other reasons you might consider using vSATA controllers, such as the need to exceed 60 virtual hard disks per VM, but for performance reasons, we recommend using vSCSI controllers only. vIDE-based virtual hard drives are not recommended due to performance considerations.

CHOOSING A vSCSI CONTROLLER

There are four different vSCSI controllers available in vSphere 5.5. The vSCSI controller options are BusLogic Parallel, LSI Logic Parallel, LSI Logic SAS, and VMware Paravirtual. BusLogic Parallel, LSI Logic Parallel, and LSI Logic SAS are there primarily for compatibility with specific operating systems. Just as with virtual network cards, VMware provides standardized vSCSI controllers that are compatible on a wide variety of operating systems without any modification or drivers required. This makes installing operating systems easy because you do not need to install a driver to make the OS recognize the virtual disk, but it does so at the cost of performance. To make a vSCSI controller that offers great performance in a virtual machine, VMware developed the VMware Paravirtual controller. The VMware Paravirtual controller, or PVSCSI, is a paravirtual SCSI controller that is optimized to run in a virtual machine. It requires a driver, included with the VMware Tools package, so the operating system can recognize it and the disks attached to it. It was designed for high I/O workloads and provides better I/O throughput at a lower CPU cost.

For most workloads, using the PVSCSI controller can offer solid performance with lower CPU utilization even if the virtual machine is not generating large amounts of I/O. Under low I/O conditions, the performance difference between the PVSCSI and LSI Logic vSCSI controllers may be similar, but as load increases, the PVSCSI controller offers better performance. In the past, the PVSCSI controller was not supported on boot volumes and also actually offered worse performance with very low I/O workloads. Both of these issues have been resolved and now the PVSCSI controller is safe to use for all workloads that support it. To find out which guest OSs support the PVSCSI controller, see http://kb.vmware.com/kb/1010398.

If you wish to use the PVSCSI driver for a boot volume, you'll need a way to present the driver during OS installation so that the virtual hard drive is recognized. VMware provides virtual floppy images that include the driver and make it easy to present the driver during OS installation. To attach the virtual floppy image to a virtual machine, follow this simple procedure:

1. Launch the vSphere Web Client and connect to vCenter Server.

2. From the Home view, select either Hosts And Clusters or VMs And Templates.

3. Locate the virtual machine you wish to use, right-click, and select Edit Settings.

4. Change the drop-down box next to Floppy Drive 1 to Use Existing Floppy Image to bring up the file browser.

5. Expand the vmimages folder, browse the contents of the floppies folder, and select the appropriate virtual floppy image based on the configured operating system, as shown in Figure 7.20. Click OK to mount the virtual floppy image, and then proceed with your operating system installation. Make sure the check box labeled Connect is checked next to Floppy Drive 1 before powering on your virtual machine.

NOTE   As you might have noticed in Figure 7.20, there is no PVSCSI floppy disk for either Windows Server 2008 R2 or Windows Server 2012. VMware has never updated the filename of the floppy image labeled pvscsi-Windows2008.flp, but it does work with newer versions of Windows. If you want to use the PVSCSI controller with Windows Server 2012, for example, select this floppy image because it contains a compatible driver.

FIGURE 7.20
Selecting the appro-
priate virtual floppy
image with the PVSCSI
driver

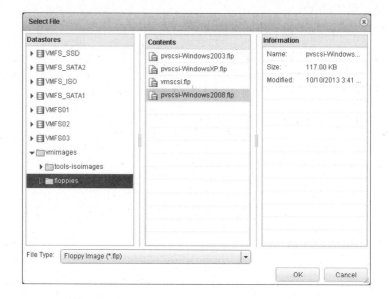

CONFIGURING vSCSI ADAPTERS ON VIRTUAL MACHINES

Each vSCSI adapter can support up to 15 virtual hard disks, providing a total of 60 possible virtual hard disks per VM. Does that mean that you should configure only one vSCSI adapter until you reach 15 virtual hard disks and then add another and so on? Though it may not seem obvious, the answer is actually no.

Virtual SCSI controllers work just like physical SCSI controllers in that each controller has its own set of queues for handling storage traffic. If you assign a large number of virtual hard disks to a single vSCSI adapter, all traffic must utilize the same queues, and in situations where I/O activity is high, those queues could fill up and performance could be reduced. Instead, if you have high I/O demands on virtual disks, it makes sense to allocate multiple vSCSI adapters. Consider the example of a virtualized database server that has separate virtual disks for the operating system, installation binaries, databases, and logs. In periods of high I/O, there could be congestion if all of those virtual disks were attached to the same vSCSI controller. By configuring three separate vSCSI controllers, you could place the OS and installation binaries on one vSCSI controller, the databases on a second controller, and the logs on a third controller. Using multiple controllers increases the number of queues available and decreases the chance of contention for I/O resources on a single controller.

Since you have some granularity over which vSCSI controllers each virtual hard disk is assigned, spreading disks out evenly across the controllers can also help improve performance. Remember, you can assign up to 15 devices per vSCSI controller, so there is no need to overload a single controller when you can evenly distribute your disks across up to four controllers.

Guest OS Disk Alignment

The issue of disk alignment has been around for years and has historically been a problem on physical servers. In general, disks need to be aligned so that additional I/O operations are not required on the backend storage for each I/O generated in the guest. Extra I/O operations may be required because the sector size in the OS, or the minimum amount of data that can be read to or written from a hard drive, does not match the sector size of the underlying physical hardware.

Newer operating systems, such as Windows Server 2008 and Windows 7, are automatically aligned at the 1 MB boundary and do not experience performance problems. Older operating systems, such as Windows Server 2003, were not automatically aligned and so performance was degraded. This scenario can become exacerbated in virtual environments where many virtual machines, all with unaligned partitions, are running on the same backend storage and generating extra unnecessary I/O.

Partition alignment may vary depending on the configuration of your backend storage. Working with your storage vendor is a good way to determine the proper partition alignment for your environment. In modern versions of Windows, the default alignment is typically acceptable for most scenarios.

Unfortunately for older operating systems, fixing alignment issues has historically not been a simple task. Though some tools exist to resolve the issue, it is generally a destructive process, so fixing misaligned disks has not been a high priority. Thankfully, when these workloads are virtualized, you have a relatively easy solution. VMware Converter, a tool designed to perform physical-to-virtual (P2V) migrations, can automatically align partitions during the conversion process. VMware Converter doesn't perform only P2V migrations, it can also perform virtual-to-virtual (V2V) migrations against your existing virtual machines. If you have older guests that contain misaligned partitions, using VMware Converter can be an easy way to resolve the problem with very little downtime.

You can download the latest version of VMware Converter from `www.vmware.com/products/converter/`.

IMPACT ON vFLASH READ CACHE

Another possible side effect of a misaligned disk is reduced effectiveness of vFlash Read Cache. vFRC will not cache a partial block to avoid inefficient use of the cache, so misaligned disks can have very low cache hit rates. To make vFRC perform optimally, disks should be aligned to at least a 4 KB boundary. Newer operating systems like Windows Server 2008 and Linux 2.6 align to this boundary automatically, so this is likely to be applicable only on older workloads. Correcting misaligned partitions can help improve the cache hit rate of vFRC and improve performance.

A WORD ABOUT VMFS ALIGNMENT

While we're on the subject of guest OS disk alignment, let's not forget about alignment of VMFS volumes too. By default, all VMFS volumes created in the vSphere Web Client (or the vSphere Client if your vCenter Server is not yet available when deploying ESXi) are automatically aligned along a 1 MB boundary. VMFS volumes created at the console are not automatically aligned, but this scenario is far less common today than it was when the full ESX Server product was available. All VMFS volumes should be created through the vSphere Web Client or vSphere Client to ensure proper disk alignment.

If you have a VMFS volume that was created prior to vSphere 5.x using the VMFS3 format, it is aligned to a 64 KB boundary. Upgrading that VMFS volume to VMFS5 will not change the alignment. Instead, you'll need to delete the volume and re-create it from scratch as VMFS5. Luckily, Storage vMotion is a nondisruptive process and this can be done without any virtual machine downtime.

Troubleshooting Storage Performance Issues

Despite all of the advances that VMware has made into virtualized storage, you can still run into performance problems in your vSphere environment. Before we dive into methodologies for troubleshooting common problems, it's important to discuss the capabilities of the vSphere platform itself. VMware has tested storage performance on every version of ESXi and has proven, as of vSphere 5.1, that a single virtual machine is capable of sustaining over 1 million IOPS; see

```
http://blogs.vmware.com/performance/2012/08/1millioniops-on-1vm.html
```

for details on the performance testing. If nothing else, this proves that vSphere can handle even the highest I/O workloads available today and is capable of working with the fastest backend storage on the market today.

What does that mean to you? It means that it is unlikely that storage performance problems are caused by ESXi itself, or by limitations in the capabilities of the ESXi storage stack. Despite the fact that virtualization is now a mature and accepted technology, many application owners or folks not familiar with its capabilities might simply blame ESXi for any perceived storage performance problems. Though misconfigurations and issues can result in degraded storage performance, the ESXi platform in and of itself is not likely to be the cause of any performance problems.

THINK OUTSIDE THE BOX

There is an expression most commonly used in the medical field that goes, "When you hear hoofbeats, think of horses, not zebras." It means that you shouldn't look for uncommon explanations to problems when common explanations are much more likely. That often applies to troubleshooting performance problems in vSphere too.

Though that logic holds true, you shouldn't rule out uncommon explanations if you cannot properly diagnose your problem. Having a good understanding of all aspects of vSphere performance, not just storage, will help you when you encounter those situations where an uncommon explanation just might be correct.

Author Matt Liebowitz remembers a situation just like this a few years back when he was called in to help assist a colleague who was having some issues running Microsoft Exchange Jetstress. Jetstress is a tool to validate storage performance for an Exchange deployment, and Matt's colleague was running it for a customer who had just purchased a brand-new high-powered storage array. Each test he ran resulted in a failure despite the fact that almost nothing else was running on the array. Since Jetstress only tests storage performance, this seems like an obvious storage-related issue, right?

Matt was luckily able to find the problem very quickly, and it actually had nothing to do with storage. Someone had accidentally configured a 4 GB memory limit on the vSphere template from which all Exchange VMs were deployed. This Exchange Mailbox server had 24 GB of configured RAM but was limited to use just 4 GB, resulting in significant memory ballooning and swapping. Once the limit was removed, the Jetstress tests passed.

What is the moral of the story? Understanding the full scope of vSphere performance troubleshooting (not just storage) will help you diagnose problems and find those uncommon, but correct, explanations.

Storage Latency

Of all of the storage performance problems you may encounter, perhaps none is more visible to end users or applications than high-storage latency. Latency can best be explained from the virtual machine's or application's point of view. Storage latency is simply the time it takes for an I/O operation to be acknowledged back by the application or operating system running inside the virtual machine. If you consider the I/O path for a virtual machine running on SAN storage, there are multiple places where that I/O must pass through in order for it to be completed and acknowledged back on the SAN. It first must go through the vSCSI adapter, then to the storage stack of the ESXi host, and from there it traverses the network (either fibre or Ethernet) back to the storage and must finally get committed to disk. Flash storage can help here because it can absorb the I/O very quickly and acknowledge it back faster than spinning disks can, which is why flash is frequently used as a cache layer.

As storage latency builds, the application must wait before it can continue to process new I/O. If you consider a multi-tier application with a front-end web server, a middle-tier application server, and a backend database, you can see that small delays can cause delays through the entire application stack. Though latency is typically measured in milliseconds (thousandths of a second), these delays can add up and become visible to the applications and ultimately the end users.

Storage latency has very little to do with IOPS. You could have an application that is generating a lot of IOPS but also at a very high latency, which would most likely result in poor application performance for the end user. Don't be fooled into thinking that storage isn't the cause of a performance issue just because you see a high amount of IOPS. If you're also seeing high storage latency at the same time as the high IOPS, then it's more than likely you've got a problem.

INVESTIGATE HIGH STORAGE LATENCY

If your virtual machines are experiencing performance problems and you know that CPU, memory, or network are not constrained, then looking first for high storage latency is a good idea. Before you investigate your latency, however, it is a good idea to know what is a "good" or "acceptable" latency level for your particular storage array. Many storage vendors provide guidance on acceptable latency levels for their arrays, so it is a good idea to work with these vendors to determine an acceptable value. If you can't get a value from your storage vendor, a good generally acceptable maximum value for storage latency is around 20 milliseconds (ms). This value can change considerably depending on the disks you're using (and would be considered very high for flash storage) or the applications you're running. Don't forget to work with the application owners to determine their storage latency requirements. For example, some applications can tolerate storage latency better than others.

In vSphere, you have several ways to determine your storage latency and also what the latency value is for several different objects, such as virtual machine, datastore, storage adapter, and storage path. Latency statistics are available in both vCenter (via the vSphere Web Client) and esxtop. As with other statistics, vCenter has a sampling period of 20 seconds, whereas esxtop shows the data in real time. For deeper troubleshooting, esxtop is often the better tool, but vCenter is often easier to access and a good first place to check.

To view the storage latency at the datastore level in vCenter, follow these simple steps:

1. Launch the vSphere Web Client and connect to vCenter Server.

2. From the Home view, select Hosts And Clusters view and select the ESXi host you wish to monitor.

3. Select Monitor, and then click the Performance tab. Select Advanced to view the more detailed performance counters.

4. Change the drop-down box next to View to Datastore to bring up latency statistics for each datastore. Note that you can also select Storage Adapter or Storage Path to view additional storage latency statistics.

5. Find the datastore in question in the performance chart legend and view the columns Latest, Maximum, Minimum, and Average. They will tell you your current storage latency for reads and writes as well as the values over time, as shown in Figure 7.21.

As you can see in Figure 7.21, the datastore VMFS02 is experiencing high write latency with a value of 94 ms, though the average over the monitoring period (1 hour) is only 3.922 ms, which is well within the acceptable range. That may indicate that the latency value is a brief spike since the overall average is normal. Esxtop, however, can provide more real-time data that can be used to pinpoint storage latency problems as they're occurring. Just like vCenter, esxtop lets you view latency and multiple levels. You can view storage latency at the device level (such as the HBA level), the datastore level, or the storage path.

FIGURE 7.21
View storage latency per datastore in the vSphere Web Client.

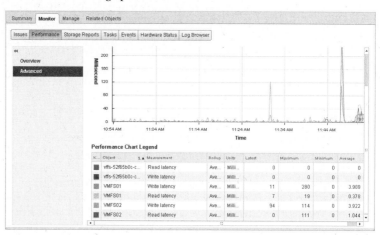

The esxtop tool displays storage latency in multiple ways, but three specific counters are the most important. These counters are described in Table 7.5.

TABLE 7.5:   Storage latency counters in esxtop

COUNTER	DESCRIPTION
DAVG/cmd	Device Average Latency per command, defined as the latency that is coming from the physical hardware (HBA, NIC, or storage array)
KAVG/cmd	Kernel Average Latency per command, defined as the latency at the VMkernel level or the vSphere storage stack
GAVG/cmd	Guest Average Latency per command, defined as the total latency as seen from the virtual machine's point of view

The value of GAVG/cmd is the sum total of DAVG/cmd and KAVG/cmd and provides, from the VM's perspective, the total storage latency that is being experienced. You will not frequently see KAVG/cmd values very high because the vSphere storage stack is capable of handling very high I/O.

To view storage latency at the device level through esxtop, use the following procedure:

1. Connect to the console of your ESXi host and log in as a user with elevated permissions. Launch the esxtop tool.

2. Once in esxtop, change the view to device storage by typing **d**.

3. View the statistics in the columns listed in Table 7.5. The output for a storage adapter that is experiencing high storage latency values is shown in Figure 7.22.

FIGURE 7.22
View storage latency per device in esxtop.

Looking at Figure 7.22, it's pretty clear there is a storage latency problem if those latency values are sustained over a long period. By looking at the DAVG/cmd counter, we can see the latency is 155.41 ms, which would be too high for almost any application. It isn't abnormal to see momentary spikes of storage latency within this range, but if these values are sustained over time, then you have identified a clear storage performance issue.

RESOLVE HIGH STORAGE LATENCY

At this point you've figured out that you've got a problem with high storage latency. More than likely applications are not performing as expected and end users are complaining. How do you resolve the issue? And "update your resume" is not an acceptable answer!

There could be many reasons storage latency is high, so it's impossible to review them all here. Instead, we'll focus on some of the more common causes.

Overloaded Backend Storage

Perhaps the most common cause of high storage latency is simply a backend storage system that is not capable of delivering the I/Os required by your vSphere environment. Remember earlier when we spoke about the I/O blender effect? If your storage array was sized with one type of workload in mind and now you're running many different virtual machines all with different I/O patterns, it's possible that it simply doesn't have the capabilities to deliver the required I/O. It sounds simple and obvious, but it's surprising how often this is the case. Remember that virtualization changes the way we size and design our storage, and not properly accounting for all workload types can lead to poorly performing storage.

If your backend storage is not capable of delivering the required I/Os, your choices for resolving the issue are somewhat limited. Here are some suggestions for working around this problem:

◆ Purchase new backend storage, either additional disk spindles or entirely new storage array(s). This is the easiest way to resolve the issue if high storage latency is being caused by an overloaded storage array.

◆ Reduce the number of virtual machines running on the disk spindles.

◆ Utilize vFlash Read Cache to help offset read I/Os from the array, allowing it to focus mostly on write I/O.

◆ Introduce a flash caching layer to your storage array if it is supported.

◆ Enable Storage I/O Control to try to enforce fairness in storage utilization on all hosts within the cluster. If the array is completely overloaded, then SIOC may not be able to help, but it offers a good first line of defense.

Incorrectly Configured Storage

It's possible that your storage array is capable of delivering the I/Os required but is configured in such a way that it can't perform as well as it's capable of performing. A simple example of this would be a RAID configuration that does not lend itself well to the primary workload type of the virtual machines that are running on it.

For example, if your workloads are write heavy and your storage array is configured with RAID-6, it's possible that is contributing to the problem. Instead, consider a more write-friendly configuration like RAID-10. As we said earlier, caching layers and other storage array technologies can help offset the write penalty for certain RAID configurations, but it is still worthwhile to investigate.

Bandwidth Saturation

The path of I/O from the virtual machine to the backend storage needs to traverse a network, either Ethernet or fibre channel. The network cards and HBAs that are used to transmit this data come in various speeds, such as 1 Gb or 10 Gb for Ethernet and 4 Gb or 8 Gb (or up to 16 Gb) for fibre. It's possible that your backend storage array is more than capable of handling the I/O and vSphere is more than capable of handling the I/O but the NICs or HBAs are not.

A good example of this would be when using IP storage over 1 Gb network cards. Let's say you've got two 1 Gb Ethernet NICs dedicated to iSCSI storage. You're using round-robin multipathing, so you're effectively utilizing both NICs, and you're experiencing performance problems. Taking a look at esxtop, as shown in Figure 7.23, we can see that the column MbTX/s (megabits transmitted) for both vmnic0 and vmnic3 is over 1,000, which is approaching the maximum capabilities of a 1 Gb NIC. If this amount of network bandwidth is consumed regularly, it is possible that you're consuming all of your available bandwidth for storage traffic and that is causing high latency.

In this instance, using 10 Gb Ethernet NICs instead of 1 Gb could help reduce this problem by providing more bandwidth for storage traffic. The same situation could occur with slower fibre channel HBAs, so upgrading to 8 Gb can help resolve that issue as well.

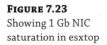

FIGURE 7.23
Showing 1 Gb NIC
saturation in esxtop

If you're using the physical NICs dedicated for IP storage traffic with other functions, such as virtual machine traffic or vMotion traffic, you can run into this scenario much more frequently. Always try to isolate IP storage traffic onto dedicated physical NICs, especially when using 1 Gb uplinks.

Other Potential Causes

If none of the items listed previously are the cause of the storage latency you're seeing, here are some other things to consider:

◆ Very high CPU usage on the ESXi host could cause storage latency to increase. Just as with networking, the processing of storage traffic can put a burden on the host's CPU. If the host is already consuming a large percentage of its CPU resources, processing of storage traffic will have to contend with other tasks for CPU time. This could lead to an increase in the time it takes to process storage information and subsequently higher storage latency.

◆ High storage queuing inside a virtual machine could lead to high storage queuing in the ESXi storage stack. If you have multiple high I/O VMDKs all attached to the same vSCSI controller, this could lead to queuing inside the virtual machine. As we discussed earlier, separating high I/O VMDKs into separate vSCSI controllers can help reduce queuing inside the guest and subsequent queuing in the ESXi storage stack.

It's possible that you've explored all of these options and are still experiencing high storage latency. At this point it is often a good idea to open up a ticket with VMware support because they are trained in helping to diagnose and resolve storage performance problems. Calling your storage vendor is also a good idea to help investigate the root cause.

Misconfigured Storage for Your Applications

Knowing how your applications work so that you can provide them with the best possible storage solution is key to delivering solid performance. Combining the details from a capacity assessment with deep application-level knowledge from the application owners, you can design a proper storage layout for your virtual machines.

Unfortunately, that scenario doesn't always play out like that, and virtual machines can get put on the wrong storage for the applications that are run. Let's take the example we used earlier of a large database workload running Microsoft SQL Server. That server will likely have a separate VMDK for the operating system (and possibly the application binaries), databases, logs, and tempdb database. If the vSphere administrator wasn't aware of what was running on that virtual machine, the VMDKs may have unknowingly been put on VMFS datastores that are not optimized for that workload profile. Combining the database, which likely is more read heavy, with the logs, which are more write heavy, on the same datastore could lead to I/O contention and ultimately poor performance.

Knowing your workload can go a long way toward delivering solid storage performance. Work with application owners and vendors to determine the storage requirements so that you can properly configure and allocate the required storage.

Storage Queues

Throughout the storage stack, from the virtual machine all the way up to the backend storage array, there are queues. In vSphere there are queues inside the virtual machine as well as at the ESXi host itself. The queues in the ESXi host allow multiple virtual machines to share a single resource, be it an HBA or a LUN, without reducing performance.

Think of being in a queue as waiting in a line. In real life we have to wait in line for lots of things: to get through airport security, to get into a concert or sporting event, or, our favorite, renewing our driver's license. At a sporting event we form a line so that we can fit through the doorway because everyone trying to cram through a small doorway at the same time would result in almost no one getting through. Why we have to wait so long to renew our driver's license unfortunately remains a mystery.

For storage traffic through the ESXi storage stack, queues are there for the same reason. In the ESXi storage stack, there are three main queues:

◆ Virtual machine queue (sometimes referred to as the world queue), or the amount of outstanding I/Os that are permitted from all of the virtual machines running on a particular LUN (per ESXi host)

◆ Storage adapter queue, or the amount of outstanding I/Os that can pass through the HBA (or NIC in the case of IP storage)

◆ Per LUN queue, or the amount of outstanding I/Os that can be processed on each individual LUN

Each queue has what's known as a queue depth, or the number of I/Os that can fit inside the queue. Each of the queues just described has its own default queue depth. These values can be increased to improve performance in certain situations, but in general you shouldn't change them unless you've been directed to by VMware or your storage vendor. The default queue depths are typically good enough for most workloads.

MONITORING QUEUES

You can monitor the size of the queue as well as how much of the queue is being used with our old pal esxtop. Just as with storage latency, there are several esxtop counters that are valuable to understand when monitoring the usage of storage queues. Table 7.6 lists the important storage queue counters found in esxtop.

TABLE 7.6:   Storage queue counters in esxtop

COUNTER	DESCRIPTION
ACTV	The number of I/O commands that are currently active
QUED	The number of I/O commands that are in the queue
%USD	The percentage of the queue that is currently in use

To view the size of the queue and, more important, monitor the usage of the queue, use the following procedure (in this example we'll view the LUN queue):

1. Connect to the console of your ESXi host and log in as a user with elevated permissions. Launch the esxtop tool.

2. Once in esxtop, change the view to disk device by typing **u**.

3. View the statistics in the columns listed in Table 7.6. The output for a storage adapter that is experiencing high storage queue activity is shown in Figure 7.24.

FIGURE 7.24

View storage queue usage in esxtop.

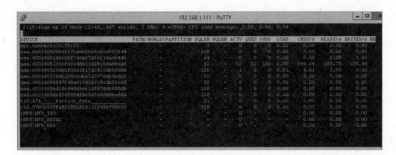

In Figure 7.24, we can see that for the storage volume *naa.60014051c60fdc1d8b11d3815da8bdd8* (fourth row down) the values for ACTV and QUED both equal 32. Next, the counter DQLEN (disk queue length) shows the queue depth for the LUN queue is 32. Not surprisingly, since the ACTV value shows the number of I/O commands as 32 and the size of the queue as 32, the counter %USD shows as 100 percent. This is a situation where increasing the LUN queue depth may help improve performance.

If you have applications that are consistently generating high I/O, check the queue statistics to see if they are consistently maximizing the queues. These workloads may benefit from a larger queue, so in these situations increasing the queue depth can help the application drive more I/O.

> ### CHANGING THE QUEUE DEPTH IS NOT ALWAYS THE ANSWER
>
> Changing the queue depth of the various queues in the ESXi storage stack may improve performance, but you should not change these values without first working with your storage vendor (or VMware support). Your storage vendor can give you the best guidance on what the proper queue depth should be.
>
> You can view the following VMware Knowledge Base articles for instructions on changing queue depths. Remember to consult your storage vendor first before making any changes.
>
> http://kb.vmware.com/kb/1267
>
> http://kb.vmware.com/kb/1268

USING STORAGE I/O CONTROL

At this point you might be thinking, "Shouldn't Storage I/O Control help to alleviate some of these storage problems?" It's true that SIOC can help to eliminate a lot of common storage performance problems simply by enforcing fairness amongst virtual machines. However, increasing the queue depth can actually help SIOC do its job better in certain circumstances.

SIOC is able to enforce fairness in access to storage resources by dynamically decreasing and increasing the LUN queue depth. By decreasing this value, SIOC prevents a single virtual machine from monopolizing storage resources. However, SIOC is unable to increase the queue depth beyond the configured value. If the configured queue depth is too low, SIOC won't be able to dynamically increase the value to improve performance.

By increasing the queue depth to a higher value, you can potentially enhance SIOC's ability to control performance. A higher queue depth could help applications perform better during periods of heavy I/O, and if there is contention for storage resources, SIOC can simply dynamically lower the value.

End-to-End Networking

The I/O path of an I/O from the virtual machine to the storage array causes it to go through many different devices. I/Os travel through the HBA or NIC of the ESXi host to some kind of switch, either fibre or Ethernet, and then possibly on to other switches before arriving at the storage array. Misconfigurations along that path can lead to storage performance problems.

If you're using fibre channel storage, the configured speed must be the same through the entire I/O path. For instance, if the ESXi host is connected to the SAN switch at one speed and the SAN is connected to the switch at another speed, this can cause the overall speed to drop and performance to be reduced. If you think this might be the cause, force the speed to be the same across all devices in which the I/O path travels.

The same is true for IP storage. Jumbo frames must be configured end to end in order to offer any possible performance improvements. If jumbo frames are not configured at one point during the I/O path, it's possible that this bottleneck could introduce storage performance issues. Similarly, if the speed and duplex settings are not the same across the entire network path, you could encounter the dreaded but all too common duplex mismatch that was described in Chapter 6.

Summary

The vSphere platform has matured over the years to become a trusted platform on which organizations can run production workloads and even business-critical workloads. Combined with technological advancements in server hardware, the burden has shifted to the storage layer to provide good performance for virtual machines. These days, the storage layer is most directly responsible for delivering good performance, and it is the place to troubleshoot when VMs start experiencing performance problems.

A good vSphere storage design starts at the physical storage layer. Performing a capacity assessment to determine your storage requirements is key to designing your physical storage. Choosing the right RAID levels based on these requirements is also important in making sure your storage is sized to meet the demands of your virtual machines. Following good practices to make sure you're dedicating NICs for IP storage and using the proper multipathing to ensure performance and availability are also key in designing your storage.

With each new release of vSphere, there are more and more storage-related features being added to help address storage performance. You can help improve the performance of several vSphere storage tasks by choosing a storage array that supports VAAI. Using technologies like Storage I/O Control, Storage DRS, and datastore clusters can make managing storage easier and help to solve the "noisy neighbor" problem where one VM consumes too many storage resources. You can also help improve both read and write performance by using vFlash Read Cache to offload read I/O to faster flash storage, allowing your storage array to focus mostly on write I/O.

You learned that virtual machines themselves can also be tuned to improve storage performance. Using eager zeroed thick disks can help improve first write performance by pre-zeroing blocks. Using the paravirtualized PVSCSI vSCSI controller can improve I/O performance and also reduce CPU utilization on your virtual machines. And you can reduce unnecessary I/Os on the storage array by aligning guest OS partitions, which also has the benefit of improving the vFlash Read Cache hit ratio.

Finally, we covered some common storage performance issues you might encounter in your environment. Of all of the issues, high storage latency is likely to be the one that is most visible to end users. Reducing storage latency is key to maximizing storage performance. Adjusting the various queue depths inside the ESXi storage stack can also help, provided your storage vendor has given this guidance based on the requirements of your particular hardware.

By properly designing your physical storage, utilizing vSphere storage features correctly, and maximizing virtual machine storage performance, you can all but eliminate storage as a bottleneck in your environment. Though flash storage can help mask performance problems, it is better to design properly from the beginning and use flash strategically to improve performance. Following the steps listed in this chapter can help you create a vSphere environment that is not limited by storage performance. Once you eliminate storage performance as a bottleneck, there are practically no workloads that can't be virtualized. The rest, as they say, is up to you.

Index

Note to the Reader: Throughout this index boldfaced page numbers indicate primary discussions of a topic. Italicized page numbers indicate illustrations.